# QUEEN OF CUBA

# QUEEN OF CUBA

## An FBI Agent's Insider Account of the Spy Who Evaded Detection for 17 Years

PETER J. LAPP
with Kelly Kennedy

Post Hill Press

A POST HILL PRESS BOOK

Queen of Cuba:
An FBI Agent's Insider Account of the Spy Who Evaded Detection for 17 Years


ISBN: 979-8-88845-549-4
ISBN (eBook): 978-1-63758-960-1

Cover design by Cody Corcoran
Interior design and composition by Greg Johnson, Textbook Perfect

All people, locations, events, and situations are portrayed to the best of the author's memory. While all of the events described are true, some names and identifying details have been changed to protect the privacy of the people involved.



**Post Hill Press**
New York • Nashville
posthillpress.com

Published in the United States of America
1 2 3 4 5 6 7 8 9 10

*In accordance with my obligations as a former FBI employee pursuant to my FBI employment agreement, this book has undergone a prepublication review for the purpose of identifying prohibited disclosures but has not been reviewed for editorial content or accuracy. (The blacked-out portions were redacted during that process.) The FBI does not endorse or validate any information that I have described in this book. The opinions expressed in this book are mine and not those of the FBI or any other government agency.*

*Some names and information in this book have been changed to protect people and programs. Finally, Ana Montes told me about her life and her motivations during the several-month period when my partner and I debriefed her after her arrest.*

*For Ethan, Emma, and Katelynn.*

*By far, my greatest accomplishments.*

# Contents

# QUEEN OF CUBA

# INTRODUCTION

# I Should've Known I'd Leave Alone

On a spring evening in 2001, Ana Montes adjusted the antenna of her shortwave radio by the window in the bedroom of her quiet Cleveland Park apartment in Washington, D.C.

Cherry blossoms had reached their peak and fallen in pink piles. Pandas Mei Xiang and Tian Tian had just made their home at the National Zoo, which sat a couple of blocks from Ana's home. She could see the city's odd black Canadian squirrels, which had infiltrated D.C. after escaping from that same zoo more than one hundred years before, engaged in their annual spring rituals in the grass outside her building.

Ana also hoped for love.

She had tried dating, perhaps once dreaming of a big Puerto Rican family like the one in which she had grown up. But three times a week, she pulled the Sony radio, which looked like something any shortwave hobbyist would pick up at RadioShack, from its spot next to her radiator. In her closet sat a professional-looking leather-ish document holder—ubiquitous in the days before everything went online—from which she pulled a piece of paper with a series of letters set up like a matrix. Had she gotten the paper wet, it would have disintegrated.

She kept a go-bag in the closet next to the radio. It contained money and maps for several big cities around the world. If she wanted to run, she could.

She lived in a co-op like a thousand other city apartments: hardwood floors, high ceilings, and marble entranceways. Like those other eighty-year-old dwellings, the thick brick walls prevented any signal from getting through. She placed the antenna close to the window.

Then she waited.

In that apartment, she kept a picture of her family: her brother Tito's graduation from the FBI Academy. He stood with his then-wife Joanie, a fellow FBI agent. Ana's dad was in the picture. He had served in the US Army as a psychiatrist. And Ana's sister Lucy was there. She worked as a translator for the FBI, helping to break up a notorious ring of Cuban spies.

It's difficult for me to look at this picture. It represents why it took almost twenty years to stop hating Ana Montes. I graduated from the same academy, took the same oath, and believed with all my heart

Photo by Joan Andrzejewski

*Ana with her family from Tito's graduation from New Agent Training at the FBI Academy in February 1988. L to R: Ana's father, Alberto, Ana, Lucy, Joan Andrzejewski, and Tito.*

that, even with its problems, the United States would always be the first of my commitments.

Each of Ana's family members, except for her brother Carlos, also took this oath seriously, putting country ahead of just about everything else, often including family. But by the time Tito graduated from the FBI Academy, Ana had already been to Cuba illegally—twice. The Cubans had already arranged for her to meet Fidel Castro to receive an award for her espionage, though their schedules didn't align. And I believe—but can't prove—she offered intelligence to Cuba about El Salvador that resulted in a 1987 ambush in which a Green Beret, Staff Sergeant Gregory A. Fronius, was killed. But that was through no fault of hers. In her mind, he was responsible for the actions that might have caused his path to cross with hers.

Ana's dreams differed significantly from those of her family, and her cause was more important to her than how her actions might affect those she loved. She risked not only spending the rest of her life in jail but also ruining her family members' lives.

There's some irony there: Ana wrote that her father was abusive and that she felt guilty she could not protect her three siblings. From then on, she advocated for the underdog, but she left her mother, brothers, and sister to deal with the aftermath.

Ana had started out as an idealistic young woman, passionate about her beliefs. In school, everyone knew she hated the Americans' interference in Central America. It wasn't that she thought their governments were better than her own, she just didn't think the United States should involve itself in other countries' affairs. The Cuban people should rise up to overthrow their own government—without the help of the United States, which had tried multiple times to get rid of Fidel Castro. The Reagan administration poured money into El Salvador—$1.5 million a day, at one point—to defeat the leftists in a stand against communism. After a training course in counterinsurgency techniques provided by US special operations troops, El Salvador's army rounded up men, women, and children in a tiny village and massacred 1,200 people.[1] You could legitimately argue that the US government was wrong to do this, but you don't fix American policy by handing over information to Castro, Cuba's leader from 1959 to 2008 who was known for banning free speech, executing thousands of opponents, and keeping most Cubans in a constant state of poverty.[2]

Ana didn't support that—didn't support the poverty and the executions and the lack of freedom. But she hated the colonialist feel of US involvement.

She saw the US government as the enemy. In fact, she kept not a trace of herself in her cubicle at work: no pictures, no postcards of sunny beaches, no posters of cats offering motivational phrases. But there hung, at eye level on the wall in front of her desk, a quote from Shakespeare:

*The king hath note*
*Of all that they intend,*
*By interception*
*Which they dream not of.*

But I think, by the time she hung her antenna out the window that balmy evening in 2001, Ana Montes had begun to understand that she had betrayed not only her family and her country, but also herself.

When you picture spies, you may think of martinis, sweet cars, and sexy clothes. That wasn't Ana. She didn't go out with coworkers. She behaved awkwardly at parties. She hadn't had good luck dating. She filled her apartment with academic books about South America and traveled often to the Caribbean for "work" vacations, but her coworkers found her intellectually arrogant—always the smartest one in the room. Often, she was, in fact, the smartest person in the room, but some people handle those situations with more grace than others. She treated colleagues' ideas with boredom or annoyance.

She couldn't be friends with the people at work because she disagreed with what they did for a living. Her attitude was, "I'm not going to be friends with you, Bob, and I'm not going to your kid's christening or your birthday party because I really hate you, and I hate what you stand for, and I hate that you believe in what you're doing."

Instead of hanging out with her coworkers, she socialized with her handlers: she saw them as friends.

The Cubans had known her for more than sixteen years. I think they cared about her, and not just because she was an asset. For all her social oddities at work, she had changed the game for her handlers. She wanted nothing to do with dead drops. Robert Hanssen—the FBI agent who spied for the Russians for more than fifteen years beginning in the late 1980s and who was also known for being smart and standoffish—used a park in Fairfax, Virginia, as a drop site. Ana wanted none of that. She could easily have met her handlers in nearby Rock Creek Park, a lushly wooded area with lots of turns and hiding spots, but she knew better. No woman would have wanted to be alone in that park for long. Even as Ana sat in her kitchen window playing with the antenna, congressional intern Chandra Levy, who lived nearby in the Dupont Circle neighborhood, had already disappeared that spring after going for a run in Rock Creek Park.

Instead, Ana insisted her handlers meet her face-to-face. Dead drops? No. She ate lunch with them in the middle of the day, often handing off classified discs like she might a music CD she wanted to lend to a friend. The tradecraft? Brush passes in the middle of a tunnel or a subway entrance that happen so quickly they're barely visible. She didn't bother with that.

She was hiding in plain view.

At the same time, she built relationships with her handlers and absolutely considered them her friends.

Still, she kept thinking about her future. She craved companionship. A loud house. Nieces and nephews and nonsense. Lots of Puerto Rican food—fried plantains, rice and pigeon peas and cilantro, pastries stuffed with beef. *Café con leche*. And flan.

The work—the constant vigilance, the watching to make sure no one followed her, the fear that someone would find her out—

stressed her to the point of bad health. She exercised almost daily, a regular at the local gym. She listened to the anxiety tapes she kept in the nightstand of her bedroom. But still she lay awake at night, worrying, her thoughts circling over the details of the day as she tried to suss out whether she had missed anything. Did anyone notice that she'd left early?

Beyond that, she worked a lot of hours between the two careers. Her bosses at the Defense Intelligence Agency (DIA) saw her as one of the best—the "Queen of Cuba"—and she advanced quickly. Then she came home, typed out from memory everything she had learned that day, and waited for word from her handlers.

It was too much. She thought about a relationship—someone to help ease the load—often enough that she came up with a plan. In 1998, she asked the Cubans to set her up with a mate. It seemed perfect: he'd already be in on the game. She told them she wanted someone Latin, smart, good-looking, and athletic who didn't smoke—from a country known for its cigars and 60 percent smoking rate. But Castro's food rationing and a gas shortage had caused people to lose weight and get more exercise.[3] Her odds seemed good. Sure, they told her, they could find her someone.

They had her travel to a Caribbean island to meet her match. The guy undoubtedly worked as an intelligence officer. The Cubans weren't going to pull some random guy off the street and say, "Hey. You're going on a date."

But after a couple of days together in paradise, Ana realized she would have to find someone for herself. Her new Cuban friend was overweight. He smoked. He was not athletic.

She felt no spark.

Ana had always put the Cubans first. They had comforted her, nurtured her, and allowed her to contribute to a cause she believed in. It sustained her, to a degree, intimately—at the friendship level. But she wanted more, and she sensed she didn't have a lot of time. She needed to get out before she got caught.

Being a woman had helped her. It's not like she was wearing a mustache and fedora, but the word "she" just wasn't coming up anywhere in the missives from the Cubans. Had we known ...let's be honest, there weren't a lot of women working as intelligence analysts at the time. There weren't a lot of women working for the DIA period then. Knowing her gender would have narrowed our search significantly—and we did know there was a spy. But nothing pointed toward a woman.

American women don't spy against their country. Either they're too smart to try or they're smart enough not to get caught. They have kids, and it's hard to spy when there's often a small child in the vicinity. And it's stressful—people in the intelligence community tend to drink a lot.

It's not like you can go home and tell your spouse what you've been working on.

Except, if women do spy, they're usually part of a couple. Of the 148 Americans-who-spied cases from the 1940s to 2001, seven of the twelve known women spies were recruited by their boyfriends or husbands.[4]

Ana's motives also made her unusual. Most spies do it for at least a couple of reasons: they might be communists who also like nice boats. Or they may have a gambling problem but also think their boss is an asshole and have a grudge against a whole agency. They may want to be James Bond—yearn for the excitement and adventure—and also be dealing with an addiction.

Ana was different. She saw her spy craft as altruistic and morally just: she accepted no money. She did it purely because she believed the United States was wrong—she betrayed her country out of the goodness of her heart.

One man's freedom fighter is another man's terrorist, but to me, it was the epitome of betrayal.

She had already outlasted the majority of spies. Almost half of them make it about five years before someone catches them. She had been at it for sixteen years.

Maybe, because she was so stressed out and so ready for a relationship, she opened her heart to the enemy: Roger. Dark hair and eyes, like hers, a big grin, and smart. Fit. He worked as an intelligence analyst against Cuba for the Defense Department's Southern Command near Miami.

She knew she couldn't date a Cuban watcher, or, frankly, anyone, and spy for Cuba and make the relationship work. He was either in on it, or he was going to notice that Tokyo Rose was hiding in the closet three nights a week with her radio.

That spring, she made up her mind. She would quit her job at DIA because working for the American government felt like torture—she didn't want to work for the war machine. And she planned to tell the Cubans she was done.

She wanted to have a life.

But she was about to become Cuba's most important spy and one of America's greatest enemies.

# 1

# Someone That You Think That You Can Trust

I'm a pretty analytical person: I like facts. I like to break things down until they become smaller facts. And then when those facts become small enough to become actionable items, I like to deal with them quickly.

I've been dealing with Ana Montes for decades.

In some ways, you'd think our upbringings were similar: We both had dads who served in the military. We both moved around during our formative years, causing us to learn how to build new relationships just as we dealt with the angst of puberty. Our fathers were both brilliant. Both had strong personalities. We both had mothers who did everything they could to keep us safe.

But somewhere, she went in the furthest direction one way while I went completely the other. (I'm not even going to try to figure out who went left and who went right here.) I, and people much smarter than I, have all combed over the data, looking for the why of it, but even if I hit on a theory—or the [redacted] does—there's a deeper why behind that: genetics. Abuse. Crossed brain signals. Birth order.

All of the above.

She would undoubtedly say—well, and has said—that she simply fought for the rights of the Cuban people. But *why*? I mean, the Cubans aren't the first to hold a grudge, legitimate or not, against the United States. And Fidel Castro? I'd put a lot of people on a heroes list ahead of him.

For me, it comes back to that photo. Ana and her family. Her smile even as she betrays them.

She was born on a military base in Nürnberg, West Germany, in 1957. Her father, Alberto Montes, served there as a US Army physician. He had gone to medical school in upstate New York before joining the army in 1956.[5] After the family moved to Topeka, Kansas, while Ana was a child, Alberto worked at the Menninger Clinic for seven years.

When she was ten, her family moved to Towson, Maryland—just north of Baltimore—a university town with historic buildings dating to the 1830s, a mall, and a theater. There, her father began a psychiatry and psychoanalytic practice, and his family lived in a nice home, and his children went to good schools.[6]

On the outside, it doesn't seem like such a bad life. But the more I learn about people, spies and otherwise, the more I realize how many people face trauma at some point in their lives and how differently it affects each of us, even within the same family.

Ana's parents were from Puerto Rico. It has been reported that her dad supported the Puerto Rican separatist movement, and that he expressed those views in letters and articles, according to research by the DIA.[7] But Ana's sister Lucy says this is absolutely incorrect: "Dad always supported commonwealth status because Puerto Rico was so poor," she said. "He was always a moderate about this and politics in general."

He sent a letter to Vice President Al Gore and the governor of Puerto Rico asking that the territory be allowed to make some of its own decisions, but Lucy said most Puerto Ricans believe that should be the case.

"He was never a separatist, as in 'secession,'" she said. Fidel Castro, however, had other ideas.

The separatist groups have sought independence from the United States since 1898: Puerto Rico has a long history of trying to gain independence from somebody. Before the United States, it was five hundred years of Spanish rule. Puerto Rico was part of the trade pipeline from Spain to the American colonies, which meant it was important to all of Latin America. It remained in Spanish hands until the end of the Spanish-American War in 1898, when both Puerto Rico and Cuba came under US control.[8]

Cuba gained its independence from the United States in 1902, but only after agreeing to allow US control over the Guantanamo Bay military base. Many in Puerto Rico hoped they would also gain independence. So, a group of nationalists launched small attacks at home,[9] attacking and killing shady cops and going after government offices. Some of those nationalists were then executed.

They decided to take the fight to the mainland. In 1950, two of the nationalists attempted to sneak into Blair House in Washington, D.C., to try to kill President Harry Truman as he slept there during renovations to the White House. One Secret Service agent and one Puerto Rican nationalist died during a shootout with the men guarding the Blair House. Pedro Albizu Campos, who led the revolt, was sentenced to eighty years in prison. In 1954, the separatists tried again: they sneaked into the US Capitol and began shooting members of Congress, wounding five of them. After that, support for the movement fell off, for the most part.

Fidel Castro, of course, played on the similarities between Puerto Rico and Cuba as a publicity campaign to gain support for Cuba and against the United States. As Ana was growing up, Fidel Castro told Barbara Walters that he supported the independence of Puerto Rico, which undoubtedly would have been a topic of conversation in the Montes household.

But Ana's sister Lucy told me she doesn't remember her parents being involved in that movement.

"My parents voted in all the elections, but they weren't politically active," she said.

They did care about Puerto Rico—cared that it was poor with the median income in 2018 at $20,000, while 44 percent of the population lived in poverty, according to the US Census[10]—and that it didn't get the resources it desperately needed. Cared that people in the United States didn't seem to care about it or even understand that it's part of their country.

"They both were highly educated, very knowledgeable, and they knew what was going on in the world," Lucy said. "And they definitely had strong opinions about things that were going on." Dinner conversation might have been limited, she said: everyone knew better than to talk about anything touchy when they discussed the latest news.

"He didn't accept differences of opinion," Lucy said of her father. "Maybe that's inherited."

In some ways, Ana's childhood was typical: she liked the beach, soccer, Stevie Wonder, and chocolate chip cookies, according to her high school yearbook.

But as the oldest of four children, Ana had some typical birth order trappings: perfectionism and a need for control. She saw herself as responsible for her two brothers and sister. She told investigators that there had been abuse at home, and that she felt guilt for not being able to protect her siblings.

"It was the belt," Lucy said, "when Dad lost his temper."

Ana was only a year older than Lucy, two years older than their brother Tito, and five years older than Carlos, so she could hardly protect her siblings against an adult man. Still, she stepped in when she could.

"You know, she was the oldest," Lucy told me. "She helped us all at one point or another. She was a little protective in that way. But as far as intervening or protecting us from abuse? No, she couldn't do that. She was a child."

Her father hit all the children, Lucy said, but she only saw him hurt her mother, Emilia, once. At the time, Puerto Rico had a higher rate of child abuse—though mostly neglect—than the rest of the United States, according to the National Child Abuse and Neglect Data System.[11] That is, in part, cultural: gender roles tend to be rigid and dictated by a conservative political system, talking about domestic violence is taboo, and police response is slow or nonexistent, a 2020 series by Type Investigations shows.[12]

But in Towson, the neighbors might have been surprised to learn the respected Freudian psychoanalyst who lived down the street—the man who helped people work through adulthood difficulties brought on by childhood trauma and who was "well regarded"[13] in the community—was the cause of trauma in his own family.

"No parent can emotionally abuse a child like a disturbed mental health professional," Dr. Eric Shaw, an experienced psychologist and recognized expert on insider threat, told me. "In addition to carrying the authority, dependency, and gravitas of a parent, they also carry the professional status and knowledge of a mental health professional. When they lash out, they are likely to cut to the core, indicting the intimate personal characteristics of their kin. They don't just make the child feel guilty about something they have done, they make them feel ashamed of who they are."

But the family no longer lived in Puerto Rico, and Ana's mother wasn't having it. Based on my experience with her, I'd call her a firecracker, and I wouldn't want to get between her and one of her children. As Alberto worked at his practice, Emilia worked as an investigator for a federal employment anti-discrimination office, the Equal Employment Opportunity Commission, and she became well known in the Hispanic community.[14]

In fact, long before Ana listened on a shortwave radio for messages from Havana, her mother had developed strong opinions about the country in the mid-1970s.

"The Cubans and I had our encounters," she told the *Miami Herald*. "They don't fight clean."

Emilia had worked to gain a slot for a group of Hispanic immigrants in the Showcase of Nations city festival in Baltimore. The festival was a big deal: a mayor had worked to bring the international neighborhoods downtown for parties that would bring tourists into the city. Folks could drink German beer, eat kielbasa and gyros, and watch Irish clogging. Italian fest. Greek fest. Korean fest.

Emilia's entourage included people from all over Latin America. But a group of Cuban exiles believed it should have the slot. Emilia didn't see "Cuban Fest" as particularly inclusive.

"They had a knock-down, drag-out fight," fellow activist Javier Bustamante told the *Miami Herald*. Emilia won.

She won against Alberto too. The couple separated when Ana was fifteen, and Emilia divorced Ana's father in 1978, just after the girls left the house for college. Emilia got custody of the younger children, as well as the house, the car, and alimony.

Ana wasn't having it either.

"She was very defiant," Lucy said. "She was the only one. She had a lot of courage."

Ana disobeyed him, but she didn't hide it. Once, when Ana was in college, she wanted to go to Ocean City with her friends for a week during the summer. Her father told her she couldn't.

"She said she was going, and he slapped her," Lucy recalled. "Then she got in the car with her friends and she left."

But Lucy doesn't remember Ana getting in trouble when she got home—she thinks her mother talked her father down, or that perhaps he realized he shouldn't have slapped his adult daughter—that perhaps she was old enough to make her own decisions about a trip to Ocean City.

From a young age, Ana saw herself as a protector. She liked to fight for the underdog, and she always took control. "Monte's childhood made her intolerant to power differentials, led her to identify with the less powerful, and solidified her desire to retaliate against authoritarian figures," the US intelligence community (USIC) wrote in its psychological profile of Montes.[15] Much has been made

Photo by Joan Andrzejewski

*Ana with her mother Emilia, sister Lucy, and former sister-in-law Joan in December 1986.*

about Ana's relationship with her temperamental father, and there's truth to it.

"Even as kids, she didn't share much," Lucy said, then laughed. "I think I was always just the pesky little sister." She never felt close to her sister.

But she remembers that Ana could be compassionate, as do others. Her cousin Miriam Montes Mock remembered that once, when a friend was getting married, Ana pulled money from her wallet to donate because she knew the young couple was low on funds. Ana didn't know them, Miriam said. Another time, Miriam asked Ana why she wore all black that day. A friend had just lost her father, Ana told her, and she wanted to be with her in spirit.[16]

She kept herself neat and was affectionate with her family, Miriam remembered—and she loved Ana's sense of humor.

But life in Ana's family could feel small. Her father paid for Ana and her sister to go to college, but there were only a few jobs he saw as acceptable for women: child psychiatrist, teacher, pediatrician, or nurse. Three of her father's aunts and his sister went to college—and they were all teachers.

"He said that women didn't need to go to college, because they raised the children," Lucy said. "If they went to college, it was to educate their children."

Tito got married while he was in college, Lucy said, but he didn't tell his father for more than a year. "When my father found out, he cut him off," Lucy said. "He refused to pay for the rest of his college." Tito, his father told him, was responsible for his own family.

"Ana seemed to have a need to punish," Lucy said. "My father did too."

Ana inherited her father's "very rigid" moral code, Lucy said. "She can be harsh. She has a few of his negative qualities; she has a few of his positive qualities. She can be very compassionate."

Lucy believes that the Cubans were able to "manipulate" her sister using psychology as a tool.

But I'm not sure. There's nothing that makes me believe Ana did not leap willingly to her fate.

# 2

# It's My Life

Picture this: A beautiful town laid out in 1869 to support a railroad. Minooka. Potawatomi for "good land."

Population? Fewer than five thousand. Everybody knew everybody, and everybody needed somebody to talk about. It's a suburb of Chicago, but it felt like a suburb of Mayberry. Siding and brick buildings. Sprawling fields with pick-your-own corn. Soybeans. Big yards. Sidewalks.

Casseroles from the neighbors, who desperately wanted to see what kind of housekeeper your mother was.

When we moved there, I was in culture shock. So was my mother.

We'd just come from Franklinville, New Jersey, where Mom had worked as a nurse in Camden, Dad had taught physics, and we lived on a dirt road in the sticks. My best friend's dad worked at a refinery across the river not far from South Philly, and the rest of my classmates' dads were blue-collar too. Franklinville was tiny—unincorporated—but it still had a bar, right next door to my best friend's house. My dad and his dad frequented it. Neighbors? Well, there were peach trees in an orchard across the street, where my sister Heather and I played for hours, building forts, climbing trees, and generally getting by without parental supervision.

But Minooka? They meant it when they said, "It takes a village," and we—my sister, my parents, and I—suddenly found ourselves surrounded by typical Midwestern neighborhood scrutiny. We had moved on up to the middle class, and Mom planned to make the best of it.

Now picture this: Dad out in the tidy new yard next to one of the laser-straight sidewalks pouring concrete for a fifty-foot ham radio antenna. The roof of the house hit about halfway up the shaft of the antenna. He used his ham radio—and the towering antenna—to communicate with people around the world.

Wait, your dad didn't do this? Huh.

The neighbors were not pleased, and neither were my sister and I.

Just after we moved, Dad made one of his many unilateral decisions about our lives: Heather and I would also get ham radio licenses so that we, too, could talk to strangers from around the world. After school and on weekends, Heather and I listened not to Bruce Springsteen and Madonna and all the things the other kids listened to, but to Morse code on tape.

*Dah, dit dah dit, dah dit dah...*

Sometimes, whether we wanted to or not, Heather and I sat in Dad's office while he "talked" to strangers around the world in Morse code.

When we weren't memorizing dashes and dots, we learned radio theory in preparation for our ham radio license exams—like why certain messages needed to be transmitted at certain frequencies to be heard in certain parts of the world. Honestly? I didn't care.

But I couldn't argue with my father. Ever.

"You'll need this one day," he said.

Why on earth would I need to know radio theory? People were already using brick-sized car phones. Dad's antenna did not seem like the wave of the future.

Dad would prove to be right.

*Damn it.*

In Jersey, my parents had struggled on the salaries of a nurse and a teacher, so Dad used his physics background—and his incredible intelligence—to get a job in 1980 training engineers how not to melt down the reactor at Commonwealth Edison's nuclear power plant. In 1979, Three Mile Island in Pennsylvania partially melted down, leading to a "voluntary evacuation" of the town—and the twenty-mile area around the meltdown—and costing an estimated $2.4 billion in 2021 dollars to clean up. In response, the industry decided to bring in smart people to train engineers to make sure that never happened again.

So yeah, Dad trained nuclear technicians and engineers.

Mom was a bit easier for me to relate to—calm, caring, and kind, like she came out of central casting for a TV mom. But if Dad worked to keep the region safe, Mom had her hands full with us. Before we left New Jersey, Heather and I spent a lot of time playing on our own, like most kids of that generation. When the streetlights came on, thousands of members of Generation X headed home for dinner or risked being grounded from watching TV.

Heather and I were pretty much inseparable. We slept in the same room and, because our tiny house didn't have air conditioning, often slept on the floor with our heads in the hallway so we could catch some breeze from the family's one fan.

One day, as we played in the peach orchard, genius struck: I would use a magnifying glass to see if I could light a plastic garbage can on fire. I caught the sun just right and hit the can. And then the bush next to it. I screamed in terror as I imagined burning down the entire orchard, and Mom came running. She put out the fire before it got too bad.

Saved.

Except, she wasn't done with me.

She grabbed my wrist and dragged me to the sink. She forced an unlit match into my fingers as she held my wrist. She lit the match and continued to hold my fingers over the base of the match as the fire crept down. Just as the fire licked my finger—the very instant I could feel the heat—she doused my small hand with water and extinguished the match.

"There," she said. "Now you'll never play with fire again."

She was right. For the most part.

Mom hit us with the practical while dad stuck with the academic. They tag-teamed morality by sacrificing financially to send Heather and me to Catholic school. Mom supplemented her nursing income by helping at school and with bingo nights, and often came home smelling of cigarette smoke from the dauber crowd on their big night out. When Mom worked, Dad made dinner—usually fried hot dogs and baked beans.

Yum.

Civilian women taught at St. Catherine's of Sienna, while nuns ran the show as administrators. My biggest memory? Being thrown through the air as I saw black, then white, then grass, then sky. It was a playground fight, and I don't even remember why it happened, but I do remember a heavyset nun pulling me from the fisticuffs and flinging me away. She suspended me from school, and then, when I got home, Mom and Dad punished me again with a grounding.

Ultimately, it was a typical 1980s upbringing—strict but also based in freedom: the freedom to play without direction. The freedom to make decisions, bad or good, and face the consequences. The freedom to learn through hard work. The freedom to figure out how to get the things we wanted because probably Mom and Dad weren't going to spring for a new pair of Levi's jeans—and nobody wanted to go to school in JCPenney's Plain Pockets. In retrospect, that probably set us up pretty well for life.

But I remember some tough moments. My father, without question, is brilliant. I could have studied for twenty hours a day and still never understood the beginnings of his job. To be fair, nuclear science did not interest me. I worked hard at school, but academically, I wasn't an overachiever. And Dad, as brilliant as he is, couldn't always see around his need to explain a thing: if I tried out for the baseball team, he would explain how to play ball—even if he had never donned a glove.

Sometimes Dad got so involved in his own thoughts that it was as if no one else was in the room.

In Minooka, Heather and I loved that we got to walk to school—it was only a mile—except in the northern Illinois winters. Gray. That damp cold that settles in your bones and stays until June. And the wind encountered no obstacles as it blew across the plains. One night after basketball practice, I walked home in the snow in the dark. As I crossed the railroad tracks, my dad drove past...and didn't stop. I walked the rest of the way home, flexing frozen fingers to try to warm them and grumbling under my breath.

"Why didn't you stop?" I asked as I came in the front door of the house.

"I honestly didn't see you," he said, looking confused.

It was dark and snowy. I'm sure he was deep in thought about some nuclear meltdown problem.

Between the household struggle to make ends meet and my dad's absent-minded professor tendency, I became independent quickly.

But Dad's lectures shut me down a bit. I knew I wouldn't be heard, and I'll admit that it gave me a bit of an inferiority complex. It turns out that I'm a fighter, even if I didn't know it then. I needed to prove him wrong, but I also needed to learn to do things my own way. Being shut down as a kid means that, as an adult, I'm a good listener, a good observer. It also means I know how to get a point across when I need to.

But at twelve, as I worked to prove myself, I started as a paperboy for the local rag. The route started a mile from our house, but I didn't mind the distance. I ran cross country and track, so I thought of it as part of my workout. But Sunday mornings? Remember the ads that, pre-internet, used to take up half the paper? Mom cutting coupons and kids digging through the Toys "R" Us pages? On Sundays, I had to combine the ads with the rest of the paper, which meant I had to get up way too early. The ads doubled the weight I carried the rest of the week, so I had to head out twice because I couldn't carry it all at once.

It was uphill, but only one way.

As a shortcut, I crossed a grassy area and went over the semi-abandoned railroad tracks that ran through town. In its heyday, the trains moved grain from the farms to the cities. One snowy morning, as I cut through the field, I caught sight of something odd. It looked like a gun. I picked it up but realized immediately it was not a toy. I put it down, marked the spot, finished my route, and then went home and told my parents.

A couple days after I took the local police to the spot, Dad showed me an article in the newspaper—the same one I delivered every day. "Minooka Teen Finds Loaded Gun," the headline read. I didn't understand how the reporter knew. Reluctantly, Dad admitted that he called the paper.

He wanted to tell the story of a young kid taking initiative and making good decisions.

In 1983, Dad's dad died suddenly. By Christmas of my freshman year of high school, we had moved back to Jersey to be closer to family. We lived in Ocean County—the Jersey shore, though back then, in Jersey, we just called it the "Shore."

Oddly, my cool-kid status—I was shy and dorky, but now armed with a sweet ham radio license—didn't improve after moving halfway through my freshman year. In fact, it's possible that the chip on my shoulder had started to develop into a boulder. I settled in as an outsider.

In homeroom, I sat behind a cute girl named Lora. She loved the hair metal band Night Ranger, and she was nice. And she liked me. Which caught the attention of a big, stocky kid with a bad haircut. Lineman on the football team. "Jimmy," because it was, after all, Jersey. His dad was a state trooper, and Jimmy was, well, a bully. He and his buddies in homeroom harassed me relentlessly, typically by misidentifying my sexual orientation.

I mean, I was fourteen and in a new school. I wasn't dating anybody, male or female.

I was afraid to stand up for myself because I knew Jimmy would kick my ass and it would hurt. A lot. And then my dad would kick my ass again after I got suspended from school for fighting.

I figured there had to be an alternative. The summer after my freshman year, I convinced my mom to let me play football. With Jimmy. One day, lying on the floor of the locker room, mostly undressed except for the athletic tape that pinned my arms to my body and my legs to each other, one of the coaches walked in. He shook his head and kept walking.

Being "taped" was a commonly accepted hazing ritual in high school football—almost like the "Code Red" from *A Few Good Men*. But that didn't make it, or me, cool.

So that whole football thing worked out well.

Music kept me company during those awkward years in high school. Edward Van Halen on MTV. Eddie was a guitar god. And it's damned hard to hear a lecture over a guitar solo. My parents paid for my guitar lessons, and I suddenly knew what color my parachute was. But being a teenager in the late '80s in New Jersey could mean only one thing: Bon Jovi. *Slippery When Wet*. Obviously, I would be the next Jon Bon Jovi. Fuck you, Jimmy. Fuck you, Jimmy's bully asshat pals. And yeah, Dad too—though I still can't quite bring myself to type the words. He's my dad; the thought was fleeting.

I waited to be discovered. Probably I should have practiced while I waited. And it might have helped to have some actual musical talent. I did play in the church folk band (there were cute girls in the "band"), but that would be the extent of the screaming crowds.

Oddly enough, between the ham radio and the bully Jimmy, as well as my dad's formidable personality, I was set for life.

# 3

# Those Spies Hide Out at Every Corner

Revolution always speaks to romantics: Ernest Hemingway. Victor Hugo. James Baldwin.

Ana Montes.

Of course, some romantics pour out their ideas in novels, treatises, or even lyrics. Others get so caught up in a story of their own making that they can't see beyond their personal bit of the tale. The saga of Ana's betrayal begins with a romance not long after the spring break showdown with her father, the rebellion still heating her blood.

During Ana's junior year of college at the University of Virginia, she studied in Spain. Francisco Franco, the military general who had led the Nationalist uprising in the Spanish Civil War and became the country's dictator in 1939, had just died. You could call him "fascist light," as he evaded allying himself with the Axis during World War II, but he still took on much of their language and methods. He ruled cruelly: concentration camps, forced labor, and thousands of executions. He restricted the rights of women, determining they should serve in traditional roles. He made homosexuality illegal. He made deals with Adolf Hitler.

In the 1960s and 1970s, students began to protest—efforts that were shoved down by the police. But before Franco died in 1975, he restored the monarchy. And Juan Carlos, the new king, led the country back to democracy.

It was early days when Ana arrived: in January 1977, tens of thousands of people protested in Madrid against the violence that appeared to be spread by the neo-fascists angered by the king's changes[17]—the nationalists of Spain and those who didn't want to see any move toward the left. The police arrested "seven Argentines, three Cubans, two Australians, an Englishman, a Colombian and a Lebanese" for the violence, according to the *New York Times*. They were all believed to have fascist ties.

In June, the country had its first elections. The new constitution was approved in 1978, so Ana was there for the discussions about what a democracy should look like—and how the people could decide it. The political left supported the king. The king legalized the Communist Party. It felt like a new beginning.

And Ana fell in love. She was young; he was handsome; they were both off-the-charts smart with a strong dose of passion. He was from Argentina, a leftist from a country with a long history of leftism. He talked with her about US support of authoritarian governments—and in Spain, everyone protested against the Americans.

As the Argentinian wooed Ana, Silvio Rodriguez's silver-voiced calls for revolution began to make their way across the ocean. Americans knew they loved the sound, even if they didn't understand the Spanish words.

The year after Ana's study-abroad program, Rodriguez's song "Rabo de Nube" would become an international hit, with The Pretenders eventually recording a cover. Revolution had made the mainstream, and Ana was there for it.

*Ana on her twenty-first birthday in Spain in 1978.*

Ana wrote letters home from Spain to her sister Lucy about her newfound interest in Cuba. She had previously never mentioned the country—at least not more than in passing, her sister said. But in 1978, she realized she liked the idea of the social-communist parties in Europe that she learned about. She began to call herself a "leftist": she supported, generally, social equality—though she didn't consider herself to be a "Marxist," or someone who supported nationalism of the economy and welfare system.[18]

Ana began to hang out with a woman, Ana—or "Mimi"—Colón, who was also from Puerto Rico and who became a close friend. By then, Ana was already against the United States—its policies, its history, and its politics—Mimi remembered.[19] Their friends in Spain were all anti-American.

The two wrote each other letters after they returned home.

While Ana's romance with the Argentinian fizzled with the end of her year abroad, it left its mark. By the time she met her first spy, Ana had already fallen for the cause.

In graduate school at Johns Hopkins School of Advanced International Studies, Ana focused on Central American history. It was the early 1980s, and many of her classmates and professors felt as she did about US involvement there: they saw it as unjust. She believed the US government was killing innocent people.

Ana became friends with Marta Velazquez, who also enrolled at Johns Hopkins in 1982. Marta and Ana began to hang out at school—they had the same classes. Marta was another extremely intelligent woman: she went to undergrad at Princeton, got a law degree at Georgetown.

She and Ana talked about the things that interested them both: President Ronald Reagan's involvement in Iran-Contra—where US officials secretly sold arms to the Iranians to raise money for the Contras, a group of anti-Sandinista rebels hoping to overthrow the socialist Nicaraguan government, but also with the hope of getting Iran to release seven American hostages being held in Lebanon. The US government denied the deal, but also destroyed a whole bunch of documents to try to cover it up. Reagan finally owned up to US involvement while denying personal knowledge of it, allowing Oliver North, a National Security Council staff member, to take the blame.

(Random: Oliver North lives down the road from me now, and I've met him several times. Seems like a regular ol' retired guy.)

Ana wasn't the only American pissed about that, but the list she made with Marta was longer: Ana was also angry about US involvement in El Salvador. The Carter and Reagan administrations gave the country a whole lot of money during the Cold War—about $1 million a day,[20] at one point—and the US military helped with key decisions. In the meantime, El Salvadoran security forces attacked civilian targets and committed 85 percent of the atrocities during the country's civil war between the leftist FMNL and Salvadoran military forces, according to the United Nations.[21] We, the United States, supported the government. Because of communism—the domino effect and all of that. If we didn't take out every communist government, the US government, going back to about 1945, believed communism would spread to neighboring nations, and that would be bad. China and Soviet Union = bad.

There was reason to be angry, and when the United States invaded Grenada in 1983, Ana's views were simply reinforced.[22]

Reagan sent 1,900 US troops to the Caribbean island after a faction of Grenada's Marxist government seized power and killed the prime minister. Suicide bombers had just killed 241 US servicemembers and fifty-eight French peacekeepers in Lebanon, and about one thousand Americans lived in Grenada. Reagan feared they were in harm's way, as well as that the Soviets, and the Cubans, would use the island to launch attacks against the United States. During the US attack, nineteen Americans, twenty-four Cubans, and forty-five Grenadians were killed.

Grenada's government was replaced, and Reagan proclaimed a victory against communism. Some questioned the need for interference and military action. But, in a democracy, there's recourse: You vote. You protest. You debate. Hell, you can even run for office. Ana, instead, was heading toward treason to help a dictator in a country where people don't have those basic rights.

Ana and Marta wrote letters to each other, traveled together, and spent their time talking about Latin American politics. Marta worked as a legal aid at the United States Agency for International Development (USAID), but by 1983, she had begun to work for Cuba. She traveled to Mexico City to meet with Cuban intelligence agents.[23]

At Johns Hopkins, she sniffed out potential spies. Yes, you could send your beloved child off to college only to see agents from foreign governments—or ours—enlist them as spies. In fact, while Marta and Ana were at Johns Hopkins, Kendall Myers and his wife, Gwendolyn, also worked as spies for the Cubans—or had, until they went sleeper. Myers, a blueblood whose family line included Alexander Graham Bell and William Howard Taft, liked to spend his not-spying time on his $300,000 yacht.

Remind me to tell you some time about how the FBI caught him....

In any case, Marta recruited spies for the Cubans. And she worked for the Cubans for free, which is their MO: they aren't a wealthy government, so they rely upon people who believe in the myth. At the time, Marta probably did not have access to classified information, so she wasn't "spying" in the traditional sense. She spotted and assessed and groomed potential candidates.

And Ana brought her right to the family home several times, Lucy remembered.

"They seemed to be very good friends," Lucy said. "She brought her on a few holidays. She was at the birthday party we had for Ana once."

One night, Marta told Ana she had a friend, a Cuban, who wanted to meet her. He worked for the Cuban government at the United Nations, and Marta had told him about her.[24]

"Of course," Ana told her.

I think it was a genuine friendship. Marta didn't use her, and Ana had already expressed her antigovernment views. On December 16, 1984, they took a train trip to New York to meet Millan

Photo by Joan Andrzejewski

*Marta Velazquez with Joan and another Montes family member at a family event in an undated photo.*

Chang-German, a Cuban intelligence officer moonlighting as a diplomat at the Cuban Mission to the United States. Chang, who is Cuban, went by the nom de guerre "El Chino."

Ana went willingly to meet the Cubans. Over the course of a dinner spent talking foreign policy and the wars in Central America, Chang teed up this idea of, "You seem to have a visceral empathy for what we are trying to accomplish in Cuba: Would you mind reading and translating English newspaper articles about the war into Spanish?" It was a soft pitch. Although her employer at the Justice Department may have taken issue with Ana's moonlighting translation gig for the Cubans, Chang didn't ask her up front to commit espionage.[25]

It's a classic recruitment tactic—this soft serve.

But Ana pushed back, "Don't you have people for that? This seems sort of menial." She's a UVA graduate, a master's student. She had more to offer.

Lucy would make a career of translating recordings, documents, and interviews from Spanish to English for the US government: no one would accuse her of "menial" work.

"How about you provide your analysis about what the US government is doing?" Chang said, or something along those lines. Playing on her ego, he sold her.

And then, on the train ride down from New York to Washington, Ana had an epiphany: "You know what? This translating project isn't going to help the Cubans. If I'm really going to help the Cubans, I've got to get a job working in the intelligence community."

Until that moment, Ana planned to finish her master's degree, and then to take that and her UVA degree off to do good around the world with a non-government agency, like Amnesty International or Human Rights Watch. These groups do a lot of work for suffering and oppressed people around the world—including here in the United States—who need help.

Instead, over the course of a three-hour dinner in New York City, the arc of her life changed forever.

"Yup, I'm in."

She and Marta had more meetings, more letters, more glasses of wine—just two students hanging out together, talking about guys, figuring out homework, planning to tell Fidel Castro America's secrets. Marta told Ana the Cuban agent had said Ana would be one of the best, and then she gave her a typewriter and asked her to write a detailed autobiography.[26]

Chang's boss in New York was Mario Monzon Barata, more commonly known by his nom de guerre—or as the Cubans said in Spanish, "seudo" for pseudonym—"Aquilles" According to former Cuban intelligence officer Mandy Gamboa, a pseudonym, whose nom de guerre was "[redacted]," Aquilles deserved most of the credit for recruiting Ana, and probably Marta, as two female agents at a university. Gamboa learned from his friend "Fidelito" that Aquilles received an apartment and awards. At the time of the dinner meeting between Ana, Marta, and Chang, Aquilles was in charge of the Center at the Cuban Mission to the United Nations. In 1984, Aquilles [redacted] significantly altered his appearance to conduct some kind of operational activity in [redacted].

Aquilles died in Cuba around 2004.

On March 29, 1985, Ana and Marta traveled to Madrid, where they met with a Cuban man who gave them false passports. They flew to Prague using those passports and met with two Cuban men, one of whom was an intelligence officer. They went to an apartment, and the men gave them more false passports, as well as clothing to wear to disguise themselves. Then, with the intelligence officer, they flew to Cuba, where everyone called Marta "Barbara."[27]

In Cuba, they learned how to receive encrypted high frequency messages over a shortwave radio and how to beat a polygraph exam. Ana worried about passing the exam because she knew a job in the intelligence community would require it. She pestered the Cubans to teach her how to beat it, despite their clear beliefs that polygraphs are voodoo.

The Cubans told Ana they would never refer to her by her real name again. She would be called "Sonia."

Ana/"Sonia" and Marta/"Barbara" came back home through Prague, then Spain—stopping long enough for Ana to take a picture of Marta in Madrid to prove they had vacationed there.

"Dear Tito & Joan," Ana wrote from Spain, as directed to by the Cubans, "Greetings from Madrid! Marta and I are having a wonderful time and plan to stay 2 weeks…Love Ana."

To be clear, Ana used her soon-to-be FBI agent brother and sister-in-law for operational cover choosing a new—and illegal—relationship with the Cubans over blood.

They returned to the United States April 13 using their real passports.

It was as easy as that. Her sister believes the Cubans manipulated Ana—that they chose someone with something to prove, someone with a save-the-underdog mentality, and probably someone with a bit of a chip on her shoulder as far as her need to be smarter than everybody else.

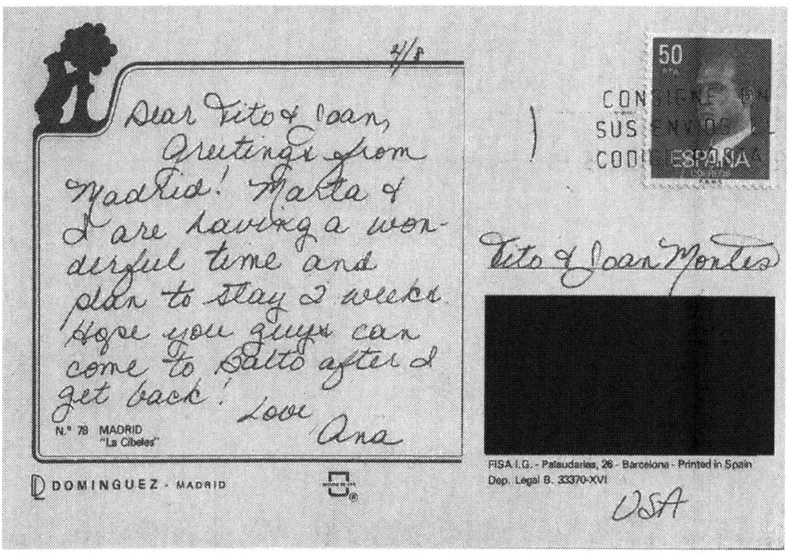


Photo by Joan Andrzejewski

*Postcard sent by Ana at the direction of the Cubans to Tito and Joan, both future FBI agents, to cover for her illegal and covert trip to Cuba with Marta Velazquez in 1984.*

Here's the thing about people with narcissistic personality disorders: They can be quite charming at first. They often are the smartest people in the room, IQ-wise. They can spin tales of adventure and appear to have the confidence to own the room—or suck the energy from the room, depending on your take. But those with a true narcissistic personality disorder also often have a clinically low self-esteem. The charm? It's an act, a need. Underneath the act is constant chatter: *People will see through to the real me and they won't like me. Nobody's as smart as I am and that's why I don't have any friends. People need to be manipulated to my needs because I know what's best.* Their need to come first can preclude them from feeling much of anything about anybody else—about anybody else's views or feelings or even safety.

Only about 1 percent of the population is a true narcissist, and those folks often exhibit a trait that throws off their friends and families: they love to help in grandiose ways. You might call it martyrdom.

They're usually men.

And if you're an expert in spotting people who might make good spies, as the Cubans are brilliant at, you can spot a narcissist—or someone with some of the characteristics of a narcissist—from a mile away.

Ana was ripe for the plucking.

On July 31, 1984, after the two women had completed their coursework, Ana received a book with an inscription from Marta, Lucy said.

"It has been a great satisfaction for me to have had you as a friend and comrade during this time we've spent as students," Marta wrote. "I hope our relationship continues outside the academic sphere."[28]

From now on, Ana and the Cubans used a parole, or the equivalent of a spy handshake, anytime she met a new handler. Upon arriving as a stranger to their first meeting, the Cuban would say "are you a friend of Barbara's?" To which Ana/"Sonia" would reply "no, I'm a friend on Sonia's." Even if the friend part of the first-time greeting got jumbled, the key to part to ensure Ana wasn't meeting with an FBI undercover was him knowing the names "Barbara" and

"Sonia." Once assured, Montes got down to business and the parole wasn't necessary until the next new guy. This is a highly common practice in espionage.

In early 1985, Ana learned she had been hired as a research analyst by the DIA. It's the CIA for the Department of Defense, but it focuses on defense-related collection and analysis targets. Ana despised the CIA and their mission, especially in Central America. The Cubans likely would have loved for her to go there, but the CIA was out of the question for Ana.

But she was surprised by how easy it was for her to get into the DIA. Marta helped her get the job. It was an entry-level position, and she would spend her days combing through documents and media reports—including those coming out of Central America—and handing off what she had gathered to analysts above her, who would then use the information to assess the military environment and advise defense officials.

Two weeks after returning from Cuba, Ana met with Mimi, Mimi recalled recently. Ana bragged about her "vacation" in Cuba, which included visiting Cuban military bases. She gushed about her Cuban chaperone. And she told Mimi the DIA had just hired her.

"What's that?" Mimi asked.

Ana explained.

"You?" Mimi said. "That doesn't make any sense at all. It's pro-US, then?"

She thought Ana planned to become a schoolteacher, just as her father had wanted.

"Yes," Ana told her. "I've realized I'm an American girl, and this is the center of where everything is happening."

Mimi was stunned. Ana Belen—Mimi always referred to her friend with both her first and middle name—had said no country felt like home, including the United States. Mimi thought her friend had grown patriotic—growing conservative with age—and that she had visited Cuba as part of her job at DIA. Today, Mimi understands the seriousness of Ana's naïve disclosure. Ana realized her slip up—if DIA questioned Mimi, the gig would be up—and quickly broke off her relationship with Mimi. They never spoke again—and that was unusual.

"She was a Puerto Rican girl, like Ana, and all of a sudden she just vanished," Lucy said. "And their friendship ended." But Ana keeps her friends, Lucy said, "holds tightly" to them, so she remembered that it seemed odd that their friendship would blow up so suddenly.

"My mother asked what happened, and Ana said, 'Well, we don't talk anymore,'" Lucy said.

Lucy and her family couldn't begin to suspect that, by the time Ana walked into DIA in September 1985, she had already become a full-fledged spy for Fidel Castro.

Every day that followed would be torture for her.

# 4

# You'll Never Get Rich

I applied to Saint Joseph's University because my dad went to Saint Joseph's College. Dad had a physics degree from St. Joe's, and he started out as a high school physics teacher. He did that for ten years, and then he took a job with Commonwealth Edison in Illinois to teach the engineers how to make sure the nuclear power plant didn't melt down.

The smartest guy in the room.

We moved back to New Jersey for a job at the Oyster Creek Nuclear Plant, which is how I spent my high school years falling for Cinderella, Bon Jovi, and Van Halen.

And so it was that I applied to study at my father's alma mater. I didn't know what I wanted to major in, but I knew I wanted to be on "Hawk Hill"—the nickname for dad's cherished school.

But…

My grades weren't stellar and my SAT score didn't have a comma. Still, I thought my alumni connection would count for something.

I didn't get in.

Not long after, I got my acceptance letter from West Chester University. I knew it was a state school on the other side of Philly, that it sat in a cool college town, and that it was the home of the summer training camp for my Philadelphia Eagles.

But my roommate—Joe Ashman. That dude changed my life. He had a close relationship with his dad. In fact, they were more like friends. His mom, Barbara Ann, reminded me of my own mom. His family treated me like a son, like they enjoyed my company, and like they were interested in what I had to say. It's amazing what that will do for a fellow's self-esteem.

Get this: before Barbara Ann dated Joe's dad, she went on a date with Mike Love from The Beach Boys.

Joe's mom isn't *the* Barbara Ann, but it's still a cool story.

I struggled through my first semester. Joe and I took a required Algebra I class, and the professor was brutal. Half of the class started failing early on, and Joe dropped the class right at the deadline. But my dad said I had to muscle through.

I failed.

I also had to take a gym class. Since I had been a lifeguard at our local lakes during my summers in high school, I figured advanced life-saving would be simple.

I puked after each of the first three classes.

Our instructor, a former Navy SEAL, had served in the Vietnam war. Most of my classmates were on the swim team. I was so far out of my league. The instructor could hold his breath for days, which I learned when he held me underwater, grinning, to recreate the feeling of a panicked drowning victim.

After my fourth day of swim-and-puke, I called Dad crying to beg to drop the class. Not an option. I signed up for it, so I would complete it. I passed—barely.

But even as I struggled, Joe already knew what he wanted to do with his life: he wanted to be a Maryland state trooper. Now this intrigued me. I had been initiated into the world of state troopers by Jimmy, my childhood nemesis. His dad was a Jersey state trooper. Jimmy was an asshole, so I figured his trooper dad was also an asshole—but the Jersey state police still fascinated me. They had impressive uniforms, and their single emotion seemed to be impassive.

I also told Joe my dream: rock star with a minor in business.

That way, I could open a music store and sell guitars as a backup. My friend and confidant laughed in my face: he knew how little I practiced.

Maybe I needed a backup for my backup.

"Hey," I asked him one day, "don't cops get free coffee?"

"Yeah," he said, "I guess so."

"And don't cops just walk into car dealerships and tell the salesman they're not paying sticker price because, you know, 'We're cops'?"

Joe hadn't heard about that perk.

Though I would eventually drink plenty of free coffee, my ethics improved.

The biggest perk? I wouldn't have to compete with my dad.

Thanksgiving of my freshman year, back when I was still thinking I wanted to be a rock star, Dad and I drove down High Street past West Chester University in his Plymouth Horizon. It was a sunny, gorgeous fall day, and we cruised toward Mom and a big family meal in Jersey. I told him that if I didn't become the next Bon Jovi, I was thinking of getting a business degree and opening a guitar shop.

"I have bad news," Dad said.

*Whoa. Mom all right? Did the dog die?* My head spun with the possibilities.

"You need to start thinking about joining ROTC."

The what?

The Army Reserve Officers' Training Corps.

The army was the furthest thing from my mind. I was trying not to fail algebra and not to be drowned by a maniac former Navy SEAL. And even if I had a backup plan or two, I still believed I would eventually play in front of thousands of people on MTV.

Dad had served in the National Guard as a commissioned officer, but he'd never even hinted that was the path I should take. He enrolled in the ROTC at St. Joe's. Mostly, it kept him out of Vietnam. But none of that had anything to do with me.

"I just lost my job," he said. "I can't pay for college."

At that point, I had paid a couple grand for my first semester, and we had split it.

I would have to pay for my own school.

So, I went to basic training between my freshman and sophomore years of college in 1989. I was infantry, so I went to Fort Benning, Georgia, and it sucked. I mean, it was just miserable. A lot of people love that shit—they want to go to the field to get away from their spouses, and they want to cook SPAM over a potbellied stove, and they like to play in the dirt and be stinky and challenge themselves to do all the things we're no longer required to do in modern society.

I am not that guy. I want my bed. I want my fan. I want my blackout mask. And I need my eight hours of sleep. I mean, I'll do it, and I did do it, but I won't say that I ever embraced the suck.

Probably for that reason, I never felt like I quite fit in with the grunt crowd. I'm pretty sure they weren't impressed.

After I got back from basic, I worked—loaded boxes at UPS at five o'clock in the morning, which also sucked. And drill weekend always inevitably happened while everyone else got ready for the homecoming game, or the night of a big party, or during spring break as my buddies headed anywhere but a Pennsylvania base camp in March.

I know. But this was long before the wars in Iraq and Afghanistan, and my weekend sojourns didn't quite feel as if they served any purpose—I wasn't taking on the Taliban.

However, I did learn, like everybody else who makes it through boot camp, that I could do a lot of things without breaking, even if I didn't like the bugs and the mud and that damned cot. Grown-ass man sleeping in a bunk bed. No.

I also developed a strong sense of patriotism. I think you'd be hard-pressed to find someone who has served who doesn't tear up a bit during the national anthem, no matter their politics. That's because, in addition to whatever your personal feelings are about what that flag stands for, veterans know that it stands for all the people who served before them—the people who died for that flag and this country—as well as all the people we served with ourselves and those who followed us in taking the oath.

I appreciated that feeling, and I found I had a deep, and maybe unexpected, need to serve.

I decided I wanted to join the FBI. I wanted to be all that I could be—outside the army, because of the army. After basic, I knew I didn't want to settle for being a local cop. It's a great gig, especially if you're a hometown kind of person. But I wanted to serve in the greatest law enforcement agency in the world.

After joining the army, I went to Airborne School and, later, made plans (which didn't pan out) to go to Ranger School. I believed in all that "Be All You Can Be" shit. Still do. All of that was a building block to the FBI.

If I got into the FBI, well, that was a big fucking deal.

And the accomplishment would be completely my own.

5

# Nobody Does it Better

No one was more surprised about Ana's new gig than Ana—not that she'd snatched up some primo job, but DIA leaned heavily on testosterone in the mid-1980s, and she didn't have any experience in the defense sphere.

"I didn't know the difference between a corporal and colonel, and I'm not kidding," she later said. "I didn't even know which service was wearing the green uniform and which service was wearing the blue."[29] Her father would have worn the green one.

About a third of Defense Intelligence Agency employees wear a military uniform, while the rest are civilian employees of the army, navy, air force, marines, or Defense Department. DIA provides intelligence to the military for both combat and noncombat missions, and it often uses human intelligence to do so, including covert agents.

Because she had no military or intelligence background, Ana believed DIA hired her because she was a Spanish linguist, because of her degree, and because she was a woman.[30]

She worked as a researcher: she read all the news coming through, in both English and Spanish, and all the intelligence she was eligible to see, based on her security clearance, and then she passed the important things to an analyst to format into information that could be given to the higher-ups.

But she was good at it. She had the academic pedigree, and she was book smart, well-spoken, and well-versed in her subject area. She drove to her office at Bolling Air Force Base—now Joint Base Anacostia-Bolling—sat down at her desk, and went to work. She didn't hang out at the water cooler. She didn't make friends. She worked. She was into *Star Trek*, and she liked to watch *Law & Order*. But otherwise, she spent her downtime reading everything she could about Central America. Dream employee, right?

For Ana, in those early days, it probably seemed too easy: she had joined DIA before a polygraph became a requirement for the job. Instead, DIA randomly selected employees to take the test—and she never made that list.

Ana was cocky. She was cocky to the point that her coworkers hated her. When you think about the time, some of that could be explained away: she was a woman working in a man's world, and brass balls came with the job. But a lot of it was just Ana. It's what her sister described from her childhood. It's the defiance that appeared when her father told her she couldn't go to the beach.

She was so good at her job that by 1986, after just one year on the job, she moved from researcher to analyst. Her bosses praised her every move. She started working El Salvador/Nicaragua, staying on that beat until 1992. While Ana didn't see herself as a communist, she sympathized with the goals of the Cuban and Nicaraguan revolutions.[31]

In January and February of 1987, she spent five weeks in El Salvador and one in Guatemala to orient herself to her new job—it was her first DIA trip.[32] It may have been her most lethal, her proving ground for the Cubans. I believe she got a Green Beret killed, but we can't put her directly in a meeting with him. But she would have been negligent in her duties at DIA had she traveled to El Salvador and not met with the senior expert on El Salvador: Staff Sergeant Gregory Fronius. Fronius would have said to her, "This is where I'm going. This is my mission. This is what I'm doing." And somebody told the Farabundo Martí National Liberation Front—the FMNL—exactly those things. Ana had the account at the time.

She went to El Salvador with a different Green Beret—she worked with him. And...she dated him. All muscle and completely not what you would have expected as her type. In any case, as they were gallivanting around El Salvador, it seems like he would have said, "Hey. There's this guy I want you to meet." Fronius. The Green Berets are a tightly knit community, and the two were likely pals or at least acquaintances: they would have been in meetings together, likely would have trained together, and certainly would have known somebody who would have said, "Hey. Ana should hook up with Fronius while she's in El Salvador." There would have been no reason not to introduce Ana to Fronius—it would have been negligent if Fronius didn't meet with her: she had the clearance and it was her job. And he was an intelligence specialist. She did visit the base where he was stationed in El Paraíso.

Fronius, along with one other American, worked as an adviser at the base. At 2 a.m., March 31, 1987, the other soldier was away. As everyone slept, FMNL, the Marxist rebel group, started to fire mortars and rockets at a headquarters building on the base in El Paraíso. That morning, only a quarter of the usual one thousand troops were there, as everyone else was out on operations or training.

Ana would have known that.

And the rebels knew exactly where to aim. Ana would have known where the important buildings were too.

As the explosions began, Fronius tried to launch a counterattack. By that time, the rebels had entered the compound. As Fronius worked to rally local forces to fight back, he was killed.

Fronius, twenty-seven, died along with sixty-nine Salvadoran soldiers. He had a wife and two kids, Gregory, who was six, and

Francine, who was one. The Salvadoran soldiers undoubtedly had families as well, who had never heard of Ana Montes, but who likely died because of intelligence she provided.

In the background, Castro encouraged the rebels.

Scott Carmichael, who worked counterintelligence at DIA and would place the blame for Fronius's death on Ana, allowed that rebel forces could have received the information from other sources and the attack might have taken place without Ana's help. That's probably true, but Scott probably wouldn't have known about Ana's affair with the other Green Beret. And "allowing" isn't the same as "believing." He believed she got Fronius killed.

The years that followed only deepened Ana's beliefs that she was doing the right thing.

In 1989, President George H.W. Bush sent troops to Panama to get rid of General Manuel Noriega. Oddly enough, Noriega had been an informant for Bush's CIA, and he'd also supported the United States against the Sandinistas in Nicaragua and the FMNL in El Salvador. But Noriega, not surprisingly, worked as a double agent,[33] and the CIA cut ties. In 1988, US courts found him guilty of drug smuggling and money laundering. At the time, President Ronald Reagan had refused to hit Noriega because of his US ties—and particularly because of Bush's ties, as well as Bush's chances in the 1988 presidential election. But Noriega started to change his alliances to the Soviet side. He started to get some help from Cuba. He lied about election results in Panama, blaming his loss on the United States. Finally, he, and his general assembly, declared that Panama was at war with the Americans.

The next day, December 16, 1989, Noriega's troops opened fire on several American service members when they went out for dinner at a Marriott in Panama City. Marine Corps First Lieutenant Robert Paz died from his injuries. The day after that, Bush sent in the troops: Operation Just Cause. Ana feared the same would happen to Cuba.

"If the United States could invade Panama for no justifiable reason, then they could just as easily invade Cuba and take advantage of their weakness," Ana said.[34]

As many as one thousand Panamanians died, as well as twenty-three Americans, including four Navy SEALs who were trapped on the airport tarmac as they disabled Noriega's plane so he couldn't escape.[35]

Noriega sought refuge at the Vatican's diplomatic mission (embassy), so US troops blared rock music—U2, The Clash, Van Halen…and Bon Jovi's "Wanted Dead or Alive"—until Noriega gave himself up on January 3.

By this time, Ana had already voiced some divergent opinions about Central America. She believed Bush was wrong to go in, but she wasn't alone in her beliefs: the United Nations General Assembly said the move violated international law. But her outspokenness would come back to haunt her.

She still didn't see Cuba as a threat. She believed Castro had gone to the Russians only to protect itself against the United States.[36] And as the Soviet Union fell in 1991, she feared the United States would attack "the Pearl of the Antilles." She felt the country needed her help to protect itself, because the Soviet Union was no longer there for them. That's when she grew into her role as an expert.

At this point, and for her first seven years at DIA, she spied for Cuba but didn't have access to US information about Cuba unless it had to do with Nicaragua or El Salvador. But she happily shared what she had with Cuba, and they happily shared it with the Sandinistas.

In 1992, Nicaragua died down because we were no longer there. In 1990, Nicaragua elected Violeta Chamorro president in a democratic election. Ana could let her outrage against the US's Nicaragua policy go.[37]

Eventually, there would be a new war, a new enemy, a new need for information. Ana fit into classic Soviet-era tactics, now embraced by Cuba: they play the long game. Ana was a slow-moving pawn in a decades-long match.

She worked hard for it. She was well-accomplished, and she got some pretty significant awards for her work as an analyst on Cuba. She earned her way into a fast-track program for managers, as well as the Exceptional Intelligence Analyst Program, which allowed her to work on projects she chose. Already in 1988, her bosses said she was one of the most capable analysts in the office and had high potential.[38]

She also paid for it. At work, she had no friends. They had an occasional laugh—her coworkers say she had a quick wit. Her coworkers also said she was "frigid" and superior.[39] She rarely left her cubicle, even for lunch. She ate at her desk. At office birthday parties—sheet cake and small talk—she fidgeted, as if she couldn't wait to get back to her desk.[40] They called her *la otra*, or "the outsider," but not to her face.

People talked to her because they had to: "Hey, we're going to work on this project together," versus, "Hey, let's go grab lunch together."

She was intellectually arrogant. She was a bully in meetings. If you disagreed with her, she'd beat you down—and worse, she was often right. But you can be right without being an asshole.

Again, you think about James Bond and how charming he was—but he was a raven: his job was to charm information out of people. Ana fit a different kind of profile. Robert Hanssen, the former FBI agent who spied against the United States for Russia, had a nickname that fit a similar profile: "the mortician." He was weird, a little creepy, and highly religious of the Opus Dei variety. People just got a bad vibe from him. People got a bad vibe from Ana too.

It makes sense, when you think about it: these are people who believe they've got it right and everybody else is an idiot. It doesn't lend itself to "Let's be pals."

Hanssen handed off the names of Russian KGB agents secretly working for the United States—the Russians killed three of them—and managed to live with himself. His dad had been emotionally abusive, but man, a lot of dads were emotionally abusive and their kids didn't grow up to be secret agents for the bad guys.

Ana worked people over on a daily basis, like Gordon Gekko was her spirit animal. She manipulated information to gain an advantage over her colleagues for competitive positions, winning spots she probably shouldn't have had from people who should have, simply by making sure they didn't hear about it. Games. She worked her networks and the system and got access that caused everyone to believe she was amazing at her job.

I'm not going to try to tell you the United States has always been an angel when it comes to the Cuban government—so I won't make that argument here. But I will say the Cuban propaganda machine, and Ana's role in it, has led to our collective idea of the island as a paradise filled with universal healthcare and 1957 Chevys and beautiful pink houses.

When thousands of people rose up in 2021 to protest human rights abuses, we got a better taste of what life in Cuba was all about: black market goods, government censors, indiscriminate punishment, and a healthcare system that features recycled needles and used catheters for all. Is that partially our fault? Undoubtedly—that US policy left Cubans feeling so desperate to get rid of a dictator, Fulgencio Batista, who killed thousands of people and embezzled money from the government and who was backed by the United States, that they launched a revolution. But did they know Fidel Castro would ditch his nationalist robes for communism and an alliance with the Soviet Union?

Nope.

(They never do. But that's what always happens.)

Did they know they would be cut off from the rest of the world, unable to speak to—let alone visit—friends and family?

They did not.

Landowners and religious figures, as well as much of the middle class and Castro's former revolutionary allies, fled the country. The United States hit the country with an embargo—economic sanctions—in the 1960s. The United States also wanted compensation for the US companies, mostly sugar plantations and cattle ranches, Castro had nationalized during his takeover. And they weren't super happy about his having a Soviet ally—and the Soviets' nuclear missiles—fewer than ninety miles from Key West. The embargoes increased after the Soviet Union fell because the United States hoped increased pressure would cause Cuba to collapse, or at least move toward democracy.

That didn't pay out, just as, decades earlier, neither did the Bay of Pigs, when President John F. Kennedy sent 1,400 CIA-trained Cubans to invade the country. They surrendered to Cuban troops within twenty-four hours. Someone, it turned out, had tipped off Castro that they were coming.

Someone like Ana?

Cuba's government blames the United States for its problems even as it represses its people, mismanages money, and takes advantage of workers. And other countries still do business with Cuba—there's always a loophole that keeps renegade countries afloat.

Human Rights Watch reported that Cuban police "arbitrarily" arrested, beat, and abused—including sexually—the 2021 protestors. Cuba shut down the rallies. At least one person was killed. And hundreds of protestors have simply disappeared. This isn't new. Castro was known for tossing people who caused problems in jail or harassing them.

White men, for the most part, rule in Cuba, even though Afro-Cubans make up at least one-third of the country. Women? Right. They are expected to fill traditional roles. The protestors have been mostly people of color.

But...

In 1980, Castro let a lot of people leave Cuba, and many of them came to the United States, under President Ronald Reagan, and they voted based on strong embargos. It's hard to get elected in Florida without a strong anti-Castro push.

Even so, by the time President Bill Clinton came into office, there weren't enough good reasons to keep the embargo. The relationship started to warm, until, in 1996, Cuba shot down two American planes over international waters.

We'll get to that.

Every day Ana went into work, she arrived promptly at 8 a.m., and she went immediately to her desk. Computer on, head down.

She would have a topic the bosses wanted her to research, analyze, and write about. That would get published within the intelligence community. She looked constantly at all the intel coming in from different sources—Cuban media, US media, satellite images, whatever military intelligence brought in—and then summarized it from a military perspective. She wrote about the political environment, the stability of the regime, the accumulation of new weaponry, the possible intent of their movements.

She might write an article about force protection at Guantanamo Bay. She might say, "I think the Cubans are going to do this. I think the Cuban military is going to do that. Based on my analysis, I don't think they're a threat." Other analysts throughout the community might have disagreed, which isn't unusual: reasonable people disagree all the time. But Ana likely would have shut them down.

Prickly.

Brittle.

Her primary audience was the Defense Department, but the CIA would also have been interested.

"She certainly had a reputation for arrogance but was deemed an expert," recalled Randy Pherson, a career CIA analyst and the national intelligence officer for Latin America from 1996 to 2000. But he didn't find her impossible to work with: "Montes had strong opinions but showed flexibility."

If she hadn't been brilliant at her job, she wouldn't have gained the access she did, and she could have been fired. Because she was the "Queen of Cuba," people invited her to their meetings, which meant she had more access. The more she produced, the more doors opened. She absolutely was the most senior Cuban analyst at the Defense Department.

She never took anything home—no discs, no documents, no notes. She didn't take pictures with a miniature camera or scan documents with the end of a pen. At lunch, with her tuna sandwich and her *Henry V* deception quote where she could see it, she memorized three things she learned she thought the Cubans needed to know.

And then she went home, every single night, and wrote up on her laptop what she had learned.

She should have thrown that laptop in the Potomac.

# 6

# Ain't No Cure for Love

On Wednesday nights my junior year at West Chester, I took an international relations class at the south campus with Dr. Polsky. I figured the class could help in my bid to get into the FBI.

The second or third Wednesday of class, this tiny, beautiful blonde woman with big hair and a white Eric Clapton T-shirt—Jersey girl—showed up. It had rained. Oh Jesus. I fell hard immediately. She was a freshman, a smart one.

It was probably three-quarters of a mile back to the main campus, and I, as BMOC, had a car. "Hi there. My name is Pete. Would you like a ride in my Geo Prizm?" I'm not sure why, but it worked. Soon after that, we went on a nice date. We went to a movie, and after the movie, we sat on a couch.

That was on my front porch.

For me, it was love at first sight.

And then she told me about her boyfriend.

I was devastated. I had listened to enough long-haired '80s rock to know that if I didn't keep her, I'd probably die. He was a guy she had dated in high school, which I learned from her roommates when I was with one of them crying about losing the love of my life.

Six weeks later, after much persistence on my part, we started dating. And then we were steady, never apart in the way that you are with your first love. Everything was life-or-death. I didn't even know who I was—hadn't even developed a taste for good beer yet—but here I was certain I could pick a life mate.

Honestly, I didn't do too badly: Jen was smart and career-oriented—she planned to get a business degree and spent much of her time planning for her MBA. And she supported me in all my endeavors, as much as she could. But neither of us could have guessed how much of a strain Ana Montes would place on our relationship.

I was two years older than she, so I graduated first. When she graduated, about two years later, we wanted to move in together, but my parents were strict Catholics and not as into the idea as we were.

"Look," my mom said, "we will help pay for the wedding."

Jen and I had already talked about marriage and knew we were heading that way, so, in November 1995, on Veterans Day, we got married in West Chester, Pennsylvania. I was working on my master's degree, and she was working on her MBA.

At the time, I was pushing the army thing—this quest to prove myself started early—and I wanted to go to Army Ranger School at Fort Benning, Georgia. But Jen quickly killed that idea: "That's not the lifestyle I want." This was pre-9/11, and there hadn't been a lot of conflict or deployments, so it wasn't that so much as she didn't want to move every three years from some base in the middle of nowhere to another base in the middle of nowhere. Military spouses have a tough time building their own careers, and she had worked hard. And I wanted the Ranger tab, but I don't know that I wanted to *be* a Ranger.

Bed.

Pillow.

Instead, we decided to jumpstart our careers. We would wait on kids. She would finish her MBA and I would finish my master's, and we would live happily ever after.

Jen—my Jersey girl with big hair and a love for alt-rock—would prove to be my only emotional connection to Ana Montes.

# 7

# Lies Can't Disguise What You Fear

At first, Reg Brown just didn't dig Ana Montes. But that wasn't unusual: nobody liked Ana Montes.

By 1996, she served as acting division chief for an important DIA shop. But instead of taking a prestigious—and better-paying—management position, she told her bosses she loved her job as an analyst too much to move up.

It allowed her to stay in the weeds reading raw intelligence. The higher she rose in management, the more "boss stuff" she would have to do that would take her away from her daily memorization practice.

But to aid the cause, she stole prime assignments—assignments meant for people in other departments—and she did it through underhanded means. She could manipulate information like no one else, and she had a particular penchant for making sure it didn't reach the people it needed to reach.

Reg and Ana worked together at Bolling Air Force Base, where Reg was a counterintelligence agent who specialized in Cuba for the

DIA. Ana's job was to see how Cuba's military could affect US operations, so their work overlapped. In fact, she saw everything he did, and he saw everything she did.

One could chalk it up to jealousy: she was a superstar. And, like everyone else, if he questioned her, she shut him down. But Reg didn't think that was it, and the more he watched Ana, the more his gut told him something was off.

So, he reported some of her behavior to Scott Carmichael, who wrote about it in his book, *True Believer*. Scott also worked at DIA, but as one of the agency's two mole hunters: he and his partner looked for people within DIA who spied for other countries. Scott's best sources had always been DIA employees who sensed something was off with a coworker, so he arranged a meeting with Reg.

Some of Reg's concerns about Ana could be attributed to a woman who knew how to do her job. She met with Cuban faculty members from the University of Havana; was aggressive in her efforts to get sensitive information from agencies outside DIA by networking, attending conferences, and getting in on special projects—even attending meetings that no one from DIA had been invited to; and was involved in a series of coincidences related to the Brothers to the Rescue shooting.

That last bit? That was national news, and Ana had definitely been involved.

Castro always needed a boogeyman to stay in power, and the boogeyman was the United States. He was fighting the imperialists, and that story helped him oppress his own people. So the United States would try to improve relations—President Clinton tried to improve diplomatic relations—and Castro would torpedo it. He didn't want good relations. He needed to be seen as the victim to the bully: the United States.

But Cuba had been working on its international image after the fall of the Soviet Union, playing on nostalgic images of classic cars and Ricky Ricardo, as well as the humanitarian needs of its people after support from the Soviets dissipated. For a couple of years, the

United States allowed some humanitarian aid to the country, but by 1996, US policy had stopped the flow. Cuba needed a win—a way to play itself as a victim who faced harassment from a global leader, even in Cuba's time of need.

Ana could help.

In 1995 and early 1996, an organization called Brothers to the Rescue flew above the waters around Cuba, ostensibly looking for fleeing citizens on rubber rafts trying to make their ways to Miami. The Brothers would save them. But they also flew straight over Cuba and dropped propaganda pamphlets about Castro's government.

In early February 1996, retired US Navy admiral Eugene Carroll, along with other retired officers and diplomats, met with representatives of the Cuban armed forces in Cuba, including Cuban general Ulises Rosales del Toro, the minister of agriculture. Del Toro told the Americans the Cuban government would shoot down Brothers to the Rescue if they entered Cuban air space. Carroll reported this message back to US Congress members. Ana arranged the meeting.

One of the Brothers to the Rescue's pilots, Juan Pablo Roque, had previously flown for the Cuban air force. In Miami, he worked with the FBI. But on February 23, 1996, he hightailed it back to Havana.

Weird.

On February 24, a Cuban MiG-29UB shot down two Brothers to the Rescue Cessnas over international waters as they returned home from dropping pamphlets over Cuba. The Cubans killed four people: Carlos Costa, Armando Alejandre Jr., Mario de la Peña, and Pablo Morales.

And on February 25, 1996, retired US Navy admiral Eugene Carroll sat down with CNN.

"They asked us, 'What would happen if we shot one of these down?'" Carroll told Catherine Callaway about his visit to Cuba. "'We can, you know.' And my response was it would be a public relations disaster."

He said the United States would see it as proof that Cuba was led by a violent regime and as a reason to get tougher with them.

But he also said the US government wasn't following its own regulations because Brothers to the Rescue had been filing false flight plans, which led to Cuban resentment against the United States.

But then he took it one step further, leading to what many saw as a Cuban public relations coup: "I'll give you an analogy," Carroll told Callaway on CNN. "Suppose we had the planes flying over San Diego from Mexico, dropping leaflets and inciting against Governor [Pete] Wilson. How long would we tolerate these overflights after we had warned them against it?"

Suddenly it seemed as if Brothers to the Rescue had been doing Cuba dirty, and like the Americans could have prevented it and didn't.

Cuba saw it as a public relations disaster—for the United States. And Reg Brown saw Ana's fingerprints all over it.

Ana had arranged Carroll's meeting with the Congress members and the DIA on February 23. It could have been a coincidence, but she had waited three weeks from the time she called the admiral to the time she set up the debriefing, which gave Cuba time to plan an operation. Roque disappearing the day before the shooting seemed awfully odd. And the debriefing occurred the day before the shooting: the Americans had been warned but undoubtedly believed they would have time to think about it.[41]

Roque showed up on Cuban television on February 26. He said Brothers to the Rescue wanted to deter any good relations between Cuba and the United States.

As Ana drove from her Cleveland Park apartment to DIA after the shooting—past the midcentury bungalows and fifty-year-old oak trees and the seventy-five-year-old Italian restaurant on the corner—and as she turned right onto Connecticut Avenue, she saw her handler, "German," standing on the corner.[42]

He flagged her down, in plain view.

So, she pulled over.

"We're in crisis mode here," her handler said, or something along those lines. "We shot down a Cessna."

It would have been public by that point, and it seems as if Ana would have known before just about anybody. But Lucy said Ana didn't know. "I was the one who called and told her about it after I saw it on the local news," she said. "I was surprised she didn't know yet—she seemed stunned." But the Cubans knew Ana would be pulled in to help deal with the fallout. They needed to meet every night, he told her—the Cubans needed to know what the US government had planned.

The Pentagon called all hands on deck. That meant DIA analysts working Cuba needed to be nearby. President Clinton was thinking about attacking Cuba in retaliation, and Ana was an analyst—a top analyst—on the Cuba team. She could have said, "You know, Castro needs a boogeyman...."

She could also have sat this one out, given that her team, Cuba, had just shed American blood.

But at some point, a coworker saw Ana answer a personal phone call. Generally speaking, folks aren't taking personal phone calls when it's all hands on deck in a crisis situation. But Ana did, and she seemed flustered.

If the Pentagon is in a crisis situation, early could be midnight.

She said, to everybody and nobody, "I have to leave at 8 p.m."

What the fuck?

To her coworkers, it didn't sound as if she was asking permission to leave early during a crisis. She stated a fact.

She had no kids. She had no dog. She didn't even have a goldfish. Everybody canceled any plans they had that day, but she found a way to leave. She managed to dictate her own terms and did it effectively enough that no one questioned it.

And she had to. Every night, she met with Ernesto. She had an amiable relationship with him, of course, but by this point, she was also dealing with some serious anxiety. She couldn't sleep at night. She worked out like a madwoman at the gym in Cleveland Park. Cardio. Constant cardio. She was seeing a therapist.

Picture this: Ana's lying on a couch, shrink behind her scribbling in a notebook.

"Well, you see, I'm spying for Cuba...."

I don't imagine that's how it went down. But over Ana's every action hung the threat that the Americans would catch her if she made a mistake.

Reg Brown could have been it, the man who brought her down. And Scott Carmichael thought Reg made some good points. Scott could investigate—he could look for moles—but he couldn't arrest. He needed the FBI for that.

But...Ana had been a model employee. Not just "model" but "*the* model." She was highly respected and had moved on up quickly without even a blemish on record. She had passed a polygraph just two years before. She emitted golden light, and the FBI would not have been impressed. (This was all pre-Pete: I wasn't even in the FBI yet.)

In fact, Pherson, the national intelligence officer, put together an interagency task force to work on a sensitive intelligence challenge relating to Cuba. This task force had an off-site location where each member had their own computer. People often worked after hours or on weekends.

After one such weekend, Ana arrived early on a Monday and promptly notified Pherson of a security violation she discovered while "working" over the weekend. And told Pherson she found one of the other member's computers unlocked—good cyber security practice includes logging out when you walk away from your computer. Ana managed it perfectly. She took advantage—no doubt—of the unlocked computer to look at intelligence from another agency, and then reported the computer's assignee for a security violation in case someone learned she accessed it.

Perfect.

But Reg nagged Scott: "She's no good. If I'm right, it's bad, real bad."

Scott remembered his mantra about trusting people's instincts about their coworkers, and he went back to the FBI with information about how Ana had manipulated her way into a special Cuba project by making sure no one else was even considered for it.

"Go ahead," the FBI told Scott. "Interview her."[43]

# 8

# I Walk These Streets

I graduated from West Chester in 1992 with my undergrad degree in criminal justice and an army commission as an infantry officer and second lieutenant in the Pennsylvania Army National Guard. I had to go back to Fort Benning for the infantry officer's basic course.

Although I had been back to Fort Benning for Airborne School, the officer's basic course wouldn't involve sixty men to a room and a drill sergeant who told me I looked like I shaved with a cat/that his pimples were older and wiser than my dumb ass/that I smelled like failure and corn chips. Instead, we would be treated like gentlemen. I had my own room and my own bathroom. And I had my fan. The suck was tolerable.

Two hardcore guys got me through: Lance and Joel.

Although they both came from similar military backgrounds—they became officers after they had been enlisted sergeants—their personalities were completely different. Lance grew up in Kentucky, trained as an Airborne Ranger, and then added snake-eating Green

Beret to his resume. He had an EF Hutton-like quiet—a calm, "been there, done that" demeanor—and projected that he had either already killed in combat or could easily kill in combat.

Joel is Jewish, a rarity in the army but especially in the infantry. And he grew up in New York City. Although he, too, was an Airborne Ranger and had been an instructor at the army's elite Ranger school, he had a refined, cosmopolitan persona once out of uniform. With him being from New York and me being from Jersey, we shared a love language: sarcasm. In Georgia, Joel drove as he did in Manhattan, honking and yelling at all the slow southern drivers to "get da fuck outta da way."

Lance and Joel had both jumped into Grenada in 1983 with the 75th Ranger Regiment during the invasion. That was a shitshow. The United States and a handful of Caribbean countries went in after the People's Revolutionary Government took over and executed Grenada's prime minister. And the prime minister—Maurice Bishop—had helped take over the previous government just four years before as part of the Communist New Jewel Movement.

In 1983, President Reagan sent in troops after the other island nations asked for help, but also because there were a couple hundred US medical students in Grenada. And because it was two days after the US Marine barracks were blown up in Beirut. The United Nations disapproved, saying it was a violation of international law.

We lost four SEAL Team Six guys who died after a helicopter drop went wrong. The 75th Rangers jumped in on the first day and took over the airport. But there were several instances of friendly fire—our guys accidentally shooting our guys—as well as a couple of helicopter accidents, among the US forces, who hadn't been in a major operation since the Vietnam War. Nineteen US soldiers died and 116 were wounded. Twenty-four civilians were killed, including nineteen who died when the US accidentally bombed a mental hospital.

But 7,600 US troops went in and defeated the resistance, as well as freeing the US backed governor general, Paul Scoon.

Oddly enough, in Grenada, they found Cubans—about eight hundred of them—most of them ostensibly working on construction teams. The Cubans had been issued firearms and were forbidden from surrendering to US troops. About sixty of the Cubans worked as advisers to the People's Revolutionary Government.

Joel and Lance, for their service in Grenada, were awarded and—with an equal mixture of pride and humility—wore their Combat Infantryman Badges and their jump wings, which sported gold stars for making a combat jump.

I looked up to Lance and Joel immensely—even more than Jon Bon Jovi.

Joel and Lance were the real rock stars.

Lance and Joel had already been in harm's way. I won't lie and claim I had this great epiphany then that a counterintelligence failure—one like Ana Montes—could put troops in danger. But I will say my respect for those who serve increased.

After I finished at Fort Benning, I returned to West Chester to apply for cop jobs: Atlanta PD, the New Jersey State Police, and several small municipalities around Philly.

And Coatesville.

Coatesville is an old steel town in the western part of Chester County. In its prime, Coatesville was known as the "Pittsburgh of the East." Coatesville is a city rich in industrial history and poor in opportunities for its residents. And its history of racial violence affected everything the police force did in a community physically and mentally divided into black and white neighborhoods.

In 1911, the last man to be lynched in Pennsylvania was killed in Coatesville when a mob kidnapped a Black man named Zachariah Walker. He moved there from his home in Virginia, leaving his wife and children behind, to seek better work in the thriving steel town, as did numerous white immigrants, many of whom believed their rights outweighed those of Black citizens. As Walker walked home from work one day—he'd been drinking—he came upon a couple of Polish immigrants. He fired a gun, hoping to scare them away. Edgar

Rice, a popular deputy constable and iron mill policeman—popular because he was known for trying to help people home, rather than arrest them—told Walker that if he didn't come with him, he would hit him over the head with his club. Walker later acknowledged that he had been acting "sassy."[44]

They began to fight. They both drew their weapons. Walker shot Rice several times, killing him, and then ran into the woods. Rather than face punishment, Walker tried to kill himself by shooting himself in the head—but he lived and was hospitalized. Doctors removed the bullet from his jaw. He told the police he had acted in self-defense. Then, a crowd of at least two thousand people dragged Walker from the hospital. They set a fire in a field just outside the city. They threw Walker on it, on a Sunday afternoon, then settled in to watch as he burned alive. But he escaped, running away from the pyre. The people beat him and returned him to the fire. He escaped again. They beat him once more, pummeling his charred skin. They looped ropes around his neck and returned him again to the fire.

His screams filled the night.

Afterward, people gathered his charred bones as souvenirs. Fifteen men and teenage boys, including two police officers, were indicted, but all were acquitted at trials for Walker's murder.[45]

The NAACP opened three offices in Pennsylvania after Walker's death, and by the time I got there, eighty years later, the story still felt close to the surface. Locals had grown up with it, perhaps had even witnessed it. They certainly felt the repercussions, the fear. The wounds had not been healed by time and social justice progress.

In the meantime, the Lukens Steel Company, formed in 1890, employed most of the city's residents. But an economic downturn fueled by an OPEC oil embargo and the Iranian revolution led to more than three hundred thousand US steelworkers losing their jobs between 1976 and 1986.

Coatesville slowly became home to the county's largest population of "Section 8" residents. After the Oak Street housing project was built on the hill, open-air drug markets appeared in the projects and in the city's East End. In 2007, the *Philadelphia Inquirer* wrote that Coatesville, "a city of about 11,000, remains one of the state's most impoverished municipalities in its wealthiest county."[46] The Oak Street housing project, built on the highest point in the city, provided the best place for criminals to look down on Coatesville's residents—and Coatesville PD headquarters.

Sweet. I think I'll apply for a job there.

After my first polygraph and a psychological examination, I was sworn in as a police officer in January 1994. In May, I graduated from the police academy and started shift work.

And immediately, I felt like a fish out of water—one that couldn't swim well to start.

Coatesville had about twenty-five police officers, but few had a college degree. The other officers saw me as a "college kid." Worse, I had applied to St. Joe's for graduate school. I was drawn to the more senior officers who believed in working on—and especially in trying to make a dent in—the city's main export: drugs. I had a lot to learn about the street. But I also spent my midnight overtime shifts up in the housing project going through my textbooks with highlighters. Some of the guys called me "schoolboy."

I spent most of my time in the city's East End working the drug beat and as a community police officer. My partner, Marty Brice, and I set up a substation on the main street and opened the door for the neighbors to come in. When we weren't arresting guys for selling dope, we handed out baseball cards with officers' faces to the kids.

There were open-air drug markets and shootings, but it was a geographically small area, so I knew if I needed backup, someone would arrive instantly. Ironically, I never felt unsafe.

Being young and in good shape, I couldn't wait until my first foot pursuit. The thought of going "man to man" felt like a challenge. I ran to stay in shape for the army and, I hoped, one day the FBI. Being young and fast helped convince the veteran officers that "college boy" had something to offer.

One evening, Duron Peoples was out after curfew. When I went to grab him, he ran. So, I ran. Duron, unlike his track-star brother Omega, was slow. I caught him quickly, cuffed him, and brought him back to the station. After writing him a citation, I called his mom to come get him.

About a year later, while walking foot beat in the East End, I saw Duron standing on a street corner widely known for drugs. By now, he had graduated from curfew violator to suspected drug dealer. Confirming Duron had an active bench warrant for his arrest, my buddy Darren Sedlak and I decided we would arrest him for the warrant and because we suspected he was holding dope for sale. Darren—who is not an aerodynamic guy—got the jump on me when Duron took off running. Catching up with Darren, I got next to him and gave him a little Three Stooges "wup, wup, wup…"

"Come on man," Darren yelled, laughing. "I'm trying to run."

After a couple blocks and some stopped traffic, I caught up with Duron and cuffed him. He was, in fact, holding drugs and a lot of cash.

This time, I didn't call Duron's mom.

Several years later, after the Montes case, Duron Peoples, aka "Gotti," was convicted for the murder of Jonas "Sonny" Suber—a former mentor—and sentenced to life in prison without parole.[47] The kid who violated curfew shot Suber eight times at point-blank range, all because Suber had cheated with Duron's girlfriend while Duron had been in prison on another charge.

Now there are two mothers without sons.

Such was the cycle in Coatesville. And neither kid had anything close to the blessed upbringing of our Cuban spy.

But I loved working in Coatesville—loved the adrenaline and the comradery. I loved getting to know the neighborhood characters. Loved feeling like I was making a difference.

I'm lucky that I once again found a brotherhood—of shared values and of being able to depend on each other and of working as a team. I can't imagine any experience that would have served me better going into the Ana Montes case, though the crimes and criminals were worlds apart.

I wanted to make my version of a difference: Catch the bad guys. I wasn't necessarily thinking about improving conditions so that there would be fewer bad guys. I certainly wasn't thinking of any historical conditions that caused people to be stuck in a "bad" neighborhood on a hill. We were community police officers, and we went out and met the neighbors and played basketball with the kids, but there was still a strong sense of "us" and "them," rather than simply "us." And I can't say being in that neighborhood helped me see that in any immediate way.

Especially after I got shot at by a suicidal man who wanted me to participate in his death. That was a tough day.

Generally, I was still thinking in terms of black and white—not necessarily in terms of race, although Marty, myself, and the drug buyers from the surrounding areas were often the only white people in this neighborhood. I was thinking right and wrong. Selling drugs was wrong, period. And the socio-economic conditions that led to it were beyond my control.

Eventually, I realized I had to get out because Coatesville was going to suck me in. On the hill, I needed to be alert at all moments, and I felt myself growing used to the job, building expectations when I should not have expected anything, good or bad. I think I did my job well, but I don't know that any of us were equipped, either by training or by experience, to make change. The place felt as if it would always be a shooting gallery.

(In 2001, Coatesville tore down the last building in the Oak Street housing project.)

In 1995, an officer in another city left for a job at the FBI, so I applied for his position. After I passed a written test, I sat for an interview with the elected board of supervisors. One of the board members—who was a defense attorney and had crossed-examined me on the stand once when I arrested his client in Coatesville for aggravated assault—asked me perhaps the most ridiculous question.

"You're sitting in your police car on a dark, rainy night, and a speeding car drives by that you don't recognize," he said. "You pull over the car, and go up to the driver's side window, and there you learn it's your mother driving.

"Do you write her a ticket?"

"Are you asking me whether I'm going to write my mother a ticket?" I said, trying not to lose my shit at this "real world" hypothetical.

"Yes," he said.

I paused for a moment: *finger… sink … match … ouch…*

"Sir, if I ever want a good Thanksgiving meal again, I'm not writing my mother a ticket."

But I was thinking, *We're not in fucking Coatesville anymore, Toto.*

Wealthy defense attorneys and shopping malls filled the bedroom community of West Whiteland. I may, or may not, have used the country club golf course to practice my short game on midnight shifts. But I didn't feel as safe in West Whiteland. Because it was a larger area, it could be several minutes before anyone responded to a call for help, and the comradery just wasn't the same as it was in Coatesville: officers didn't face the same extreme situations that build trust.

That didn't mean there wasn't violence.

One night, we got a call about a shooting in a home. Arriving first, I learned a woman had shot her husband. Domestic violence is a factor in all socio-economic areas, but this was a twist. I arrested the wife and took her back to the station to book her for attempted homicide. She was drunk, and as I fingerprinted her, she wouldn't stop talking.

"Did I kill him?" she asked.

"No, ma'am," I said. "And by the way, you should shut up because everything you say can and will be used against you."

"Did I shoot him in the balls?" she asked. "I meant to shoot him in the balls."

"No, ma'am," I said, "you shot him in the stomach."

"Damn," she said, "I meant to shoot him in the balls."

*Maybe a tad less booze and some target practice, ma'am,* I thought.

The next day, Scotty, my detective buddy, and I went to the hospital to interview her husband, the "victim." By this time, we knew this wasn't his first conversation with the police. He was usually the aggressor.

We gave the husband—balls still intact—an opportunity to tell us what happened.

Silence.

After a few minutes, I asked him whether he wanted to press charges against his wife.

"I don't know what you're talking about," he said.

"Your wife tried to shoot you in your balls," I said, "and you don't want to cooperate?"

More silence.

No victim = no crime.

And they lived happily ever after.

Me? Well, the push and pull of my life caused challenges. Working my shifts, taking graduate school classes, and doing the one-weekend-a-month national guard thing was wearing me out. Was I a cop? Was I a grad student? Or was I a light infantry platoon leader? I was all of them at the same time, and I was burning out. And it certainly wasn't helping my new marriage.

After five years of working as a police officer, I felt tired and, to a degree, bored.

It was time to pursue my dream.

9

# A View to a Kill

On November 7, 1996, Scott brought Ana in for an interview. "Got to be out of here by 2 p.m.," she said, as soon as she walked in the door. Just like in (almost) every aspect of her life, Ana had decided she would control the meeting. But Scott was on to her. This was hardly an original move in an agency full of egos and power plays.

"Look," he said, "I have suspicions about your involvement with Cuban counterintelligence. This will take as long as it takes."[48]

Quick question: If someone were to accuse you of being a spy, how would you respond?

Me? I'm pretty sure my jaw would drop to the floor. And then I might laugh. *Is this a joke?* When I realized it was not, my mind would race: *Holy shit. What did I do? What could ever make them think this?* And then I might get scared: *Oh god. Am I going to lose my job? Did someone set me up? Will my wife believe me?* I'm pretty sure I would then get pretty pissed: *How dare you question my patriotism!* Or something to that effect. How many stages of grief are there? I would have hit them all.

But I'm pretty sure that each and every one of those emotions would come with the same response: You got the wrong guy. Nope. Not me. You gotta believe me. I can prove it!

Ana? She acted shocked, but she didn't deny it.[49] She did not appear afraid or panicked, Scott said—and he acknowledged that, because he didn't actually believe she was a spy, he missed some red flags. In fact, she pulled out another name—tried to lay the blame on someone else. It was almost as if she had been thinking about what she would do should she ever find herself accused of being a spy.

Scott was a pro, of course, so he got right into it. He brought up a couple of things that seemed problematic.[50] Ten years before, one of Ana's Department of Justice coworkers had complained about her: Ana had said she disagreed about how the United States had handled Cuba.

"So?" Ana essentially said to Scott when he asked her. Americans are allowed to have an opinion. True that. In fact, she still disagreed with US policy in Cuba, she told Scott. But she had stopped talking politics when she realized her coworkers might question her patriotism—and whether she was the right person for the job.

Scott asked her why she had lied on her resume: she had completed her coursework at Johns Hopkins, but, because she hadn't paid her bills, she hadn't yet received her degree. No big deal, she said. She'd done the work and she knew it would eventually get paid.

Here's a fun fact: when the Cubans found out about this kerfuffle, they insisted that she pay off her loan so she wouldn't get fired for it.

Scott asked her about Admiral Eugene Carroll's debriefing after he returned from Cuba. Oh that, Ana said. It hadn't even been her idea. A son of a DIA employee had traveled with Carroll, and the employee knew an acquaintance of Ana's, and the acquaintance mentioned to Ana that the admiral should be debriefed.[51] February 23 was the best day for everyone to meet.

Welp. That pretty much ended that.

She had answers for everything, good answers. Except, when Scott asked her who called her that day at the Pentagon, she lied: She said she didn't receive a call. She didn't announce that she was going to leave early. And she said she left early because she had arrived at 6 a.m. and she was stressed out. Anyone who has worked at the Pentagon knows that's the wrong answer. But she also knew that Scott would check her story, just as he did the story about the DIA acquaintance's son. He couldn't check "I was tired."

Still, Scott reasoned, she might have received a personal call that embarrassed her: Her cat was sick. Her boyfriend dumped her. She had bad health news.

He didn't have anything. Every boss praised Ana, and she had passed her polygraph. By the end of the year, Scott closed out his case.

Malcolm Gladwell called Scott out for this in his book, *Talking to Strangers*, and I don't think it's fair—even though it's based on Scott's own account. Gladwell says Ana was a terrible spy because she hid in plain sight—he calls it "amateur hour." But that was the brilliance of it. And he said Scott wanted to believe Ana, because it's hard to believe bad things about people.

That's nice, and certainly often the case, but this is the United States: Scott didn't have evidence that Ana had done anything wrong. She didn't do any of the typical spy stuff. She hadn't deposited any large amounts of money. She didn't drive a flashy car or live in a killer apartment or wear Chanel suits. She drove a sensible car and wore sensible shoes. She showed up early for work. She ate lunch at her desk. She was arrogant with each and every one of her coworkers. And she left at the same time every day, usually going straight home or to the gym or to the grocery store. Nada. Scott didn't have a damned thing but a bad feeling about a phone call and a coworker who thought her actions were fishy.

It takes a hell of a lot more than that to get a search warrant.

Ask me how I know.

(We'll get there.)

Ana appeared cool as a mojito as she met with Scott. But, the meeting rattled her.

She decided she needed a lifestyle change.

# 10

## Dazed and Confused

As Ana proved herself to Fidel, I worked toward getting into the FBI.

Nothing else had grabbed my attention until then. Cop? Yeah. Excitement. Do-gooder. Opposite of my dad. And make my doughnuts of the Krispy Kreme variety.

But FBI agent? It was like I suddenly had a reason not to go to Ranger School: I could still be the best of the best, but I didn't have to rough it out.

Everything I did was meant to make me more competitive—I aimed straight toward that bright, shining star. I made it to Quantico, and I spent the whole time thinking I'd be working drugs or gangs. Violent crime. I wanted to kick in doors and wrestle down fleeing suspects and do what I had been doing as a local cop, but as an FBI agent.

*Miami Vice.*

I would look so cool in a pink jacket.

Or *The X-Files*.

That had been my ten-year ambition, and suddenly, here I was.

I was an FBI agent.

Obviously, the FBI would send me to some crime squad. You know, work the cool stuff.

Being from Philly, I wanted to get close to home, but in no way did I want to go to New York: too big, too congested, too expensive. I put Washington at the top of my wish list knowing that, as a big office, they would have to staff it with lots of my classmates. Six weeks in, we received our office assignments.

I was heading to the Washington Field Office.

A little while later, my new boss, Diane Krzemien, gave me a call at Quantico. She said, "I'm your new supervisor." Cool. Awesome. Tell me more. And she did. "You'll be working Cuban counterintelligence."

I'll be what?

"What the hell is that?" I asked.

"Do you speak Spanish?" she asked.

No. They didn't teach us that at Quantico.

"So, what will I be doing?" I asked.

"I can't tell you over the phone."

"Well," I said, "I guess this is going to be a short conversation."

I hung up not knowing a thing about a thing, but it didn't sound like I'd be chasing down drug lords or Mafia, and it felt like a gut punch. *I thought I was gonna do cool stuff.*

As it turned out, there isn't any rhyme or reason to how people get assigned in the FBI. Basically, the Washington office got a call: "You're getting five people." Then, as far as I can tell, they let a monkey throw darts to figure out where we would all go. "So, Pete, you've got a background in drug crime, and you don't speak a lick of Spanish. We're putting you to work on Cuban counterintelligence."

I called Jen, all pissy.

"What am I getting myself into?" I said (whined). "My boss won't even tell me what I'll be doing over the phone."

In context, the FBI has two houses within the same organization: law enforcement and national security. And back then, national security wasn't the cool stuff. They work counterterrorism, national security, and counterintelligence. Back then, we were like all these misfit toys stacked in one toybox. Now there are boxes for cybersecurity and counterintelligence and so on. Back then, had I known anything about anything, I might have been pretty excited about it—except I still couldn't speak Spanish. And I didn't necessarily know what it meant. What's the goal? Are we going to arrest people? "Protecting national security" sounded, well, vague and secretive. I was not intrigued.

I probably could have pointed to Cuba on a map, and, during my sixteen weeks at the Academy, we had learned a *tiny* amount about counterintelligence, but my brain went straight to Russia and China. Even that was in the historic sense: the wall had come down; the Cold War was over. As much as I was thinking "counterintelligence," I was not thinking Fidel Castro.

Luckily for Jen, I had another few weeks at Quantico to stew in my own juices before joining her in the nation's capital.

We had moved into our little apartment in Virginia for Jen's MBA program in the fall of 1998—two years after Ana's encounter with Scott—and in September, after Quantico, I had one week of home leave before I started at the FBI. As I geared up for the new gig, we watched on CNN as a case broke in Miami. The FBI had arrested ten people, five of whom were Cuban intelligence officers—Gerardo Hernández, Antonio Guerrero, Ramón Labañino, Fernando González, and René González. They were part of the Wasp Network—*La Red Avispa*—and eventually, ten members would be arrested. (The media called them "The Miami Five.")

Castro had sent *La Red Avispa* illegal officers to infiltrate Brothers to the Rescue, as well as Alpha 66, the F4 Commandos, and the Cuban American National Federation—all Cuban exile groups in Miami. Castro saw the organizations as terrorist groups that wanted to invade his country. He denied that the five were spies and said they weren't spying on the US government—just the para-military groups. He'd sent them in after a former CIA operative had organized bombings in Havana. Cuba said the groups had killed almost 3,500 people since the 1960s—including several at tourist hotels as recently as 1997.[52]

But after Cuba shot down the Brothers to the Rescue plane, President Clinton ordered a crackdown on the spy network.

In the middle of preparing the evidence, in June, Ana headed to Miami for a visit, where her sister Lucy worked as a translator.

For the FBI.

Lucy had graduated with a bachelor's degree in Spanish and a master's in education, but she didn't want to teach in the public school system. While living in Maryland, she saw the FBI wanted to hire translators, so she applied. It had nothing to do with her older sister. When the job took her to Miami in 1985, she started talking to her brother Tito about how much she enjoyed her work. He eventually joined the FBI in 1988.

For *La Red Avispa*, the FBI brought in a team of ten translators. Suddenly, Ana's sister was working Cuban counterintelligence. She translated conversations and documents.

"The Cuban exile community had always said there were people in Miami working for Castro," Lucy remembered, "and, obviously there were. They weren't making it up, they weren't being paranoid."

Getting the job meant Lucy's bosses trusted her, but also that she would get to help with a big case—one that people like me were watching on CNN. She just couldn't talk about it.

"That was the first human-intelligence case that I worked in Miami," Lucy said.

After *La Red Avispa* case went public, and after the translators' work was done, the Cuba Chamber of Commerce presented Lucy and her coworkers with an award. Lucy didn't bother to tell Ana.

"I knew she would have no comment," Lucy said. "She would not discuss anything to do with work—my work or hers."

When Ana came to visit, they didn't talk about it at all.

Ana's family thought Ana was just being Ana, but she was extraordinarily touchy about talking about work. She didn't do it. She'd always been strange, her sister Lucy said. She didn't ask about Lucy or Tito's work—even though they both ostensibly knew the rules. They weren't going to ask for the Secret Squirrel stuff, but Lucy said both she and her brother liked to chat about how it was going generally: Well? Poorly?

Ana? No comment. "She wouldn't touch the subject," Lucy said. Lucy knew Ana was in Cuba once when the Pope was there. She knew Ana had applied to work a sabbatical-like position at the CIA—which came as a big surprise to Lucy. And Lucy knew Ana had visited Central America a few times. She just didn't know why or what she thought of it or what she saw for her future.

Ultimately, and in part because of Lucy's work (though she'd tell you she was just doing her job), *La Red Avispa* were convicted of conspiracy to commit espionage, conspiracy to commit murder, and acting as an agent of a foreign government.

The international community protested their sentences, saying they had not received a fair trial. And Netflix made a movie about the case in 2019 starring Penelope Cruz—with the help of the Cuban government.

At about the same time, the *La Red Avispa* case Ana's sister had worked on also changed Ana's world.

Cuba recalled her illegal officer handler, who she knew only as Ernesto, back to Cuba because he had been too close to the Wasp Network while in the United States—poor operational tradecraft on the part of the Cubans. Instead, Ana suddenly started going on a lot of vacations—every six months, she'd pop up someplace sunny and give a high-level debriefing of what she had learned. This was big picture stuff, rather than, "here's what I read at my desk today" stuff, but it was still a lot to get right and remember. It's not like she could write it down in her journal.

So Montes had anxiety tapes next to her bed, she was medicated because once, when she got promoted at work, she passed clean out, and she was at the gym trying to beat the hell out of a treadmill every day. And on her down time—her vacation time—she met up with her Cuban handlers.

Ana knew how to party.

At this point, she was just lonely—so lonely that she asked her Cuban handlers to find her a partner. And they did, because they liked Ana, and because an exit plan to Cuba with her Cuban boyfriend was probably better for the Cubans than Ana retiring in the United States and spilling the beans to the girls over a three-martini lunch. Or worse, getting caught.

In any case, they set her up with a man she called "Mr. X" because he apparently made such an impression that Ana couldn't remember his name. Allegedly. It wouldn't have been his real name, anyway—just as he wouldn't have known hers. I mentioned this guy earlier: she wanted a tall, dark, and handsome healthy nonsmoker. They sent her on vacation to meet her dream date: an overweight smoker.

They met and then went off together for a couple of days, courtesy of Fidel, and she felt no spark. She realized she would need to find her own boyfriend. And she realized that as all the Cuban agents went sleeper—underground until the Wasp Network fallout chilled—it might be a good time to retire from her spy duties.

Her timing might have been perfect. US intelligence had realized there was another spy beyond the Wasp Network, someone in deep as a tick: Castro seemed always to have advance knowledge of US operations, which then failed. And US intelligence couldn't get a foothold with agents in Cuba—it was as if Castro knew exactly who they were working with.

He did.

But as *La Red Avispa* went to prison, even DIA investigator Scott Carmichael had forgotten about Ana.

I, of course, knew none of this.

In fact, the first couple of months out of Quantico, I was disgruntled.

But then we started doing some things that were great. I can't tell you what those things were—how cool is that? But we were sneaking around and working with people who were sneaking around, and it was pretty neat. It was 1950s-TV-show neat. The old-school enemies were still the biggest concern: China was the No. 1 threat. Russia? No. 2. But Cuba? Cuba was a strong No. 3. And when we met with sources, we met them in a Starbucks, or somewhere else nice. Not behind a seedy motel with a crack dealer like my colleagues doing the "cool stuff" working violent crime.

We were civilized.

I got to help escort Jose Imperatori, a Cuban diplomat who was accused of conduct inconsistent with being a diplomat—a diplomatic way of saying, "We caught you spying." The United States said he had to leave. The Cubans said he was staying. Because Fidel personally put up a fight and said Jose didn't need to leave the United States, we received a letter from President Clinton saying Jose's visa had been revoked and he needed to leave the United States immediately. While providing surveillance at his apartment building in Maryland, we negotiated with the State Department's Cuban Interests Section in D.C. for him to come out so we could escort him to the airport.

I mean, President Clinton decided what I did that day.

Now you can find Imperatori on Facebook—though that may change after this book hits the bookshelves.

My teammates were also pretty cool, for the most part. Smart. Talented. Overachievers.

Like Molly Flynn. She was a fucking badass.

The FBI had been chasing the Unabomber—trying to identify him—for years. From the late 1970s to 1995, he terrorized people by mailing bombs to homes to protest technology and what he saw happening to the environment. He killed three people and injured twenty-three, and for a while there, people were too terrified to open their packages.

The guy was brilliant—a full-on math prodigy. And the FBI had spent more time and money on this case than any other. In 1995, he sent a long-winded, handwritten letter, or manifesto, to the *New York Times* and said if they published it, he'd quit killing people. Which is nice and all, but the manifesto was long, his demands were essentially blackmail, and it would be expensive to publish it. Still, the *New York Times* and the *Washington Post* put it out into the world.

This is what people did in the before-Twitter times.

The manifesto came out hard against industrialization and political correctness and how much "leftists" hate white men as well as themselves. The guy sat in a cabin by himself for twenty years writing, but this was no Walden.

Oddly enough, people were more interested in the bombs this guy sent out than his deep ideas about how women aren't as strong as men. The FBI did its analysis, looking at the paper and the handwriting and the syntax. Nothing.

Then the guy's sibling, David Kaczynski, read the manifesto. *Welp*, he thought, *that sure looks like my brother's crazy*. (Oddly enough, the manifesto served as proof of Ted Kaczynski's lucidity during his trial.) David reached out to an attorney, and the attorney somehow found Molly who was working on a violent crime squad at the time at Washington Field.

In the meantime, the FBI task force in San Francisco was getting just pummeled with leads. "My neighbor uses his leaf blower at 4 a.m. every Monday. I think he's the Unabomber." "The guy at the 7-Eleven looked at me sideways. I think he's the Unabomber." "There's a kid bullying my daughter at school. I think she's the Unabomber." Some folks went straight fascist and started ratting out their neighbors—so most of the leads were bullshit.

But David and his attorney met with Molly for coffee, and they handed over this letter Ted had sent. To Molly, it sounded an awful lot like the manifesto.

So, Molly reached out to San Francisco and said, "I think we should look at this."

"We think we'll ignore you," they said, but in mostly nicer words. Molly kept pushing. That's how she beats you—with her wicked brains and persistency.

"I think," she said, when she called again, "you should look at this."

She was ultimately such a pain in the ass that they took a look.

Then the supervisor from San Francisco called Molly and said, "We're about to execute a search warrant on a shack in Montana, and we just thought you should know," or something to that effect. None of the other theories had panned out. They had nothing left. Fine. We'll check this Kaczynski guy.

And it broke the case.

Molly flew up to New York where Kaczynski's brother lived and met with him again.

"The press is converging," she remembers telling him. "Let me tell you what's going on." She became almost like a victim advocate—David, of course, was innocent, but that didn't mean the fallout wasn't going to suck for basically the rest of his life.

The "big hero" moments are the arrest shots, where they're walking Ted's greasy ass out of the woods. But to me, the real hero moment is that tenderness Molly showed—just her ability to quietly think about the aftereffects to the other people involved. Ted's brother and his family remembered her for that, and they wrote her a kind letter when she retired thanking her for her compassion to them as well as for helping put their brother in jail.

Molly's a humble person, and she doesn't talk about this much. I didn't know this part of her career until two weeks before she retired. In retrospect, given how she cracked the Unabomber case, she probably should have been the co-case agent for Montes, rather than me. But that's how the FBI works sometimes.

That I got to be on a team with Molly was damned cool.

My new partner, Steve McCoy, was close to twenty-five years older than I was, and often reminded me of my father. He didn't always get along with people. He was witty, and witty in an intelligent way. At times, he could be dismissive of contrary opinions—except that you could usually persuade him to see another perspective. Like my dad, he was intelligent in an academic way. He was Morgan Freeman in *Seven*—like older and wiser—but Morgan Freeman was more tolerable.

Just to be clear, I'm not comparing myself to Brad Pitt.

But Steve also had a softer, tender side to him too. Squad meetings, life events, or the personalities we all dealt with were often the muse for his comedic poetry, and he delivered them from a place of love, regardless of their unintended bite. Given that he was significantly more experienced than most of us, he took on an avuncular role in mentoring the younger agents who came and, often as soon as they could, went. He treated me, from the beginning of our partnership, as a true equal, despite his decades of FBI experience. I am indebted to him.

I often dealt with Steve the same way I dealt with my dad: sometimes I just nodded along as he talked about what we should do next, and then I went and did my own thing. I wasn't disrespectful; we were just different kinds of investigators.

He didn't push back on that, at least not loudly, and I think it's because it worked for us. His strengths were in looking at all the different ways and all the different theories and postulating possibilities and digging into the background of Fidel Castro's childhood or whatever. I'm more of a bulldog: I'm going to go talk to this source, track down this piece of evidence, get into her residence, and give not the tiniest bit of a shit about who changed Fidel Castro's diapers.

I felt confident about the work I did. I had confidence in Steve, and he in me. He had worked counterintelligence for years, and he knew the Cubans well.

Fortunately, I already had some tools in place for that specific personality type—and to be honest, he tolerated a lot of my idiosyncrasies, as well as my still evolving maturity.

Who needs a therapist when you have the FBI?

Steve and I agree that we could not think of a better mesh of personalities, skills, experience, and energy then he and I had.

Ana would later decide she liked Steve much better than she liked me.

# 11

## I'd Fallen For a Lie

Ana continued to date, occasionally, but nothing felt big enough to make her give up her true love: Fidel.

Logistically, she didn't have a great setup. One might think that in a male-heavy industry, there would be no shortage of interested men, but Ana ate her lunch at her desk and avoided the water cooler. The last thing she needed was some boyfriend nosing around.

Roger also worked Cuba, but for a different area of the Defense Department. They disagreed often, but they reviewed each other's work, and it was important work. Despite the disagreements, for Roger, it was great to have someone smart—and senior—understand what he was doing and offer helpful feedback. They had a good working relationship, and she was always on her best behavior with him and with Southern Command. "We worked for the same company," he told me, "and we were two department heads. So she needed me because she supported my organization, my command—we were her intelligence customer. And I needed her help with the

Washington intelligence world, and she was my conduit to all the other agencies. So we worked closely together and we worked well together."

She was older by about seven years and had already figured out the path. She was kind about helping Roger learn the intel ropes. Roger, to no rom-com writer's surprise, saw her as a challenge. He found her intelligence and the mystery of her attractive. It became a chase. "They had known each other quite a while, and she refused to go out with him," Lucy told me. "And then, at some point, she relented."

And probably, while he may have seen it as a bit of a game, Ana saw it as, "Whoa. This dude must really like me."

Roger first considered asking her out during the fall or winter of 1999 or 2000 at a work conference, but their first official date—a group date with friends in Old Town, Alexandria—wasn't until late 2000, Roger remembered. Initially, he wanted to see where it would go, but only in the, "If this is fun, we'll keep doing it" sense. Realistically, not a lot of young men go straight to, "Let's see if this leads to marriage."

Lucy said Ana told her about a couple guys she dated, but, like everything else, she didn't talk about it much. "She told me the bare minimum," Lucy said.

But she was excited about Roger. "She thought she was going to marry Roger," Lucy said. "She never talked about having kids or getting married, which I could never understand. She was a career girl. But she thought she and Roger would get married."

As things wound down a bit with her spy activities, Ana realized she wanted out. Roger took a job at the Pentagon so he could move to Washington. As he traveled between Washington and Miami, he stayed with Ana.

They had a classic long-distance relationship, living in different cities, and would only see each other when they traveled for work. In late August 2001, they took a vacation to Cape Cod, where she met his family, and he met her family in Miami. She wanted to see where the relationship would go.

Roger liked her family but didn't feel entirely welcomed by Ana's mother. "I think her mom was skeptical of us," Roger said. "I think she looked at me and she thought, 'Oh. This isn't going to last. He's way too young.' She was nice to me, but you could kind of tell she wasn't full on-board."

Seven years, when a person's in his thirties, can feel like a huge difference: different music tastes, different sports references, hugely different life experiences.

Lucy had her doubts too. "It didn't seem like a good couple," she said. "But he loved her, so I was happy if there was someone who was going to love Ana and make her happy.

There were other early warning signs, though her family couldn't see them and Roger didn't know what to make of them.

One weekend, Roger was in Washington hanging out with friends. He wasn't supposed to see Ana that day, or possibly even that trip. But as he and his buddies drove near the White House, Roger looked across the traffic on Constitution Avenue and spotted Ana.

"There she was in her stupid little red car with her little gloves on," Roger said, adding that Ana wore driving gloves. "And I started waving at her. When she saw me, she just flipped out, like she had been caught doing something bad."

She may have felt guilt simply for driving the car: while the Cubans didn't pay her to spy, she insisted they pay for the car because she had to drive to DIA. Her plan, had she not grown up to be a spy, was to take public transportation everywhere. Her handlers gave her cash—an operational expense—and she used it to make her car payment. Roger just thought it was odd that she wore driving gloves for a cheap compact car.

She dressed primly, properly, Roger remembered. She spent hours in the gym—to the point where it seemed like an addiction. Roger and Ana didn't get to see each other often, and he would sometimes come into town after being away for a couple of months. "She'd be like, 'I gotta go to the gym,'" Roger remembered. "I'd be like, 'You gotta what? What do you mean you gotta go to the gym?' It was weird."

At work, only Roger's close friends knew they were dating. And Ana was the outlier—most of their other coworkers fell in with Roger's genuinely patriotic beliefs, which means work must have been a lonely place for Ana in ways other than the obvious.

"She was very aggressive and detail-oriented about her work," Roger said. "So she could always wear you down with detail: 'Well, Clandestine Report No. 375 shows that the Cubans don't really cooperate with the Russians.'"

Sure, but Reports 376, 377, 378 and 379 say they do—but no one else memorized report numbers. Because why would you, unless you needed to type it all up for the Cubans in the evening?

"I knew how focused she was," Roger said, "but I thought it was so she could win at the arguments at work. But even with her attention to detail, I always felt like she drew the wrong conclusions from all that information she saw."

She'd say things like, "The Cubans probably don't really even share sensitive intelligence with the Russians, despite the Russian SIGINT site in Cuba," referring to signals intelligence—or how the Russians (and Americans) try to listen in on each other. "They don't really like the Russians all that much because of XYZ."

"But it was just wrong," Roger said. "And everybody knew it was wrong; it was bias. But it was a matter of who could prove what from the available data." But suspicious? Nah. That was a popular viewpoint to have then, even as it is now—despite the recent protests by the Cuban people and the headlines about concerns that the Russians use Cuba to harm Americans with audio waves. Americans have a romanticized view of Cuba.

Ana and Roger argued at work. A lot. To the point where they would have to just stop—cut off the subject entirely. And she refused, as she did with her family, to talk about it in private. But at work? He tried to shut her down. "I wasn't going to let her get away with any of her bias, if I could help it," he said, "but it was always hard to make headway."

There were other oddities. Roger suspected abuse because of the way Ana acted with him sometimes, but she never talked about anything, including her father. We know from her sister that Ana's father used the belt on Ana and her siblings. Adults who were abused as kids are more likely to engage in risky behavior, to be antisocial, and to have difficulties maintaining relationships. They can become defiant or oppositional. And they can work to regain their power by trying to control others.

"I remember she was very proud of Puerto Rican/Latin American culture," Roger said. "She liked to point out, from time to time, how superior Latin American culture was." Kids were celebrated, rather than sent to a corner and told to stay quiet, she said. In Latin America, the kids are the center of activity. "She just had this inner narrative of self-delusion about politics and economics and culture. I would think, *Okay, that's just her bullshit again*, which is another big, contributing factor about why we could never be together." Their politics didn't align—he leaned more conservative. There was the age difference.

A few months in, Roger stepped into an early relationship trap: he tried to change her. For the young guy in the office, it was hard to know what normal should look like. She was the top. He was an up-and-comer. "She was the queen of Cuba," he said. "But I learned, like her coworkers did, that she was like the evil ice queen of Cuba."

The man felt bad for her and wondered if she simply didn't know how to act. So he decided to help her present a softer side to her coworkers—a kinder, gentler Ana. "Her office was full of great people," Roger said. "And she's like the star. But she was mean to everybody, except for a couple of small exceptions."

He would fix everything with some homemade goodness: cookies.

But he's not a clean cook. He makes a mess. "And that's what I did in her apartment: I made a mess."

Ana didn't seem grateful. Ana got up in the middle of the night and began to scrub her kitchen, including the ceiling above where he had been working. "That's just what she was like," Roger said. "I mean, I look back and think, *How could I not have read more into the idea that she was an obsessive-compulsive freakshow?*"

The cookies did not change her coworkers' opinions of Ana.

At one point, Ana and Roger traveled to Mexico together.

"Thank God my friends were there," he said. But his friends didn't like her. She couldn't relax. "She was just a really high-strung, goody two-shoes, overachiever type."

After that, he didn't go out of his way to go to D.C.—he just went up when he had to for work, and even then, he didn't always tell her when he was in town.

But Ana didn't seem to notice. Instead, she dreamed about a life with Roger, rather than with the Cubans.

# 12

# Runaway

The red of the dinghy failed to mask its profile against the ocean backdrop. A blip—barely ten feet, inflated—floating in seemingly endless blue on a moonless, late summer night.

A blue raft would have disappeared against the vast blue of the ocean. But a red one, powered with a 7.5-horsepower Evinrude outboard engine—less than what you'd put on a lawn mower—would have to do.

That, along with current, prayers, and fate.

They'd secured the boat the previous day. And they'd run out of time.

The captain, "Kevin," a pseudonym, whose nom de guerre was "[redacted]," had been a Cuban star, beginning just after high school when he'd been selected to study at a school on the Isle of Pines, the second-largest of Cuba's islands, run by the Ministry of the Interior. It also housed Cuba's Dirección de Inteligencia (DGI), the country's main intelligence agency. Seeing his aptitude, the government decided he should study math. He learned cryptology: signals intelligence, or picking up communications from foreign governments, decoding it, and translating it.

Quickly, he understood military officials and their families lived differently from everybody else—the have-nots. The people of Cuba suffered—starved—as corrupt government officials lived large. Kevin made his first mistake. As he struggled with his conscience, as he moved toward becoming a "have," he denounced, in a place with no freedom of speech, the corruption and abuses he witnessed. The government decided his math and intelligence skills would best serve Cuba in a construction job. He measured drywall and beams.

After his "rehabilitation," Kevin worked in Department M-VI, which conducts industrial espionage for the regime. He would, as an intelligence officer, recruit agents to steal microelectronics technology from foreign companies.

In the United States, this is considered economic espionage, or the theft of trade secrets to benefit a foreign power. In 1996, Congress passed the Economic Espionage Act to help defend American companies from this threat.

Kevin used his training and skills not to steal secrets from the US government, as Ana did, but to target private companies and try to steal technology in America and other foreign countries—such as from General Dynamics and DuPont. US intelligence does its fair share of spying, but it doesn't steal trade secrets from private companies. Cuba, Russia, and China attempt to do so routinely.

Oddly enough, the construction gig did little to change Kevin's attitude about the regime. He believed the corruption was so rampant that "the Cuban regime was, in reality, a lie." For the sake of his dignity, he decided he could no longer be an accomplice.

He had reached his breaking point.

But leaving Cuba wouldn't be enough: he needed to hurt the regime. For that, he needed allies. Each day at work, chafing against the system, he searched for like-minded intelligence officers. At sea, the sharks would feed his dreams, but they never terrified him as much as the possibility that someone would catch him in his search. He faced a fate far worse than a construction site should someone realize he was looking for people who shared his treacherous beliefs. But as he searched based on the clues of his own personality, there were tells: facial expressions, a slipped interest in knowledge, a breath in to refrain words from coming out.

He found two other like-minded, rebellious individuals: "Jorge Ramirez" and "Mateo Cruz"—both pseudonyms. Over time, the three stole Cuban classified documents from computers and burn bags located in their respective departments. Often, one would stand guard as another downloaded documents from secure computers.

The Cubans had their own yet-to-be-discovered insider threat problem.

Kevin handled some of the most important agents in the industrial espionage department. He got to know a couple of them when they came to Cuba. Kevin convinced them to join him to work with the US government against Cuba. Had they been caught, they undoubtedly would have been executed. Instead, with their help, Kevin made his first contact with the [redacted] in Virginia, and, later, with the US Interests Section in Havana—the diplomatic mission that replaced the US Embassy in Cuba during the Carter administration.

Kevin created a small spy network in Cuba, which included Jorge, Mateo, some of Kevin's industrial espionage agents, and even some artists. Kevin's agents left sensitive intelligence in dead drops around Havana for the [redacted] officers to pick up. Although Kevin and his crew didn't know the name Ana Montes, or the name of any other agent the Cubans had recruited within the US government, Kevin knew the information they were stealing was incredibly damaging to Cuban intelligence.

Less than a decade earlier, another Cuban intelligence officer had come to the same conclusion as Kevin: Fidel's regime was corrupt and he could no longer support it. "Mandy Gamboa," a pseudonym, was born in [redacted], just before the revolution, but he remembers only life under the Castro regime. His family was celebrated as "royalty of the revolution": his father fought alongside Che Guevara against Batista. Like Kevin, Mandy was recruited by Cuban intelligence just after high school. He, too, spent time training in the Soviet Union with the KGB.

Slowly, but as assuredly as Kevin, Mandy grew to despise his life because he believed he lived a lie. Although he didn't know the full extent of the Cuban's human rights abuses—saying he "didn't work in counterintelligence"—he saw the contrast between the haves and have nots. With a career in Cuban intelligence, Mandy had plenty, but he saw poverty all around. Eventually, Mandy would marry "Lila Cros"—another pseudonym—whose father also fought with Che Guevara against Batista, but who would later see communism as evil. Lila's father fought for the United States during President Kennedy's failed invasion of the Bay of Pigs when she was one year old—his body has never been recovered.

Mandy, too, had reached his breaking point.

Mandy was assigned to the Directorate General of Intelligence, or DGI, which is now known as Department M-II—the Latin America/Caribbean department. In the late 1980s, he was assigned to the [redacted]. Mandy performed admirably as an intelligence officer, at one point handling an agent who was Cuban but fought against communism. The agent was assigned to a high-level position within the United Nations in New York City, an establishment long penetrated by foreign intelligence agents.

Get this: the anti-communist agent cooperated with Cuba because he knew Fidel read his reports, and it was a nice, steady ego boost.

Fidel himself proved to be Cuba's most important case agent. He personally met with most of the top agents Cuban intelligence ran.

Everyone in Cuban intelligence trusted Mandy, whose nom de guerre was "[redacted]." Once, while in the office of Gustavo Carballosa Puig, whose nom de guerre was "Gaston," he saw something that looked important on Gustavo's desk. Mandy and Gustavo were good friends, in addition to fellow intelligence officers. Gustavo headed the analysis department for Cuban intelligence, where he gathered intelligence from the agents to figure out where the pieces of the puzzles fit into what Cuba knew about the United States. On Gustavo's desk sat a US State Department document stamped "TOP SECRET." Whether Cuba classified it top secret because of the source or whether the State Department did is unknown. But the document likely came from Walter Kendall Myers, who the FBI arrested and convicted in 2009 for espionage.

Mandy also knew Cuba had penetrated deeply within the US Congress.

Over the years, Mandy trained with the KGB in the former Soviet Union—the relationship between the two countries and services was strong.

In early [redacted], Mandy walked into the US Embassy in [redacted], wearing a suit and carrying a briefcase that contained his service revolver and a Colt .45 and defected to the United States. Believing in Ronald Reagan's vision of the "shining city on a hill," Mandy proudly boasted, "Ronald Reagan recruited me."

Mandy had decided to defect a year earlier.

In 1988, Castro traveled to Ecuador to attend the inauguration of the country's new president. Mandy, as the senior intelligence officer assigned in [redacted], had [redacted] in preparation for the state visit. Cuba spent millions of dollars on Castro's four-day stay, including bringing his own food, water, and entire bedroom to Ecuador to make sure Fidel felt comfortable away from home. As the Cuban people starved, Fidel Castro needed his own bed for sleepy time.

Mandy was disgusted.

Mandy was intimately involved in all the security logistics of Castro's visit. Although Fidel had countless bodyguards, José Abrantes, the head of Cuba's Ministry of the Interior and Fidel's closest confidant—closer than Fidel's own brother Raúl—pulled Mandy aside and handed him a loaded Colt .45 to protect Castro.

By this time, Mandy had a relationship with the US intelligence community. Mandy had the run of Castro's house in Ecuador, including his bedroom, and now he had a decision to make.

"Castro's life was in my hands," Mandy told me. He had the means, access, opportunity, and motive to assassinate him. All he had to do was put a bullet from the Colt .45 into Castro's head, and the future of Cuba would change forever. Nearly thirty-five years later, over two bottles of pinot noir on a beautiful South Florida night, Mandy seemed to still struggle with his decision. "But nothing would have changed," Mandy said, if he had killed Castro—except that Mandy would also be dead. When Castro died naturally, his brother Raúl took over and the regime continued its corrupt and repressive ways.

Mandy was right. Nothing changed.

"The [redacted] was pleased," Mandy said, referring to the US intelligence community, about the restraint he showed. The legal consequences of a [redacted]-affiliated agent killing Fidel in cold blood would have been tricky for the United States.

Five years later, Kevin dreamed an elaborate, James Bond-like "operation" would bring him to America. But the US intelligence community could not take on a grand exfiltration operation to get Kevin and his two comrades out of Cuba.

The timing of Kevin's decision to defect remains unclear, but in the espionage world, the decision is never "if," but "when."

In mid-1994, as Kevin was scheduled to head to Canada to conduct an industrial espionage operation, his bosses suddenly canceled the operation.

Kevin believed he and his network were firmly in the sights of Cuban counterintelligence and internal control. Some claimed Kevin spent US government cash lavishly in Havana, drawing Cuban counterintelligence attention. But Kevin told me this was "false and slanderous," adding that the United States hadn't paid him—he simply felt driven to act: "The United States is a symbol of freedom for the world."

"Besides," Kevin said, "I could not have wasted money in Cuba without being detected."

There might have been a more obvious reason: Kevin stole a Smith & Wesson revolver from the head of Department M-XIX—a man named Juan Miguel Carbonell Cordero—a couple of days before stealing a raft. M-XIX targets Cuban exiles in foreign countries. (Hmm. Why do you s'pose they needed guns?) Kevin knew he would need to be armed in case he ran into either sharks or, worse, the Cuban coast guard. Kevin decided he would not be taken prisoner. After Cuban intelligence realized the guns were gone, they interviewed all the officers in the department, including Kevin.

Jorge had his own service weapon and planned to take it with him. But now, they had to find a boat without attracting attention, which proved almost impossible. After several previous attempts, Kevin found and bought the dinghy just "eight feet from a watchman and some Canadian tourists at Varadero Beach," he said. Kevin, Jorge, Kevin's brother, and a fourth man spent the last day making final preparations: building oars and a base to hold the engine, and acquiring gas and water.

Kevin took his children and their mother to his children's grandparents' house in El Cotorro. As his children walked into the house, Kevin felt his heart break. But he knew he had to escape, as it was the best of only two options: wait to be arrested by Cuban intelligence or leave his children and risk dying at sea trying to escape.

Kevin looked to the sky and prayed.

*Please God, do not allow my children to have their father die at sea. Please let me live to enjoy freedom and to see them one day, again.*

Prayer is not taught in Communist Cuba; there is no freedom of religion.

But faced with the certainty of prison or execution, he had no choice.

On "go" night, everyone left work by 7 p.m. Kevin sat on the deflated dinghy in the back seat of an old, rented Chevrolet. Kevin watched Jorge say goodbye to his wife.

Heading to the northern part of the Cuban coast, they chanced upon a spot on the rocky beach that had a tunnel. Hiding in the tunnel, they used their acquired scuba diving tanks to inflate the dinghy. Without the aid of light, a cap on a valve on the other side of the dinghy popped off as they began trying to inflate.

*Shit*, Kevin thought, *practice would have been nice*.

With the dinghy pumped up hard as a rock, they filled it with gas, water, and the homemade oars. As they carried the dinghy to the rocks to launch, a man with a light approached: a fisherman, who had the aid of a lamp because he wasn't trying to escape. As Kevin and his crew got in their dinghy, the fisherman launched in his not far away and started to row.

At 11:30 p.m., Kevin tried to start the engine, but it sputtered. Finding a rope caught in the propeller, Kevin got out of the dinghy to untangle the rope. Free from the rope, the engine started, but it struggled against the strong waves.

Twelve miles. If they could make it just twelve miles, they would arrive in international waters.

But they didn't have a compass. In Cuba, it's illegal to own one. They couldn't see Florida, and they needed to head straight toward the Florida Keys—the shortest distance to the United States. They looked to the stars for guidance.

"That's the North Star," someone said.

"That's Mars," another testily replied.

Kevin knew a thermoelectric plant sat in Santa Cruz del Norte not far from where they launched. Using the lights from the plant as a point of reference, he steered them away from the coast. After an hour, they could still see the coast. They'd barely moved.

For hours, they drifted, unable to hear over the roar of the barely functioning motor, and unable to see much but darkness.

"Red light coming," someone whispered at about midnight.

As the craft moved closer to the four men in the dinghy, Kevin recognized the shape and antennas of a Cuban coast guard boat. They knew being caught by the Cuban government at sea would be even worse than being caught on the island: justice would be swift and immediate.

Because they were Cuban intelligence, their deaths would likely also be violent.

The four men sank low, hoping the dinghy's low profile would provide cover.

But the coast guard craft moved closer.

At about five hundred meters, Kevin could identify the Cuban flag, its white stripes and single star glowing in the boat's lights. They could see the green stern light as they ducked further down, praying.

Peering over the sides, Kevin saw the boat start to curve just before it reached the dinghy. It seemed as if it moved in slow motion. Would they send a smaller craft? Kevin and the other defectors watched.

The boat continued to turn, and Kevin and the others realized it was making a U-turn and heading back to its nightly sweep of the northern coast between Havana and Santa Cruz to search for defectors.

But the darkness that had kept them hidden also shrouded yet another danger: with the morning light, they could still see the Cuban coastline. Darkness no longer hid the red dinghy, and they didn't know how far they had traveled.

As they floated, Kevin allowed his mind to wander far from the dangers the crew faced. He thought about the beauty of the flying fish that accompanied them—as well as his desire to catch one for breakfast. The crew dangled their legs over the side of their craft and into the water, even as they scanned for another threat: sharks.

With daybreak, Kevin took inventory of their supplies. In their haste to get away, they'd left some of their water, much of their gas, and all their food on the rocky beach. And they were low on gas.

Kevin shut off the engine.

They floated silently. In the afternoon, they came across four empty rafts. No people. Kevin noticed condensed milk on one of the rafts.

"They must have been rescued," Kevin said, reasoning that the milk showed the occupants hadn't needed it.

But one of his crew disagreed: they would have taken the milk with them.

"They're dead," he said. "It's a cemetery."

Cubans had heard many tales of empty dinghies—of refugees who grew delirious after too long in the heat or without food. The water might look like safety.

The sun grew hot as they debated the mystery. Ball caps couldn't protect them from the relentless heat. With nothing to mark their movement, it seemed as if they stayed in one place.

By 2 a.m., they were still adrift. The sun had disappeared, leaving them wet, cold, and exhausted. Kevin tried to restart the engine, but learned the hard way that wet plugs don't spark. But they now sat in the middle of the Florida Straits, a strong, warm current channel that runs between the eastern shore of Florida and the Bahamas. But the beautiful blue hid sharks that monthly plucked people from tiny crafts. Sudden waves could crest at ten feet, flipping passengers into the water. The same waves could send Kevin and his crew toward the Bahamas, leaving them stranded.

Dazed and groggy, they watched as another coast guard boat approached. They had been in the water for twenty-four hours—plenty of time to think about what would have happened had the first boat seen them. Would it be better to dive into the water and face the possibility of sharks?

They waited for the flag. White stripes glowing in the deck lights.

United States.

"Help!" Kevin and his crew shouted in English. "Help!"

As the coast guard cutter came to a stop, its searchlights reached out over the water, alerting Kevin's crew that they could approach. If the ship had continued toward them, they could have capsized in its wake.

The cutter headed away with new passengers…but Kevin and his dinghy remained in the water. The cutter had stopped for somebody else and couldn't hear Kevin's cries for help.

Rain came down, soaking the men and flooding the dinghy. Their ninety-mile journey seemed like thousands.

They thought about their families, about what they had risked. Men often divorced their wives before they took the journey so the Cuban government would not torment their families. Would it be better for them if the men died?

They joined hundreds, thousands, who, since 1959, had been desperate to escape the corrupt regime. They took boats, rafts, or chugs—vessels made of Styrofoam, plastic, inner tubes.

They didn't sleep. Their stomachs had moved past the point of growling. As dawn broke yet again, they grew desperate, dreading the sun's rays and another day with little to sustain them. They stared into the vast blue for hours.

"There's another boat on the horizon!" Kevin yelled at about 10 a.m. "Look at the reflection!"

Kevin tried to rouse himself from his groggy slump. They'd seen—and unseen—dozens of spots that might have been a ship. Or a shadow. Or a wave. Kevin stared intently, hoping his brother hadn't reached hallucination stage.

But the reflection drew closer.

It was an American fishing boat, filled with Cuban Americans.

"Relax!" they shouted over the water. "You're in the land of the free! You're saved!"

Kevin boosted himself upward. "Please don't leave," he shouted, his voice hoarse. "Please!"

But they were safe. The boat moved closer, and its crew invited them to board.

As they drank and ate and celebrated, the Cuban Americans heard the screams of a pregnant woman from a blue raft with a tall mast and sail. To Kevin, it looked luxurious. His saviors headed toward the blue raft to rescue the woman and her crew.

By dinner, Kevin and his crew stood on US soil in Marathon Key, Florida. They were safe and free.

Except for one.

Photo by Kevin

*Raft that had contained passengers who were rescued by the same US fishing boat that rescued Kevin and his fellow passengers.*

Twenty years later, in 2014, the United States agreed to a spy exchange with Cuba to obtain the release of Alan Gross, who had worked in Cuba for the US Agency for International Development. The Cubans had falsely accused Gross of committing espionage for the United States in Cuba. In a press release from the director of national intelligence, the United States announced it had gained the release of an unnamed Cuban individual.

When Kevin defected, Cuban intelligence dismantled his old department, which likely led to the arrest of his friend Mateo, Kevin said. Mateo never made it onto the dinghy. Likely because his father had been a high-ranking Cuban intelligence officer, Mateo's life had been spared. He would spend twenty years in a Cuban prison.

While Cuba views Kevin, Mandy, Jorge, and Mateo as traitors, they are American heroes. It would take Kevin another twenty years to see his children again after his escape in a dinghy not seaworthy enough for a Sunday excursion on a placid lake.

The intelligence spark Kevin, Jorge, and Mateo provided would begin to turn the tables for the FBI and the US intelligence community against Cuban intelligence. Although it would take time, Kevin and his band of brothers had achieved their desired maximum damage.

Spies catch spies.

For the FBI, the difficult work had only just begun.

# 13

## You Know My Name

No one can beat the Cuban Intelligence Service at recruiting like-minded sympathizers willing to risk it all to defeat their common enemy: the United States. Think about how many headlines you see about Russian and Chinese spies. Now do Cuban spies.

For Cuba, you need only one hand.

But through the late 1980s and early 1990s, the US intelligence community had several successes with human sources, most of whom defected to the United States for a better life. Those sources hinted at Cuban agents within our borders.

Sources like Mandy Gamboa, Kevin, Jorge, and Mateo.

In the counterintelligence world, spies catch spies. Rarely—if ever—have we arrested a spy because they disclosed information to a background investigator.

"Hey, I've got this pot of money buried in my backyard the Russians gave me. Is that okay?"

When the US government investigates someone for a security clearance, they talk to that person's family, neighbors, and coworkers—past and present. But that investigation doesn't typically catch spies.

We have other sources. But it's not like Kevin and friends said, "Pssst! You're looking for Ana Montes." It was more like, "You've got a spy. That spy is causing a lot of damage."

Some call it mole hunts. (John le Carré was the first to do so.)

Some call it spy hunts.

The Bureau calls it an UNSUB investigation—short for unknown subjects.

And they are hard and complicated. Just like counterintelligence investigations.

In many ways, espionage unknown subject cases are like serial killer investigations. In the hunt for a serial killer, detectives look at a crime scene or the scene where a body is dumped and look for clues. They look for not only pieces of physical evidence—DNA, hair, fibers—but evidence that will help determine the psychological profile of the suspect. They want to narrow down the 332 million people in this country to a manageable list of potential suspects. With serial killers, detectives or FBI profilers try to determine what kind of monster—and importantly, what sort of psychological make up—would perform this horrendous act.

We use similar methods when we don't have a suspect in an espionage case: once we know the tidbits—the clues—FBI agents analyze them to come up with a profile.

But we say "matrix," rather than "profile," to avoid the negative connotation of the word.

Armed with this matrix, the FBI then compares it—discreetly—to US government employees, or almost four million people, including uniformed military personnel—to try to narrow it down to a handful of potential suspects.

Needle, meet haystack.

In the FBI's arrest warrant for Kendall and Gwendolyn Myers, they included some tidbits:

"Among the messages sent to co-conspirator 'C' was a message sent on or about December 18, 1996, in which co-conspirator 'C' is instructed to show an interest in a tumor on the shoulder of agent 'E-634.'"[53]

A message from around February 15, 1997, to co-conspirator "C" describes Cuban reactions to a "gringo" project to democratize Cuba.

A third message from around January 29, 1997, congratulates co-conspirator "C" for actions in the "heart of the enemy" and declares them a "tribute to Marti"—which, I believe, is a reference to José Marti, a Cuban national hero.

Earlier in the affidavit, FBI Special Agent Brett Kramarsic wrote, "I am aware that, during the time frame described herein, [the Cuban Intelligence Service] often communicated with its clandestine agents operating in the United States by broadcasting encrypted radio messages from Cuba on certain high frequencies.... The clandestine agent in the United States, monitoring the frequency on a shortwave radio, could decode the seemingly random series of numbers by using a decryption program provided by [the Cuban Intelligence Service]. The series of numbers would then be decoded into cognizable text for use by the agent. Once decoded, the text of the message could provide the agent with tasking for intelligence gathering, instructions about operational activities, including communication plans and meets with [Cuban Intelligence Service] handlers. Similarly, [Cuban Intelligence Service] would broadcast similar messages to its handlers."

Sound familiar?

The information in the affidavits shows the US government was able to read the encrypted messages.

This information came to us thanks to Kevin, Jorge, and Mateo.

They had more: before he defected in 1989, Mandy's friend "Fidelito" told him he was handling "two cases, involving two women."

But this early tidbit about two women committing espionage didn't narrow the suspect pool by much.

For a brief period in 1996–1997, the FBI read previously encrypted high frequency messages the Cubans sent to some of their officers here in the United States. These messages were sent to Ana and the Myers' handlers.

With the help of the intelligence the trio gave to the US intelligence community, the FBI—along with help from the National Security Agency—read a series of a couple-dozen messages the Cubans sent to "E," short for Ernesto, or Ana's handler. These now-decrypted messages provided some of the more significant "tidbits" to form the matrix in our case.

Out of all the things we did on the squad, the unknown subject cases were the coolest. This was badass—like figuring out the murderer in *Silence of the Lambs* in real life.

Here's what we knew: Cuban agent [redacted] appeared to be a man. The Cubans referred to their agent as either "Agent S" or "Sergio" in the decrypted messages to Ernesto.

The agent received high frequency communications on frequencies that could be heard from North Carolina to New England. These broadcasts began in 1992, so the agent had likely worked for our government since then. During that time, Cuban agent [redacted] received 151 valid decrypted messages.

Cuban agent [redacted]'s Tandy 1400FD laptop (made by RadioShack) had technical issues, but agents can't just call the Cuban IT help desk to get support. So, in October 1996, the Cubans told agent [redacted] to spend $2,000 to replace it with a Toshiba 405CS from an unknown store in "Alexandria"—but we didn't know which Alexandria.

If you pulled out a map and started planting pins, you'd find twelve places called "Alexandria" in the United States.

Steve didn't spend a lot of time looking for Toshiba purchases in Alexandria, Iowa.

From the decrypted messages, we knew Cuban agent [redacted] had access to a specific CIA document and had traveled to Cuba around a specific time.

The agent used a SAFE system—a computer system used within DIA (we later learned).

We knew [redacted] traveled legally to Guantanamo Bay for work during a specific period in the mid-1990s.

We knew about a refugee issue related to GITMO, which would have involved a lot of US government agencies.

And we had a password—"NELEBANIOS"—for the spy's covert communication system.

We knew an "Agent S" met with a person with the initials "WD" because one of the messages referred to something he said in a meeting.

A person called "Oscar" worked on "enemy services" for Cuban intelligence—the FBI, CIA, or Defense Department—and handled Cuban agent [redacted].

Finally, we knew [redacted] used 3.5-inch floppy disks as part of his covert communication system.

That narrows it down.

The Cubans go to great care to protect the identities of their spies. The FBI was convinced Cuban agent [redacted] was a man because that's how the Cubans referred to the agent: "Sergio." In the intelligence world, it's called "denial and deception."

We had other false leads. Because we didn't know how "Agent S" sent his intelligence back to Havana, we believed the agent had to be in the United States for each of the 151 valid messages.

We believed Cuban agent [redacted] worked for the US government, but we didn't know which agency—the CIA, the Defense Department, the National Security Agency, the Defense Intelligence Agency, or the FBI. Suspect population in the "enemy services"?: 2.5 million—not including contractors.

Steve started his search within the CIA because we knew about a specific CIA document the Cubans had received from "Sergio." We didn't know, of course, that Ana, because she had worked her network so hard, had unusual inter-agency access.

So that turned out to be a dead end.

Nearly one million federal employees live in Washington—a city near "Alexandria." And Cuban defectors had told us Washington was Fidel's top intelligence priority, just ahead of the Cuban-American community in south Florida, which hated him and his regime.

We just needed to narrow it down.

The tidbits we had were both specific and maddingly vague at the same time.

But sometimes, getting lucky is better than being good.

# 14

# A Pretty Face Can Hide an Evil Mind

Lady luck can be a fickle mistress.

But before we get to that, we need to back it up a bit.

We weren't the first to look for Cuban agent [redacted]—and the Defense Intelligence Agency was in it early too.

Beginning in late 1994—Bon Jovi's "Always" on the radio—a small group within the US intelligence community secretly tried to solve a big problem: identify—and neutralize—efforts by the Cuban Intelligence Service to penetrate the US government. We're not talking a couple of moles.

We're talking about *a lot* of moles.

Analysts and investigators from three agencies—the FBI, Central Intelligence Agency, and National Security Agency—formed a need-to-know team. This closely held team didn't have a name. The FBI led it, because the infiltrations were stateside, but each agency brought its best, and everyone worked together on one of the largest mole hunts in American counterintelligence history. The goal? Send Cuban spies to prison.

The problem? The government didn't know who the spies were.

When they defected in 1994, Kevin and his pals provided evidence to show just how successful the Cubans had been. But they also gave us a key to decrypt some of the high frequency messages Cuban intelligence personnel had sent to operatives in South Florida. The decryption disks didn't come by boat, for obvious reasons.

Instead, Kevin and company handed them off to US intelligence community agents in Havana. That's how the investigation into the Wasp Network—the one Ana's sister provided translations for and that caused *La Red Avispa* to go to prison—began. As they, legally, searched the homes of those involved, the FBI found more decryption clues, which allowed them to read the high frequency encrypted messages Cuba had sent to the Wasp Network. On September 12, 1998, as I finished up at Quantico, the FBI's Miami office arrested ten Cuban spy handlers in South Florida as the culmination of the investigation the Bureau called ROYAL FLUSH , the FBI code words for *La Red Avispa* investigation.

Kevin called it the biggest blow to Cuban intelligence in decades. Beyond handing the key to US officials while still in Havana, Kevin, or Mateo—both cryptologists—likely wrote some of the key.

And, unknown to me at the time, the secret, ad-hoc team of intelligence personnel looking for more Cuban agents had access to those clues. That meant they could read other messages sent by Cuban intelligence to some of their handlers and agents in the United States. This led to several new cases, mostly in New York and Washington, looking to find Cuban handlers and identify their networks of agents.

In particular, they wanted Cuban agent [redacted]. They knew this person worked for the US government—but was loyal to Castro.

At first, the decryption clues and documentation Kevin and company provided seemed like a windfall. But the number of new cases gained from that information quickly overwhelmed the small intelligence team.

So, the FBI opened an umbrella investigation—referred internally as the "[redacted]"—that included almost [redacted] investigations of Cuban agents, their handlers, and others. This was huge. And under-resourced.

If you think about the timing, Cuba sat far below the likes of Russia and China on the boogeyman list, as it does today, so the government didn't spend as much money on it. In my mind, if Cuba knows, Russia or China knows too.

But Cuban agent [redacted] got some extra attention. In 1998, Andy Guzman, an FBI agent on the Cuban counterintelligence squad at Washington Field, and a former squad mate of mine, opened a case he code-named SCAR TISSUE. Andy describes himself as a "veteran of the Cuban wars," having worked counterintelligence cases in Puerto Rico. And he's a proud, first-generation member of the FBI's elite hostage rescue team.

Like all of us, Andy had a lot going on. But he made it his mission to find Cuban agent [redacted]. He got close. In fact, Andy shared a strong lead with a Defense Intelligence Agency employee—an army lieutenant colonel named Francisco, or "Paco," who was a fellow Hispanic. (Paco's last name remains unknown.) Andy recently confirmed that DIA was involved in the search as early as 1998. The pair learned the Cubans knew about a refugee matter involving Naval Station Guantanamo Bay. They chased that tidbit hard, with Andy believing Paco was the best person to help him, but then Andy was reassigned to support the US government's Y2K preparation.

Remember that? All of the computers in the world wouldn't be able to handle the date rollover to January 1, 2000—they'd only been programmed up to 1999—and electrical systems would short, nuclear weapons systems would launch their missiles, and bank security systems would shut down. It would be chaos.

Except it wasn't. The computers were already smarter than we are.

In any case, the Cuban agent [redacted] unknown subject case was transferred to Steve McCoy, who continued to use the case's code name: SCAR TISSUE.

Early in 2000, after the computers didn't take over, Elena Valdez, a senior analyst and team lead at the National Security Agency, was working on the small, secret intelligence team looking for Cuban bad guys. (Elena's a pseudonym.)

Wayback machine again: Perry Como's live at Guantanamo Bay (really). It's 1962.

The shit's about to hit the fan.

Elena, age six, her parents, and her siblings are fleeing Cuba, days before the Cuban Missile Crisis. Her parents own a shop on the island. Protests against the new regime—Castro—have grown across the island. Friends in Cuban intelligence have warned Elena's father that Castro's minions plan to round up average citizens and keep them in jail "indefinitely."

Elena's father obtains a tourist visa and hotfoots it to Miami with his family. They never return home.

Elena told me her parents, part of the earliest wave of Cuban refugees, worked two or three jobs just to feed the kids. But they worked and worked some more until they were able to start their own business—a business that would not be indiscriminately taken over by the government.

Freedom.

Elena grew up surrounded by Cuban culture. Everyone she knew followed the regime in Cuba, hissing Castro's name. But Elena, decked out in dungarees, climbing trees, and devouring Nancy Drew and Hardy Boys mysteries, planned to be a police officer. She thoroughly understood her why: she would do everything she could to hurt the Cuban government. She would put the bad guys in jail.

In fact, at one point, she even applied to the FBI to be an agent.

Instead, she earned her degree in criminology, before heading to graduate school. Soon, she accepted a position at the National Security Agency.

In 1997, as a senior analyst, she transferred to the intelligence group that tracked Cuban agents, working for late-Marvin Shoop.

Take that, Fidel.

The team met infrequently and lacked a solid structure. More collaborative than organized, meetings consisted of interagency analytical brainstorming. They looked for actionable leads, I would later discover. And they wanted more "key." They needed to be able to read more encrypted messages that might reveal better clues.

Elena, Marvin, and their colleagues were working SCAR TISSUE, as well as several other unknown subject cases. And Elena told me she shared some of the tidbits with other Defense Department counterintelligence entities: the Air Force Office of Special Investigations, the Naval Criminal Investigative Service, and the Army's 902nd Military Intelligence Group.

"I shared, but I shared very carefully," Elena said. "And I was very careful not to share the 'crown jewels' of what we knew out of fear of alerting the potential suspect. Whoever that was."

She needed to fish for information, but she didn't know which agency the suspect worked for. If she fished too much, the suspect might flee. But every once in a while, Elena called FBI headquarters to check in on progress on the most significant cases. She usually talked with an analyst named John Paul Rosario. He was a program manager for Cuban counterintelligence cases, but he was an intelligence operations specialist. An earnest one. He was introspective, smoked a pipe, and kept a photo of Robert F. Kennedy in his cubicle.

During one of those check-ins, in early 2000, Elena asked about the SCAR TISSUE case, or Cuban agent [redacted]. Though John Paul didn't manage Washington Field's cases, he knew about the unknown subject cases.

"It's closed," Elena said John Paul told her.

"Are you kidding me?" she remembers saying.

"I'm serious," he said.

But it was a miscommunication or a misunderstanding: John Paul didn't oversee SCAR TISSUE, and the case had not been closed.

But Elena, hitting full Trixie Belden mode, decided she would simply solve the case herself. First, she worked her network inside the "No Such Agency." She talked to a guy named Joe, who worked a different side of the Cuba target, about figuring out the agencies that would have been involved in the Cuban-refugee-issue tidbit involving GITMO.

"You know who you should call?" she remembers Joe asking.

"Who?" she said.

"Ana Montes at DIA," Elena told me Joe said. "She's the go-to person on Cuba."

This would be the first time Elena heard the name Ana Montes.

Armed with a name, Elena picked up her secure phone and cold-called Montes at her desk at DIA. Desperate for a break, Elena thought if she could identify the agencies involved in the refugee issue, she would have a list of meeting attendees and thus identify suspects for Cuban Agent [redacted].

Elena dialed the number, and Ana's phone rang several times before eventually going to voicemail. Elena didn't feel comfortable leaving a voice message that was not encrypted, so she hung up.

"Thank God I got her voicemail," Elena told me. She had planned to play coy with Ana, since she wasn't in the "circle of trust" about the case.

By September 2000, Elena's frustration peaked. She had been working for nearly two years with the ad-hoc team to identify someone—anyone—of the unknown subject cases. Just after Labor Day, she crashed a conference hosted by NSA, figuring she could mingle. And mingle she did, with DIA analysts Paul Weber and John Kavanagh. (Paul Weber is a pseudonym.)

Paul told her he was working, as a Latin American counterterrorism DIA analyst, on a research paper involving ongoing Cuban sponsorship of terrorist activity throughout Latin America. Even though the US State Department had added Cuba to its list of countries that sponsor terrorism, the US intelligence community still found it challenging to implicate Cuba for sponsorship of terrorism in the late 1990s.

"You should totally publish that," Elena told me she remembers saying.

But Paul recently told me he had pushed to publish his paper, now more than eighty pages long, for the larger US intelligence community, but had been blocked at every turn.

"I can't," Paul remembers telling Elena. "Some bitch in DIA is blocking it from getting published."

It was the first good news Elena had heard in months.

"Who?" she asked.

"Ana Montes," Paul said.

Ana Montes.

Again.

A couple of months before, DIA analytical management told Paul that Ana had "analytical seniority and time in grade" over him, so they deferred to her in rejecting the findings of his counterterrorism paper, he told me. And although Paul knew Ana was the "DIA analytical rock star" on all things Cuba, he loathed her.

"I couldn't believe DIA analytical management supported Montes's blocking my publication solely based on her reputation, without giving consideration to the facts and findings of my work or even bothering to read it," Weber said. "It still boggles my mind how blinded by groupthink and analytical bias they were. In reaching such an absurdly bureaucratic decision, they were falling into the very intellectual traps that they constantly warned new analysts against."

"Loath" may not be a strong enough word.

That same summer, Paul confronted Ana during a meeting:

"Whose side are you on?" he remembers shouting.

But Ana—and his leadership—refused to budge. She deftly discounted his work.

Undeterred, Paul traveled to NSA that August to meet with an analyst named Marisol, who worked on counterterrorism issues involving Europe. He brought supporting documentation for his argument, as well as a sharp fellow DIA employee and counterintelligence analyst named Coleen who supported his project. Marisol encouraged Paul to publish his work, but also mentioned an important document that might support his case. But only a few people had access to it at DIA.

Including Ana.

Who would likely have to approve his use of it.

Paul told Marisol about his battles of trying to get anything past Ana.

"Oh, we've been told by the FBI not to coordinate anything with Ana," Paul told me he remembers Marisol saying.

Whoa.

Paul immediately deduced the FBI was investigating Ana for espionage, he told me. And suddenly, her seemingly irrational and visceral hostility to his paper made sense.

Based on Paul's memory of the timing of the conversation, it would have happened at least six weeks before the FBI—specifically, Steve McCoy—opened a preliminary investigation on Montes. Marisol did not respond to my requests to talk with her, so I could not verify or rectify this disparate timeline.

But Paul remembers driving down the Baltimore-Washington Parkway back to DIA after the meeting with Marisol.

"You have to tell your boss about this meeting with NSA today," Paul remembers telling Coleen, after sharing with her his hypothesis about Ana. Coleen worked for Army Lieutenant Colonel James Stuteville. Chris Simmons and John Kavanagh—the guy Elena had begun mingling with at the NSA conference—also worked for Stuteville.

A few days later, Paul ran into Coleen, who told him she hadn't shared the information about Ana with her boss. Soon after, on October 1, 2000, DIA sent Paul on an extended temporary duty assignment to South America that went well into 2001. He still doesn't know why he was selected for that assignment, he told me.

So back to Elena, who's still mingling at the NSA conference. She learned that John Kavanagh was a counterintelligence analyst, so she pulled him aside and told him about the Cuban-refugee-issue tidbit, as well as some other tidbits about the unknown subject cases. John leaned in close as she whispered the need-to-know information.

"This sounds like the Pentagon," she remembers him saying.

They agreed to meet someplace less mingle-y.

A week later, John and Coleen returned to NSA to brainstorm with Elena. They realized the Pentagon had to be involved with the Cuban-refugee-issue-GITMO tidbit. A week later, Elena met John with his boss, Chris Simmons (who also worked for Stuteville), at DIA. She told them she needed to piece together a puzzle. She began to show Chris some of the tidbits, one of which was part of the Defense Department's Secure Access File Exchange.

"That's us," Elena remembers Chris saying, his eyes widening.

"Do you have any more?" he asked.

"Yes," Elena remembers saying, "but you need to come up to NSA."

The remaining tidbits were classified, and she didn't want to reveal too much. Three days later, Lieutenant Colonel Stuteville told Simmons to "read in" Scott Carmichael, who was from DIA's security team. The next week, John and Scott headed to NSA to read more of the raw intelligence.

Elena watched their faces as they read.

"Ana Montes," both men silently mouthed, she told me.

"This could be a lot of people," she remembers John saying, "but this could also be Ana Montes." They asked if they could take notes, including about a trip to Guantanamo Bay that Cuban agent [redacted] had taken, which Elena's leadership agreed to.

Scott and John then briefed Simmons, and then Scott dove into DIA's travel database and came up with a list of one hundred names of people who had traveled to Cuba.

One stuck out.

"Oh shit," Scott said.[54]

Scott dug deeper and decided he knew it was her. He had her sized up for a jumpsuit: I think she's a small.

Scott, by the way, was no slouch. He had enlisted in the navy during the Vietnam War, then took a job as a cop.[55] In 1984, he went back to the navy to work for the Naval Criminal Investigative Service before hitching up with DIA in 1988. He had dealt with tough cases: He and a partner brought down Frederick Hamilton, a DIA spy who passed classified documents to the Ecuadorian Military Attaché office in Lima. His case was a bit different from the Cuban spy case: Hamilton hoped to ease tensions between Peru and Ecuador. He and his colleagues believed that if the Peruvians knew what the Ecuadorians were capable of militarily, and vice-versa, everybody would chill out. But a speedy approval for such a plan seemed like a long shot, so Hamilton took on the mission himself, purely for altruistic reasons—no money changed hands.

But you can't just hand over classified information to foreign governments, and Scott and his partner got Hamilton to confess.

In any case, I'm not all about the leakage on a need-to-know matter, but Elena talking to John Kavanagh out of school turned out to be a lucky break. In the meantime, Paul Weber's suspicions moved the search on a separate path toward Ana.

Like Elena, Scott knew that if Ana heard that she was being investigated, we'd be looking for her in Havana. So he worked his contacts until the head of security at DIA sent out a note to those who knew about the case to tell them to shut the hell up.

Scott went to FBI headquarters. The FBI's first response was, of course, "How in the hell did you find out about this case?"

But within days, Scott met with my future partner, Steve, a seasoned FBI agent.

"Yeah, I've got another bit of information, and it doesn't match your spy," Steve said, or something along those lines.

Scott, of course, didn't know, we thought, the extent of the breadcrumbs. And we couldn't tell him. But initially, some of the details simply didn't match with Ana, and not only did they not match, they seemed to show that Ana wasn't it.

We knew the suspect had traveled to Guantanamo B investigative lead," according to the Defense Departn tigator general's report. And we knew the Cubans callea u... "Sergio."

Which didn't match "Ana."

And honestly, that made sense to all of us: We weren't looking for a woman. We weren't even necessarily looking for a Hispanic person. Even Scott acknowledged that 93 percent of spies from 1950 to Ana Montes were men.[56] The only woman who had acted on her own, to that point, was Svetlana Tumanova. She was arrested in 1987 after offering up to the Soviets names and biographical information of army foreign language students training in Munich. Her parents lived in the Soviet Union, and she married someone from there—honestly, it seems a little obvious. The Soviets told her if she didn't cooperate, they'd hurt her family. She ended up with five years of probation.

And only 5 percent of women spies were Hispanic—and they all worked with someone else: Aldrich Ames's wife, Maria del Rosario Ames, and two women involved in the Wasp Network—Linda Hernandez and Amarylis Santos, who also worked with their husbands.

In the meantime, we received a torrent of data. The FBI gets a lot of information from a lot of sources. As we saw with the Unabomber case, we get it from the public. We get it from law enforcement. We get it from the US government. We get it from the US intelligence community. That's all great. We'll take anything from anybody. But it doesn't always—usually doesn't—pan out in the way we all hope it will. (If I had a dollar for all the people who truly, emphatically believe the CIA has taken over their brains using radio waves or implants...)

Steve and I—as well as the rest of the squad looking at unknown subject cases—had watched as Richard Jewell's life was destroyed when the FBI decided, based on psychological profiling, that he had bombed the 1996 Olympics in Atlanta. For almost three months, the media dragged his name through the mud after it was revealed he was a "person of interest." As it turned out, he was simply a professional—a security guard who had risked his life rushing people out of an area to safety after he found a backpack filled with pipe bombs.

And Brian Kelley worked honorably for the CIA as a counterintelligence officer. But in the 1990s, before the FBI figured out Robert Hanssen worked as a mole for the KGB, we investigated Kelley. The CIA actually suspended him before the FBI collectively tucked its tail between its legs and brought him back on, later awarding him a Distinguished Career Intelligence Medal for his service.

Carter Page is a more recent example: He was accused of linking the Donald Trump team with some folks from Russia—foreign interference. His name popped up in the infamous Steele dossier. Carter Page looked like a duck. Carter Page smelled like a duck. Carter Page wasn't a duck, according to the Robert Mueller investigation. Depending on your views of Russia and Vladimir Putin, you could argue that Carter Page is an asshole for criticizing the United States for being too harsh on Russia, but he still isn't a duck.

But the FBI came out of each of those cases smelling like something other than a duck.

Every case is an art and is a science: if you have no reasonable doubt that your person is *the* person, then there's no need for an investigation because you already have your evidence. But we weren't about to even open a case until we were pretty sure.

Everyone's talking about this Malcolm Gladwell book *Talking to Strangers*. Gladwell makes the same argument Reg Brown made for it being immediately obvious that Ana was the spy: she orchestrated the Brothers to the Rescue shooting to make the Americans look bad. Retired admiral Eugene Carroll had warned the government, one full day before the shooting, that the Cubans planned to shoot down planes in their air space, and suddenly the Americans looked bad for not taking heed of the warnings and keeping the Brothers safe. And not only that, Carroll said, on live TV, the Brothers were asking for it because the United States would have responded angrily had Cuban planes flown over Miami and dropped propaganda.

Photo by Wikipedia

*Unarmed Cessna 337 Skymaster, similar to the aircrafts used by Brothers to the Rescue that were shot down by Cuban Air Force Mikoyan MiG-29UB planes, murdering four American citizens on February 24, 1996.*

Gladwell writes about the coincidental timing that Reg Brown brought up, but also that Reg had written a report about senior Cuban officials involved in an international drug-smuggling ring.[57] But before Reg released the report, which Ana would have seen, the Cubans executed several of the officials Reg had named and issued a denial about the drug-smuggling ring.

Gladwell also writes about the mysterious Pentagon phone call: Reg said he called the Pentagon that day to talk with Ana. But a woman answered the phone and said Ana had left—that she had gotten a call, was agitated, and then told everyone she was going home because she was tired and "there was nothing going on."

Scott had no reason not to believe her: It was Sunday. The cafeteria at the Pentagon was closed. She was starving because she didn't eat food out of the vending machine because of allergies and because she was sort of maniacal about fitness. So she left.

But Gladwell argues that Scott should have known better because Ana was...

...odd.

Gladwell interviewed Brian Latell, the former national intelligence officer for Latin America, who said Ana was a terrible analyst and had weird reactions when he asked what Fidel Castro's motives might be—like she was nervous or didn't know what to say. Some believe she also wrote papers that didn't make sense, unless you sympathized with Cuba. Others, like Weber, believed she blocked publication on papers unfavorable to Cuba. But her boss, Marty Scheina, the chief of the Latin America Division at DIA, saw her as a solid employee. He "did not find any cases where she skewed her analytical views in favor of Cuba," he told me recently.

Gladwell suggests that Ana's brother and sister should have known. But Ana's brother and sister had grown up with Ana: she had always been…

…odd.

He brings up Roger too. Roger knew better than just about anybody else that Ana was…

…odd.

Ana had been odd long before she spied for Cuba.

Scott didn't say he believed Ana. He said the evidence checked out. She passed her polygraph. Scott also said he thought she lied about the phone call at the Pentagon, and he said he came away feeling uneasy, but he simply didn't have a case.

Our laws don't state that you are innocent until proven guilty… unless your accuser has a bad feeling about you. Body language? We pay attention to that, but the facts didn't line up, and you don't go after someone when the facts don't line up. This isn't Tom Cruise blowing one bubble through one nostril in *Minority Report*. We didn't have any psychics telling us what Ana was thinking, and we couldn't arrest her based on a prickly personality.

Scott did not have proof. He knew that if he kept a case open on Ana after talking with her it could affect her career—and that was even if he could have kept it open. He had a suspicion, and it didn't pan out. She lied about her drug use, she lied about having received her degree, and she lied about a phone call she received at the Pentagon. Everything else checked out.

Tell me this: The last time you went in for a job interview and the interviewer said, "Have you ever smoked weed?" did you say, "Yup. Every day for a year as a freshman in college"? Probably not.

Did she respond oddly to the accusation that she was a spy? Sure. Ana was odd. She liked to control the room. If she had responded by flipping out, that would have been out of character.

Our team also didn't want to put anybody's name out into the world until we knew we were right. Sometimes, the "sure cases" are wrong, and you can ruin people's lives in the process. We had to be sure. So yeah, DIA had the jumpsuit lined up, and Steve was feeling pretty confident, but we needed to have no doubts.

We had to think, "Okay, if we put this out there, who's going to get pummeled on the front page of the *Washington Post*?" Ana? DIA? Probably not. The FBI? Yup. We're the big boys and girls, and with that comes a big bull's eye if we fuck up.

We did not want to fuck up.

On October 13, 2000, Scott and his partner, Karl "Gator" James, met with Steve and Diane Krzemien, our boss.

"We need more facts," Steve remembers saying. He said that a lot. But he said he'd look at Scott's talking points. Scott verified some information he'd missed the first time around, and he faxed it to Steve on October 14. He was persistent as hell—and for that he deserves a ton of credit. On Monday, Steve asked Scott to meet with him again.

That day, October 16, 2000, the FBI opened an official preliminary investigation into Ana Montes.

Steve—rightfully so—was skeptical. But the FBI opened a case within two months of Steve hearing Ana's name.

Things got complicated after that: We had to prove in ways that took us away from how we knew—or at least strongly suspected—that Ana was our girl, because we couldn't take our top secret information to court. Our tidbits and the way we received them couldn't go into a court document, or classified information would end up in the news. Basically, we had great "proof," but we needed to find new proof that we could take to court without hurting national security. It was incredibly complex, and we faced a ton of pressure from FBI headquarters.

Scott and his partner continued to investigate Ana internally at DIA.

By November 2000, the FBI upgraded the preliminary investigation to a full investigation. This would allow the FBI the use of all of its investigative techniques, including physical surveillance and the ability to apply for a FISA.

Almost immediately, and completely coincidentally, Ana told her bosses she was leaving DIA. She had earned a National Intelligence Fellowship at the CIA under George Tenet—an incredibly prestigious position. She would continue to work for DIA, but she would essentially be on sabbatical at the CIA and would have access to everything. We needed to work fast, and we needed to keep her out of the CIA without letting her know we were on to her.

And, to get the CIA fellowship, she needed an updated polygraph. And we needed to get a Foreign Intelligence Surveillance Account (FISA) court order so we could surveil her activities, as well as search her apartment. Easy, right? Except if she passed the polygraph, the court would frown upon our surveillance activities: it would be that much harder to get the search warrant.

DIA was fully on board with figuring out how to quash her fellowship while understanding the need for secrecy. For us to do our jobs right, Ana couldn't know we were after a spy—and certainly not that we were after her, in particular.

At this point, we didn't know if she was still actively spying. The Wasp Network arrests had likely forced many agents underground. At least one handler, unknown to us, had been pulled back to Cuba, leaving Ana largely on her own, to dream about a future: about marriage, about quitting DIA for a job that fulfilled her, and about not falling asleep to anti-anxiety cassette tapes.

Photo by DIA

*Montes receiving DCI National Intelligence Certificate of Distinction from then DCI deputy George Tenet in 1997.*

In early December, Tenet met with Vice Admiral Thomas Wilson—the director of DIA—as well as the assistant director of the FBI, Thomas J. Pickard. Things were turning into a high-level crisis.

But Ana, with the help of *Soldier of Fortune* magazine, made things a bit easier for everybody: in August, she reached out to a reporter to ask about an article he had written. DIA required their employees to seek explicit permission before talking to members of the press—ever. She talked with the reporter—just curious about his work—and then set up time for him to talk with someone else at DIA. In real life, it was no big deal. But Scott used it to delay her polygraph until after we could get our FISA order.[58]

By mid-December, we were approved for a full field investigation, which meant we could use all the FBI's investigative techniques to go after Ana. DIA, in the meantime, gathered maps and blueprints of DIA's headquarters at Bolling Air Force Base, where Ana's office was, so they could monitor her after we got the FISA approved.

Gator started looking at her phone and email records, as well as her computer files.

Nada.

I still wasn't officially on the case, beyond whiteboarding with the team.

But Santa came early.

Stuart Hoyt, a retired FBI agent and Cuban counterintelligence legend, hosted our squad's Christmas party that year. Steve and I spent some time at the festivities bullshitting about the Cuban spy case.

"Yeah, we got a name," he said. I don't think he mentioned Ana at that point. We had been generally tossing around the "tidbits" in the office, but I didn't realize those breadcrumbs had potentially led somewhere.

At the party, Steve talked about trying to crack how she was sending messages and what those messages said.

"Dude," I said. "You know I had to get a ham radio license as a kid, right?"

Dah-Dit-Dah-Dit, Dah-Dah-Dit-Dah. Dit.

It's not necessarily something I bring up often—it's not the trick I use at parties to impress people.

But remember Dad's giant antenna on Mom's shiny new lawn? Dad made me get an amateur ham radio license, memorize the Morse code, and study radio theory. But the theory part would help us understand how Ana communicated with the Cubans. I had a little bit of background with the high frequency stuff—and it turned out to be kind of interesting. Once again, my father was right.

We knew Cuba actively sent high frequency radio messages to someone and had been doing so since 1992. Those messages could be picked up in a frequency range that reached everywhere from Havana to Miami to North Carolina to the District of Columbia. This was a little bit above the local DC101 radio station range, but the frequency didn't have to be 7,000 megahertz, or super high range—more like 3,000 megahertz—for the signal to reach that ninety-mile range. One of the little bits of information also showed that the person receiving messages from Cuba was somewhere between North Carolina and Maine, which really fucking narrowed it down. I mean, gee, why don't you just say, "Left of the Mississippi"? In any case, Steve needed someone who knew how radio worked.

I didn't have a ton of experience with the high frequency tech, but I had more than anybody else on the team did.

"Do you mind if I help out with that?" I asked Steve at that December 2000 Christmas party.

"Yeah," he said. "That'd be great."

As I mentioned, I had been listening in on the unknown subject cases as a member of the squad, so I knew they existed and that there were spies out there waiting to be found. But this was a specific case, and it was a big one. This felt more like what I had signed up for: taking down the bad guys.

And Steve and I became partners—something I had missed since being a cop in Coatesville.

Photo by Charlie Archambault

*Montes FBI co-case agents, Steve McCoy (L) and author.*

# 15

## Livin' On a Prayer

Now that we had a name, we could start seriously investigating Montes: physical surveillance, records checks, and lines of credit. But as with all major espionage investigations, we had a big hurdle to get over: we needed an electronic surveillance and covert search warrant.

And we needed to get inside her apartment.

To get this level of intrusive authority, we had to convince a federal judge, bound by the rules of the Foreign Intelligence Surveillance Act of 1978, that Ana was an agent of a foreign power. So far, our case was circumstantial. We certainly couldn't go to the court and say, "But your honor, Scott at DIA says Ana is a spy, and he thinks she would look lovely in an orange jumpsuit."

We had to make our case to the FISA Court.

Think about this: At FBI headquarters, we daily feel the presence of the founder of the FBI—and godfather of modern law enforcement—J. Edgar Hoover. We operate in the Hoover Building. We display his desk and globe as artifacts to the legacy of the man who formed the Bureau, and then transformed it, arguably, into the greatest law enforcement agency in the world. His name adorns what is often described by tourists—as well as occupants—as the ugliest building in D.C.

Among the plethora of Hoover stories—and there are some doozies—we learned that Hoover inadvertently sent hundreds of agents to the US borders because he wrote, "Watch the borders," on a memo. He meant the borders of the memo—keep 'em at one inch, fellas!—not the borders of the country. Who knows what those dudes thought they were looking for as they scrambled toward Canada and Mexico.

Many long-retired FBI agents speak reverently about Hoover and staunchly defend his legacy. Steve's dad, for example, grew up in Hoover's FBI. Steve followed in his father's footsteps, but on his own merit, starting as a clerk and grinding his way through law school at night. Later in his career, Steve's dad became a high-ranking bureau agent who worked under Hoover. We rarely, if ever, spoke about J. Edgar.

But Hoover has a complicated legacy.

Under Hoover's leadership, and direct orders, the FBI illegally spied against "subversive" groups, including Puerto Rican independence groups, the NAACP, the Black Panther Party, the Ku Klux Klan, communist sympathizers, and others Hoover deemed as threats to national security. He and his FBI subjected these groups and their members to "counterintelligence" investigations and techniques under the FBI's Counter Intelligence Program (COINTELPRO), though the Senate's Church Committee later found that "bureau witnesses admit that many of the targets were nonviolent and most had no connections with a foreign power."[59] Probably the most egregious was Hoover's treatment of Dr. Martin Luther King Jr., who seemed to have particularly drawn Hoover's ire. With a short-term approval by then-Attorney General Robert Kennedy, Hoover and his FBI conducted legally tenuous wiretaps of Dr. King—though Hoover's approval of the surveillance against the civil rights leader would later intensify without Kennedy's knowledge and approval.

It is a stain on the legacy of Hoover, the FBI, and our nation.

As a result of a burglary—this time at an FBI office in Media, Pennsylvania, by the group Citizens' Commission to Investigate the FBI—the world would learn about COINTELPRO. The Senate's Church Committee took on the work of exposing and reforming the counterintelligence activities of the FBI after the Senate's Watergate committee found some of the FBI's domestic activities were "constitutionally questionable."[60]

"Government officials—including those whose principal duty is to enforce the law—have violated or ignored the law over long periods of time and have advocated and defended their right to break the law," the Church Committee found.[61]

Pretty damning statement.

Congress passed the Foreign Intelligence Surveillance Act of 1978, known as FISA, to limit both electronic eavesdropping, as well as physical searches.

As an agent, FISA was the bane of my existence, but also one of the most important pieces of legislation I've ever encountered. We'll call it a hate/love relationship.

Although imperfect, FISA improves our handling of true national security threats from foreign powers and their agents, like Ana. Recently, the FBI—rightfully so—took its lumps on its FISA performance in relation to the Carter Page investigation. We talked about him earlier: he's the guy accused of linking Trump with the Russians, the one who looked like a duck but wasn't proven to be a duck. Page claimed in court that the FBI's year-long surveillance of his communications was an abuse of power. The Justice Department inspector general agreed.

During my time at Quantico, we vigorously studied our Constitution's Fourth Amendment. Of all the amendments, I believe it is one of the most important to the work of the FBI because it provides

Americans with protections from unwarranted searches and seizures. It also allows us—federal agents—to conduct physical searches and electronic surveillance:

> *The right of the people to be secure in their person, houses, and effects, against unreasonable search and seizures, shall not be violated, and no Warrants shall issue, but upon probable cause, supported by Oath or affirmation and particularly describing the place to be searched, and the persons or things to be seized.*[62]

Law enforcement holds an awesome power to protect our nation, and FISA allows the government to delve into the most private areas of our lives, including our personal communications and our homes. The law provides oversight—because we now have to prove probable cause that our target is either a foreign power or the agent of a foreign power, and not, say, the Democratic National Committee or Martin Luther King Jr.—while allowing us to keep our actions secret so we don't tip off a target that we're on to them. It's a privilege that the FBI should never take lightly.

But FISA meant we had to work harder to get the authority to dig into Ana's physical or electronic property.

In December 2000, Steve wrote up our FISA application and sent it to headquarters for their input, where after some improvements, the FBI sent it off to the Justice Department. Steve used every one of his creative writing skills—honed during his study of English literature at Duke—because our case, like most counterintelligence investigations, was circumstantial. We had the tidbits that started the unknown subject case of Cuban agent [redacted], and we had bits about how Montes matched those tidbits. We showed that the "North Carolina to Maine" information pointed toward D.C., especially as Castro had always been obsessed with Washington's policy against Cuba, and the Cubans probably wouldn't glean much from Charlotte, lovely as it may be. We also knew the Cubans had told agent [redacted] to buy a Toshiba 405CS laptop computer in October 1996 for $2,000 from an unknown store in "Alexandria."

We figured that meant Alexandria, Virginia—we just needed to find the shop. And we knew the Cubans had sent "Sergio" feedback about a CIA report that "Sergio" had provided.

You remember "Sergio"? He was Steve's main reason for initially not considering Ana as a suspect.

Kevin and company had given us this intelligence spark after they stole it from Cuba. The "key" opened encrypted high frequency communications between the Cubans in Havana and some of their illegal officers in Miami which led to illegal officers—like Ana's handler—operating elsewhere in the United States. We could read a brief series of messages from 1996 that went to Ana's illegal officer at the time, who she knew as Ernesto. The intelligence Kevin's trio stole would ultimately lead to many successful prosecutions of other agents.

After Ana became known to the FBI, there had been a "WD"—as the decrypted messages mentioned—who met with Montes at an inter-agency meeting on the topic of Cuba: William Doherty, who was the FBI's chief for the Global Counterintelligence Section at FBI headquarters.

Doherty knew we were looking for a spy, but he didn't mention the tidbits to Ana. She didn't have a "need to know." Had he shared, Ana would have fled to Cuba.

We used the "WD" tidbit as corroborating information to share with the FISA judge.

We acted pretty quickly on the Toshiba information too. It seemed easy enough: we just had to find a computer receipt from some store in some city of Alexandria in some part of the United States. Probably they did not mean Iowa.

I hoped.

But it could be North Carolina or Massachusetts. Alexandria, Virginia, sits within spitting distance of the Pentagon, so we figured we'd start there.

In October 1997, the Cubans told their agent to go buy a Toshiba laptop because the one they had been using was on the fritz.

So I called Toshiba.

"Hi, my name's Pete Lapp, and I'm trying to catch a spy," I said, or something like that. "Is there a way to determine if someone bought a specific kind of computer in a certain area during a specific time period?"

Bolo. Toshiba sent their computers to a distributor who sent the computers to stores. Back then, it wasn't just Best Buy and Amazon—there were a ton of little mom-and-pop stores. After the computers hit the electronics stores, Toshiba lost track of them.

But the person on the phone had an idea.

"Perhaps your spy filled out a warranty card?"

Right. Who in the hell actually fills out those things?

The warranty card was a dead end.

But Ana Montes bought the computer under her true name.

I'd sent a National Security Letter asking for Ana Montes's line of credit. Interestingly, in October 1996, Ana took out a line of credit for $2,000. At CompUSA.

"Can you tell me what store?"

"No. CompUSA."

Right.

In the meantime, FISA required that we tell the court both the good and the bad, so we had to disclose a strike against us. You may remember that, in 1994, two years after the Cubans started to send encrypted high frequency messages, and nine years after she began to work for DIA, Ana passed a DIA polygraph. DIA employees hadn't been required to sit on "the box" back when DIA hired Ana.

But she had dreaded the possibility from the beginning.

When she and Marta traveled to Cuba in the early 1980s, Ana nagged the Cubans to teach her how to beat the polygraph. Ana's persistence finally broke them down, and they set her up with a polygraph test to prove to her it didn't work.

"Do you intend to commit espionage against the United States?" the Cuban polygrapher asked her, or something like that.

"No," Ana responded.

Lie.

The Cubans showed her the squiggly lines and bullshitted that she had passed.

See? Voodoo.

She likely hadn't actually passed.

But in 1994, when DIA randomly selected Ana to take a test, she beat the polygraph by contracting the sphincter muscles in her anus during the control questions. Like, bear down. Her results?

I suppose Gladwell could argue the DIA did not pay close enough attention to her body language in that situation.

Her results? No deception indicated.

Years later, the government would require all polygraph takers—including me—to sit on a wired cushion, which I refer to as the "Montes Whoopee Cushion," to prevent the sphincter countermeasure trick. It measures, well, you know. In DIA's defense, the polygrapher had no indication this model employee was a spy because no one suspected anything at the time.

Despite Ana's fabulous muscle control, Steve's FISA masterpiece arrived with a pretty bow in front of a judge. The FISA court meets in a secret room in the heart of the Justice Department—what we call Main Justice. The judges, all eleven of whom are federal judges appointed by a president and then Senate-confirmed, rotate among a dozen judges from around the country. That week, the judge on rotation was from New York. Although neither Steve nor I were there, we learned he read our application with deep skepticism, telling the poor headquarters agent something along the lines of, "This is the weakest case I have ever read."

But your Honor, Scott has the jumpsuit sized and ready....

This wasn't the first time our FISA application received this kind of criticism. When the application arrived at the Justice Department's Office of Intelligence Policy and Review, it landed like a thud. Fran Townsend, who at the time was counsel to the attorney general and director of the Office of Intelligence Policy and Review, thought it was a "weak case." She and William Doherty, aka "WD," who was the senior executive at FBI headquarters over the investigation, had a pretty long conversation about the merit of our application. In the end, she agreed to move it forward and let the judge, well, judge. But let's be clear: Fran didn't have a rubber stamp at her "Counsel to the Attorney General" desk.

Reluctantly, the judge signed our FISA, but he told the Bureau it would need to go back to him in New York in ninety days for renewal. He "didn't want to have this case bounce around to other judges and just be renewed by whoever," I remember being told he said. It makes sense: Brian Kelly and Carter Page. The judge didn't want any ducks. And he wanted to see progress—significant investigative progress.

DIA had Ana all but convicted of espionage, but the court thought we may have the wrong person.

At least there was no pressure.

Back at FBI headquarters, Ana Maria Mendoza, our headquarters program manager, took issue with my investigative focus.

"This is a waste of time," she told me. "Now that you have the FISA, you need to get in her apartment."

Roger that, but I hoped a receipt would solidify our "weakest case" FISA.

On a beautiful day in early April, Steve and I went down to the CompUSA in Alexandria to see if they keep their ridiculously old receipts. "Sure. We keep a trailer out back with five years' worth of sales receipts in shoeboxes."

About twenty minutes later, we found a sales slip. Exact brand, make, and model. $1,900. Ana Montes.

That bit of paper instantly removed all doubt from my mind: She's a spy. She's a fucking spy.

I brought it in to Ana Maria and put it on her desk.

"Here. This is evidence," I said. "We are positively convinced that she's who we're looking for. She is Cuban Agent [redacted]."

Ana Maria agreed and arranged for headquarters to get in front of the head of the FISA Court. From there on, our FISA renewals were smooth and effortless.

We took it to Scott. "Hey, Scott, we got the sales slip."

"Great," he said. "Now you're where I've been for six months."

That tension was palpable and understandable. Scott was right.

We had several small victories, even as we were humbled by Ana's ability to operate in broad daylight.

One day, Tré, our squad mate, was messing around in the office.

"You know, this 'NELEBANIOS'? It's Sonia Belén." It was like, *Shit. Belén's her middle name.*

Who would have thought someone would use a true part of their name for covert communication? She was playing right under our noses. Ana's sister later told me that Ana had always loved palindromes—"Ana" is a palindrome. She wrote lists of them.

In the FBI's defense, Ana didn't use "Ana Belén Montes" at DIA—she used "Ana B. Montes."

Still, it was humbling.

Two days after the judge signed our FISA, another espionage case made the headlines: on February 18, 2001, the FBI arrested one of our own, Robert Hanssen, an FBI counterintelligence agent, on charges of spying for Russia. That one hurt.

The FBI called all surveillance personnel from Washington Field—where the Hanssen case was worked two floors down from our squad—to headquarters so Director Louis Freeh could personally thank them. Included were the teams we had on Ana. But that night would be the first since Ana had been named as a suspect that the Cubans would send her a high frequency message.

Because of the Hanssen-appreciation party, we couldn't prove she was home to receive the message because we had no surveillance team on her.

Fucking Murphy.

This would not be the last time he made an appearance.

# 16

# All-Time High

It took us months to get to this moment.

It almost didn't happen.

What I was about to do was simple: put a key into the door of a residence, open the door, and walk in. I had done this thousands of times over the course of my life, without so much as a thought. But this time it wasn't my door, and this time it wasn't my home.

Ana had no idea a group of FBI agents was about to enter her house while she was out of town visiting her boyfriend, Roger, in Miami.

Without a warrant, my team and I would have been guilty of burglary—a felony in the nation's capital. But I was about to commit the second most famous "burglary" in the history of Washington. I had a classified covert search warrant the Foreign Intelligence Surveillance Court had granted to the FBI, and I was about to lead a team to conduct a "government-sanctioned burglary"—otherwise known as a black bag job—into Ana's most sacred sanctity: her home.

Memorial Day feels like a solemn, yet highly anticipated, three-day holiday weekend. I'm a veteran, and I'm one of many who remembers the brave men and women who died for our country. And I'm also one of many who anticipates the kick-off to summer, which means getting together with friends and family to relax and re-energize.

But for me, this was not going to be the typical holiday weekend.

Before we can make a covert entry, the FBI's Tactical Operations Section from Quantico must first conduct a survey. The FBI can get through a locked door, but we also needed TacOps to make sure the keys worked because the last thing we needed was for the neighbors to see us picking a lock. I had worked for months to get a copy of her key from the co-op's key box, where all tenants were required to keep a spare in case of emergency.

On a beautiful day in early May, while Ana sat in her cubicle at DIA, Kevin Leuenberger, who was our Washington Field Office tech agent, and Don, from Quantico's TacOps, stood in front of Ana's co-op. Her door had two locks, like most old apartments, one of which was a deadbolt. Using the keys, they went inside, did a quick

Photo by Author

*Cleveland Park co-op building on Macomb Street where Montes resided. Her residence, where the FBI conducted multiple FISA covert entries, was inside the three windows to the upper left of the green awning.*

walk-around, and, after about an hour, they left, locking the doors in the same way in which they had found them.

Or so they thought.

Minutes after Ana returned home from work, she sent an email to the Cleveland Park co-op board members and the property management company.

"Hey—who was in my apartment today?" she wrote in an email I later saw. "I know someone was in my apartment today because I always lock the top lock, and when I came home, the deadbolt was unlocked. On top of that, the bottom lock is now broken, so I've had to call a locksmith. Thanks—Ana"

*Fuck.*

Clearly, Murphy had joined Kevin and Don on their walkabout. We'd finally gotten the FISA—for the weakest case ever—and now Ana knew somebody had been in her apartment.

We had access—legally—to her emails, so we saw her note about the lock almost immediately. The guy who gave me the key? Yeah, he was also on the email chain.

Peter Green was not the first person we approached as we tried to develop a source who could get us the key. We had found a co-op tenant who, as a member of the co-op board, had full access to the emergency key closet. This person had something we thought we needed: a clearance. She worked for the US government, which was perfect. Except, she didn't want to play.

*Um, excuse me? You're on Team USA, aren't you?*

I was beyond incredulous when she didn't want to be our number one source.

But when one door closes, sometimes another door opens. We looked for someone else who could help us get a key.

And that's when we found Peter.

As a businessman, he had much to lose helping us with a black bag job. Pre-9/11, fashionable folks in D.C. circles did not assist the FBI. But when I learned his father had retired from the National

Security Agency, I thought, *I'll bet we could trust this guy.* We could: Peter created reasons for us to be in Ana's co-op. (Thank you, Peter).

And I didn't take his help lightly. Holding a copy of the email, I stormed down to the third floor to find our tech squad supervisor, Dave. I barged into his office.

"What the fuck, Dave?" I said, as I threw the email at him.

"Shit," he said, Boston accent lending weight to the word. "Let me call Kevin and Don to find out what happened."

I headed back to my desk, thinking about doomsday options for our case. I knew we had blown it.

As I sat, head in hands, I got a phone call. Dave wanted me back down in his office. I tried to calm myself as I descended the four flights of stairs.

"Look," he said, as I appeared, "I talked to the guys: they were adamant she hadn't locked it."

"I don't give a fuck what they said, Dave," I said, asshole accent lending weight. "I only care about what she thinks, and she thinks someone was in her apartment. And guess what? She's fucking right!"

But…she might have dropped her purse, gotten distracted, and forgotten to lock the top lock after she retrieved it. Or, there might have been a building snoop. Or she might have locked the damned thing.

I called Peter back and apologized profusely on behalf of the FBI. Taking full responsibility, and with my hat firmly in my hand, I asked him to make a copy of the new key after Montes placed it in the co-op building's lockbox. For this unfortunate turn of events, the FBI paid him, let's just say, a lot of money.

It might just be the most expensive key ever made.

For the next three weeks, we waited. We didn't know what Ana was thinking. *Are they on to me? Am I being paranoid? Did I forgot that I dropped my purse?* We waited, hoping she added the incident to the *Huh. That was weird* category and forgot it.

I'm not here to dump on Kevin, Don, or Dave. Combined, these three outstanding FBI agents probably conducted hundreds of these operations—and most of their successes remain classified. According to Ronald Kessler in his book, *The Secrets of the FBI*, "In any given year, TacOps conducts as many as 400 of what the FBI calls covert entries."[63] In the movies, black bag jobs are either always flawlessly executed or there is some magic Hollywood trick that fixes shit that breaks.

In the real world—at the pointy end of the spear—shit happens and there is no Hollywood fix.

Murphy hadn't finished with us.

Ana's co-op offered an array of operational challenges and quirks. We knew the co-op owner just below her used his apartment as an office during normal business hours on weekdays. That made going in during the day, when most of the rest of the co-op was at work, risky. A retired couple lived across the hall from Ana. The husband liked to walk around the building during the day. He meant no harm and was likely not on official neighborhood watch duty, but we called him "nosy neighbor."

The co-op had an oddly tightly knit board—and the tenants looked out for each other. In most city buildings, people can go years without saying more than "good morning." But people in Ana's building were social, and they paid attention to the building's goings-on.

Ana's co-op, one of ten on her floor, looked down on Macomb Street from the front of the building. Down the hall, and on the same side as her apartment, one of her neighbors ran a legitimate massage business out of her home. I had toyed with making an appointment as a ruse to get into the building for a legitimate reason—but I figured getting the Bureau to approve my on-the-clock massage wouldn't be worth the paperwork.

That spring, one of Ana's neighbors had an open house one Sunday afternoon as they tried to sell their co-op. I didn't want to later be recognized, so we sent Steve to the open house to get a feel for the apartments.

Shortly after the open house started, Steve was buzzed in at the front door. He immediately encountered a sign-in sheet. Steve had lived in his home for decades by that point and probably hadn't been to an open house in just as long. Under the watchful eye of an aggressive listing agent on the hunt for her next client, Steve quickly came up with a fake name. But the sign-in sheet also asked for employment.

"FBI agent" didn't seem like the right move.

"Sod farmer," Steve wrote.

And he had, in fact, worked as a sod farmer in a previous life. He figured he could bullshit his way through a deep conversation about the ups and downs of the industry. But nobody asked.

Open houses often draw curious neighbors—for decorating tips, for comparison for a future sale of their own place, for pure nosiness. As Steve chatted with potential buyers in a bedroom of the unit, in walked Ana. He now stood face-to-face with the woman he had chased for years as an unknown subject spy case.

*Time for small talk*, he thought.

"Hey," Steve asked, cucumberly calm, "do you live in the area?"

"I actually live in the building," Ana replied, Steve recalled.

"Oh great!" Steve told me he said. "Do you like it? Are the schools good?"

"Well, I don't have kids so I can't comment on the schools, but the building is great," Ana told him. "Super quiet. And everyone keeps to themselves, which I really like."

*I'll bet*, Steve thought.

She was pleasant and upbeat, a far cry from her introverted and sour work persona.

Steve would remember the quick conversation. Ana would not.

A week before Memorial Day weekend, we learned through our wiretaps that Ana planned to visit Roger in Miami. After our surveillance team confirmed she had made her flight, we decided to go into her place during the workday Friday. My team—Kevin; Rusty Rothenthal, who was our computer forensics expert; Zach;

and me—showed up in broad daylight just before lunch. Zach had come up from Quantico and was on TacOps's "Flaps and Seals" team, which, Kessler writes,[64] "concentrates on special techniques the occupants may use to detect intruders." Flaps agents make sure you don't get caught tripping over an intentional trap or disturbing too much dust. Steve and I called Zach, our flaps agent, "Mr. Dust Bunny," because he would catch dust bunnies floating in the air and gently place them back in the spot from which they had floated away. Even though I was technically in charge at Ana's place, I knew to follow Zach's perfectionist ways.

This was, after all, my first burglary.

I had been planning this covert entry for months—so much so that Steve started to call me "the cat burglar."

I knew, going in, that we'd find something in there that would prove our case. The FISA warrant goal is explicit: collect foreign intelligence. But I wanted more. I wanted an arrest warrant.

We marched up the steps in front of her brick building. Turning the key, we entered the main entrance quickly.

Easy.

Without a word, we walked up the marble stairs to the second floor and Ana's co-op. As we approached her door and our footsteps echoed through the long hallway, my heart began to beat faster. We had to get it right.

While on probation early in my career, I rammed a door down while we executed a criminal search warrant for a drug case. As probationary agents, we worked all kinds of cases to round out our training.

It wasn't my case, but on that day, I was the third person in the stack as we hit the house at 6 a.m. with a criminal search warrant. Someone pounded on the front door. "FBI! FBI! Search warrant!" My heart pounded because I was worried about being shot.

And that's exactly why I joined the FBI.

Heart pounding. Palms sweaty. Alive.

After a few moments, the case agent gave me the nod to use the battering ram. I took aim at the door handle, and, within two strikes, the door was off its hinges and the homeowners were now awake.

As I stood in front of Ana's door, my heart raced faster than it did during that drug raid.

Up to this point, we could have made up some excuse to be in the building if confronted by a nosy neighbor. But this was blatant. Had a neighbor seen us as we entered Ana's door, we were done. This time, I didn't fear being shot—I feared being caught.

I turned the keys quickly—and yeah, I noted she always locks both locks—and we walked in. The team quickly followed, and we quietly shut the door behind us.

We were in.

And then we were miserable.

Ana didn't have air-conditioning—not even a window unit. I took this as proof enough that she was our spy: Who in the hell doesn't have air-conditioning in the swamp?

We knew the guy with the office in his apartment was likely downstairs, so we couldn't make any noise. Old apartment, old hardwood floors. I felt like I was walking around trip wires. We couldn't talk—just whisper and motion. Her high ceilings seemed to send any sound boomeranging through the building. And we certainly weren't going to use her tap or her glasses. None of us had brought water.

Ana had left D.C. the day before and left the windows open. Her co-op, about one thousand square feet, had one bedroom and a sitting room. A couple of closets were filled with clothes, old purses, wallets, linens. And there were books. Lots of books. And lots of floppy disks.

We had to move quickly—before people started to come home from work. If we tried to search it all at once, it could lead us to be sloppy. And there was simply too much. My mind raced.

*What if we put a book back in the wrong spot? Or move a purse that she placed in an exact way so that she could tell whether someone—like the FBI—had been in her co-op looking through her stuff?*

I had to think like Ana.

If I were Ana, where would I hide a laptop? Where would I hide the disks that I used to decrypt the messages from the Cubans?

After a quick walk around the apartment, I decided to start in her bedroom. Across from her bed sat a small desk with a large Gateway desktop computer with speakers. Interesting.

*Wow*, I remember thinking. *Gateway computer.*

My dad had loved that brand, but it wasn't the computer I was looking for.

But a Sony shortwave radio, in its original box, sat under the window overlooking Macomb Street. It had rained the night before, and the box was wet.

*Jackpot.*

We hadn't been able to prove she owned a shortwave radio, which she needed to listen to the Cubans' high frequency messages. Our surveillance teams had watched her make pay phone calls, but I still couldn't prove she tuned into her favorite "Radio Havana" station. The pay phone calls weren't enough for an arrest warrant. I took a couple of photos, and we carefully pulled the radio from the box. I powered up the radio and looked in the preset memory for frequencies I knew the Cubans used to send her messages. I didn't expect to find them—that would have been poor spy craft on Ana's part—and I didn't. But the radio worked.

Progress.

We searched for the frequencies. She must have written them down and hidden them somewhere in her apartment. It was too much to memorize, given that there were six different frequencies that corresponded to when the messages were broadcast—twice on Tuesday, twice on Thursday, and twice on Saturday night.

Zach and I searched for the Toshiba laptop. I prayed it was in the apartment and not at the bottom of the Potomac River. Starting with her closet, I didn't see an obvious hiding spot. Then I stood with my back toward the closet. *What would Ana do*? I tried to imagine her using the radio: She sat on the bed and took the radio out of the box. She placed the radio on the old radiator under the window. The bedroom was tiny, with barely any room around the bed. Her apartment sat at the bottom of Macomb Street, so she would have to stick the antenna out of the window to get good reception. This I knew because I had spent many nights in my Bu-car (Bureau car) with my own shortwave radio trying to hear her broadcasts.

Closing my eyes, I imagined her setting up the radio, tuning in the frequency for the broadcast, and then pulling out her laptop computer to decrypt the message.

From under her bed.

I knelt next to her bed and pulled up her comforter. I saw a blue and black backpack dead middle under her bed. I pulled it out, pleased at the weight of it. Inside, I found the laptop.

Not just any laptop. It was a Toshiba 405CS.

I knew the Cubans told her to buy a Toshiba 405CS laptop and a backpack in October 1996—this was one of our surest of our "tidbits" I also knew, through credit records and a sales slip, that she had done so.

But now, we could prove she had it. Still. And just feet from her shortwave radio. Rusty made a forensic image of the computer, capturing all its files and data, and then placed it back into the backpack, carefully sliding it to the exact spot we had found it. I had no idea what was on it.

I could see the sunlight changing. We need to move quickly. In her desk, we found a stack of floppy disks.

Let me back up here to that Toshiba computer we knew Cuban agent [redacted] bought to replace a Tandy computer that started having problems somewhere around September 1996. So Steve and I had gone on the search to find the store in Alexandria-hopefully-not-Iowa, but I was able to use that little tidbit from Kevin and crew in another way.

Back in the day, RadioShack made Tandy computers. After we got our receipt showing Ana bought the Toshiba, I sent a "SAC letter"—special agent in charge—asking them to send us a list of everything Ana had ever bought at RadioShack.

The list was long. And scary, if you happen to be worried about the security of your nation. Over the years, she bought one hundred blank floppy disks. That's a lot of lost intelligence. They also confirmed that she tried to get a Tandy 1400 FD computer fixed in 1996.

As I continued my search of her apartment, in the next drawer down, I found a twenty-five-foot mono earpiece. The earpiece was odd—it wasn't stereo, of course, so you wouldn't use it to listen to music. She didn't take it to the gym and attach it to her Walkman.

But there it was in the second drawer. She had wrapped all twenty-five feet around a large roll of tape.

I pictured her using the earpiece to listen discreetly—the neighbors mustn't find out—to her messages.

*Atención, atención, uno, dos, tres, quatro…*

In Miami, where Lucy worked, the FBI had found mono earpieces as they covertly searched the homes of *La Red Avispa*.

The earpiece was also on the list of Ana's purchases from RadioShack.

Zach and I found a bunch of wallets and purses in her closets, but we didn't have time to go through them. I still needed the floppy disks with the encryption key the Cubans had given her. She used the disks to decrypt the encrypted high frequency messages she received over the shortwave radio. The purses would have to wait.

We put everything back in place and left as quietly and quickly as we had entered. Our team picked us up down the street, and we went back to the field office. I had to brief what we had found. I knew it would get management's attention.

After I slammed some water, Diane, Steve, and I went down to brief Diane's boss, Assistant Special Agent in Charge Dan Cloyd. Dan had overseen the Hanssen espionage case. Hanssen had been arrested in February and would be on his way to pleading guilty by July. We all respected Dan—he was smart and had focused most of his FBI career working against the Russians.

Dan's spacious office had a sitting area, but there was no place for me. I sat on the floor in my jeans and sweat-stained T-shirt with my back against the wall.

I felt drained.

Dan sat in his chair caressing the top part of his now bald head. It was Dan's signature, odd move. Prior to the FBI, Dan had been a college professor, and this tic made me think of him as an academic in deep thought, almost coaxing his brain to absorb and process what he heard. He was clearly deep in thought.

I finished.

"Well," Dan said, with his slow and measured Southern drawl, "it sounds like you had a pretty good search and found some good stuff. Keep me posted on what y'all find on the computer."

It may not sound like much, but it hit me right in the feels. I admired Dan, so I appreciated the compliment.

And I knew we had done well. I'd make that judge eat his words: Ana was not only Cuban agent [redacted], but she still had the tools she used to communicate with Castro's regime to damage US national security.

Still, we faced intense pressure from DIA: they knew she was a spy and they wanted her gone. But we had to do it right—and for the right reasons. I felt the weight of the FBI's reputation on my shoulders. The Hanssen case—years of spying under our noses for the Russians—had brought us down. And I felt the pressure of Hoover's legacy and all the things he did wrong.

But I loved figuring out the details and the plan, and then executing it. I loved planning ways to get in and get out of her apartment without being caught. I loved the thrill of possibly getting caught. It hadn't been clear until we entered Ana's apartment: this was why I joined the FBI.

I loved being a cat burglar.

I rode into the holiday weekend pumped with adrenaline but deep in thought: What was on the laptop and disks? And I still worried

Ana was thinking about the key/lock issue. I was distracted as hell, like never before on a case. I couldn't get outside of my own head.

It would take us weeks to learn what the Toshiba contained.

Tom Petty was right. Waiting *is* the hardest part.

# 17

# Misunderstood

Of course, it was a Friday.

Because shit, both good and bad, always happens on Fridays.

Tom Petty songs aside, we had been waiting—patiently—for this call and hoping for good news. Finally, three weeks after our search, the call came: "Stand by the secure fax machine because we have something for you." After the covert entry over Memorial Day weekend, we had sent a copy of our image of Ana's computer to another government agency in the intelligence community. We wanted to see if there was any stenography on the computer, or evidence of spy craft.

What we got back was even better.

Inside Ana's computer, they had essentially found a journal.

*Dear Fidel,*

*Today I learned classified information about US defense capabilities regarding (fill in the blank). Good luck!*

*Love, Ana*

I took some poetic license there, but it's not far from what we actually found.

Page after page of Spanish text came in over the fax machine. In essence, it was some of Ana's communications to the Cubans, written by her as if it were her personal diary, and some of the Cubans' communications to Ana. Ana had typed it into her computer in Spanish. She then encrypted her notes using software the Cubans had given her, loaded the files onto a three-and-a-half-inch floppy disk, and handed the disk to her handlers when they met up for Chinese food at lunch. Our experts found eleven pages of it in the deleted and slack space of her computer—meaning she thought she had wiped the information from her computer. For as good as the Cubans' covert communications capabilities were, their wipe program sucked. Ana had no idea what remained on the computer she had hidden under her bed. A significant amount of the information Ana had sent to the Cubans was classified and considered national defense information. This was a critical element of Title 18 of US Code Section 794(a): Gathering or delivering defense information to aid foreign government.

Espionage.

I had read all the major arrest warrants for Hanssen, Ames, and Earl Edwin Pitts. My goal was to find evidence that fit 794.

As page after page came across the secure fax machine, Steve and I, along with Stu and Molly Flynn, who both could read Spanish, traded pages back and forth with glee and excitement.

Before the 9/11 attacks, Steve and I weren't allowed to directly work with either the Justice Department or local prosecutors to determine if we had enough to make an arrest because of the "wall" between national security and criminal cases—more consequences of the sins of the FBI's past. At DIA, Scott worked behind the scenes with Admiral Wilson to make sure something legitimate occupied Ana's time so she would not grow suspicious, but also so she couldn't hurt anything.

But this was my eureka moment. I knew we would one day see parts of Ana's "diary" in a public arrest warrant. We use FISA to collect foreign intelligence, but that doesn't mean intelligence can't also be used as probable cause for an espionage arrest. Even without the expert opinion of a federal prosecutor, Steve and I knew we were reading the essence of her eventual demise.

In one portion, the Cubans discussed with her a beeper that was public, or, "in other words, it is known to belong to the Cuban Mission to the UN, and we assume there is some control over it," the diary stated. Or, "Hey, the FBI might know about this pager, so be careful."

Thanks guys. Now we can prove the foreign power part without relying on the top secret information we couldn't expose in court documents.

In another chunk, the Cubans wrote, "Continue writing along the same lines you have so far, but cipher the information every time you do, so that you do not leave prepared information that is not ciphered in the house...." And, "This is the most sensitive and compromising information that you hold."

Ana also gave up the names of US intelligence officers heading to Cuba. In one portion of the diary, the Cubans said, "What [redacted] said during the meeting...was very interesting. Surely you remember well his plans and expectations when he was coming here. If I remember right, on that occasion, we told you how tremendously useful the information you gave us from the meetings with him resulted, and how we were waiting for him here with open arms." Because Ana identified a US intelligence officer by true name and real employer, the Cubans were able to stay one step ahead of him for his entire tour in Cuba on behalf of the US intelligence community.

Finally, we found a high frequency message that started with "30107 24624..." We could prove the message came from Cuba on February 6, 1999, on frequency 7887 kHz. The message began with a Spanish-speaking woman: "Atención, Atención..." The message, in its entirety, was on Ana's laptop. After spending months trying to prove she was listening to the high frequency messages, we had concrete evidence she had done so at least once.

Photo by FBI

30107 24624 13808 76314 23844 28995 78518 12984 06373 11369 34676
17005 43667 75210 01119 95335 32270 25937 63573 57263 68605 27525
48680 65468 98142 34012 66160 21490 31292 49410 45805 47888 89459
04498 66802 01150 93875 93870 69771 43609 42900 81505 17263 33769
76660 53601 38988 55673 03811 09860 53740 36169 40815 95743 78166
93266 91505 83084 72417 94829 15253 43112 14448 01316 17699 37162
79314 08832 84921 72404 23858 79167 39901 88476 73803 80241 79973
70524 59924 08376 48857 05380 24837 63346 27662 04249 12646 60266
07506 99681 57237 95588 30920 38862 56255 28403 40305 19323 67816
90009 95286 90080 83973 34776 53084 38634 23063 84140 75898 29389
11653 31979 57609 71881 28615 63566 52218 43075 61027 55906 37881
65586 58136 08070 16935 86866 63938 10003 89604 22588 58309 13116
00638 78248 57232 69921 06972 03808 25280 78668 56507 62895 88932
83966 71878 75365 96998 30107 24624

*Encrypted high frequency message dated February 6, 1999, found on Montes' Cuban-purchased Toshiba laptop during FISA covert search on May 25, 2001.*

The following Monday, I had Rusty, our computer forensic expert, set up our copy of her computer for me to review. Using keyword searches, I started looking for the same information that had been sent to us. I needed to find it so I could testify about what I had seen—the folks who had sent us the information would likely never testify in open court. But the files were mixed with other things she had deleted: emails to her co-op board, computer ones and zeros, basic computer stuff.

But in there, almost hidden, I found something else: four sentences they hadn't faxed to us. I figured they may have missed it. They may have seen it and decided not to send it. Or they couldn't send it because they weren't authorized to send it by encrypted fax because it was really, really classified. Or maybe they didn't want us to see it because it was too sensitive. Who knows, but I think they probably didn't see it. I checked and double-checked, and, sure enough, what I found was new: we hadn't seen it before. I went upstairs and found Steve. I showed him what I had found.

His face went pale.

"Fuck," he said. "Fuck."

The four sentences showed Ana had been read into a top secret National Reconnaissance Office's Special Access Program called "BYEMAN." The program was so sensitive that the government had classified the word "BYEMAN" as secret—just the name of the program was classified secret—for thirty years, until 2005, four years after Ana's arrest. In fact, the National Reconnaissance Office—an entire US government agency—was classified until 1991, six years after Ana started spying for the Cubans. As far as the public was concerned, it simply didn't exist.

This was some *X-Files*-level shit.

With the passage of time, the program may seem like child's play, but back then, the US government used high-flying drones and unmanned aircraft, and later, satellite systems, as well as other methods, to conduct covert reconnaissance operations on other countries—sometimes allies, when we didn't think we knew enough about their military strength or installations. The mission was top secret so our enemies wouldn't know our capabilities, but also because we didn't want to piss off our allies or embarrass our government or diplomatic forces.

We've seen how that plays out in recent years after WikiLeaks detailed that the United States spied on France, and, later, when Denmark was accused of helping the United States spy on Germany and France. Thank you, Chelsea Manning, Edward Snowden, and Julian Assange.

But Ana also would have had access to what those methods had discovered about other countries' military forces, bases, airports, weapons systems, and so on.

Ana had only been read in to the program and hadn't looked at one piece of intelligence from the program, fortunately. But telling the Cubans the program existed was enough. And if Fidel knew, he would surely have shared it with other like-minded thugs. Ana was supposed to be debriefed from the program in March 2001, but she simply didn't show up to sign the necessary documents. That meant she still had access to updated information from the top secret Special Access Program months later.

"Scott knew she had seen this," Steve said, referring to the DIA investigator. "And he was terrified that she had passed it to Cuba."

We sent it to FBI headquarters and then over to Scott. In an odd twist, Steve and I now had classified information we weren't cleared to read because, until then, we weren't read into the Special Access Program because we didn't have a need to know.

When headquarters got the fax, they yelled at us for sending it by secure fax, rather than walking it over in a courier pouch—and also because we weren't allowed to see it.

Really.

"Listen," I said, in one of the only moments when I lost my temper, "this top secret program has already been shared by Fidel to all his fucking buddies. And you're yelling at us? Is Fidel getting read in too?"

A couple days later, Steve and I went to the National Reconnaissance Office to get read into the Special Access Program. The briefing was full of doom and gloom about the consequences of the program falling into the hands of the enemy. I felt tempted to laugh—considering the program was now posted on Fidel's bulletin board—and to cry because an important, expensive program had been compromised.

The four sentences from the fax potentially made Ana eligible for the death penalty.

And she knew it.

# 18

## The Spy Who Loved Me

Despite helping to recruit her, Millan Chang-German—a Cuban diplomat who moonlighted as an intelligence officer—couldn't continue to handle Ana in case the FBI had him under surveillance.

This is where "the illegals" come in.

*La Red Avispa*, as well as the FBI's Operation GHOST STORIES—the FBI's code name for Russian illegal agents in the United States—have spotlighted this practice in major news stories, but unlike in the Netflix series *The Americans*, real "illegals" engage in far less sex and murder than Hollywood would have you believe. But it would be hard to exaggerate their covert lifestyles.

The "illegals" are the handlers, the ones who move intelligence from agent to government. If you can suss out a country's "illegals," you can find its spies.

Most "illegals" are trained intelligence officers. Cuba sends trained intelligence officers disguised as diplomats to the Permanent Mission of Cuba to the United Nations in New York City to moonlight as spies. The US State Department recognizes these diplomats, so they come to the States legally. But their intelligence work does not fall under diplomatic protection.

If the FBI discovers intelligence activities, they don't arrest the foreign intelligence workers: they expel them. In the world of diplomacy, they become "persona non grata"—or PNG'd—for "activities incompatible with diplomatic status."

Jose Imperatori's expulsion by President Clinton from the United States in 1999 would be an example.

But "illegals," and their supporting program, exist at a different level of secrecy.

"Illegals" are not officially affiliated or recognized as being with the foreign country's diplomatic establishment. "Illegals" come under false names with fake passports. Because they are in the United States illegally, they have no diplomatic immunity and can be arrested by the FBI.

Within the Cuban Intelligence Service, Department M-V runs the "illegals" department—from the [redacted] floor of headquarters—managing the "illegals'" movements throughout the world.

As with all of its intelligence operatives, Cuba looks for and recruits people even at the high school level. Cuba trains its "illegals," often side by side with the intelligence officers, both on the island and at the KGB school, going back to the Soviet era and continuing today. The trainees perfect the art of brush passes, clearing dead drops, handling agents like Ana, and learning Morse code. Cuban "illegals" use Morse code for their high frequency messages from Havana, rather than the Spanish woman's voice Ana heard. (Convicted Cuban agent Kendall Myers used Morse code because he didn't know Spanish but had learned Morse code in the US Army.)

The Cubans—with the help of the KGB—taught its "illegals" the skills needed to live in deep cover in the heart of the enemy: the United States.

Over nearly seventeen years, seven intelligence officers—five of whom were "illegals"—handled Ana in the United States. She didn't know the real names of her handlers, though they would likely know her name. Even if they knew her as only as "Sonia," they knew enough about her to help the FBI if they were, like Kevin and Mandy, to reach a breaking point.

- Eduardo Martinez Borbonet, or "Fidelito," handled Ana after Millan Chang-German recruited her in 1984.
- [redacted], or "German," handled Ana from [redacted].
- Gerardo Garcia Cabrera, or "Edwin," handled her from [redacted].
- During a critical period, German once again handled Ana from [redacted].
- [redacted].

The morning after the Cubans shot down the Brothers to the Rescue plane, Ernesto, one of her handlers, stood at the corner of Macomb Street and Connecticut Avenue as Ana drove to work on a Sunday to report to the Pentagon for the crisis. After Ernesto got her attention, Ana pulled over. Ernesto told her they would meet every night after work so Ana could tell Ernesto how the United States planned to retaliate for the shootdown. Every night, Ana left the Pentagon—early—and debriefed Ernesto on what she had learned during the crisis.

We don't know who called Ana at the Pentagon before she left—early—but it wasn't the Cubans. An illegal officer would not have called the Pentagon to speak with one of their most sensitive agents during a crisis of Cuba's making.

That would be dumb.

After Ernesto, who handled Ana from [redacted], and whose real name I don't know, was recalled to Cuba after the arrests of *La Red Avispa*, Ana had no US-based handler.

She was on her own.

Shortly after the FBI arrested *La Red Avispa* in September 1998, Ernesto intercepted Ana on her way to work. Once again, she pulled over. Ernesto told her he was being recalled to Cuba. "Oneido"—Oscar Lorenzo Mendivo, an intelligence officer—would send her high frequency messages that explained how she would be handled next. Turns out Ernesto had been too chummy with his buddies in Miami, who were now under arrest—a major security faux pas. The Cubans didn't tell Ana why Ernesto was recalled: it could jeopardize her freedom and add to her almost overwhelming anxiety.

Including Oneido, Ana had two intelligence officers over the course of her espionage career, who managed her from a small office on the [redacted] floor of Cuban Intelligence headquarters in Havana. Oneido has since died, but he spent more time working with Ana than any other Cuban intelligence officer.

Except, from a distance, Castro himself.

Whose photo, oddly, didn't appear on the walls of the twelve-story headquarters building that stands at the intersection of Línea and A streets in Havana. Perhaps it wasn't necessary—everyone knew who wore the crown of the King of Cuba.

The building itself served as a mystery to Cuban agents: none of them had entered it, yet all of their identities existed on files inside. Certainly no American, diplomat or otherwise, with the possible exception of Phil Agee—the American who defected to Cuba and then identified 250 American agents and officers—had slipped past the single armed guard in front of the building, spartan when compared to the intense security of the CIA or FBI, or past the two guards, armed with AK-47s, who stood watch at the desk inside the door.

Beige paint covered the walls, except for the propaganda murals espousing the revolution or bulletin boards celebrating "this day in Cuban revolutionary history."

Department M-I, home of the officers who managed Ana, Marta, and Kendall and Gwendolyn Meyers, occupied the [redacted] floor. Every evening, [redacted]

[redacted].

Officers rarely violated security protocol.

This constant, internal security makes Kevin, Jorge, and Mateo's accomplishments all the more impressive.

Oneido sat, with another Department M-I-2 officer named Jimmy, in a small, two-person, windowless. Oneido and "Jimmy" managed the care and feeding of Cuban agent [redacted], among others. Oneido worked in near-isolation drafting the high frequency messages he sent to Ana and then reading Ana's intelligence "diary."

Ana met with her "illegals" officer—she had lunch with him at a Chinese restaurant and handed him a floppy disk. The "illegals" officer then dead-dropped or brush-passed the floppy disk to a Department M-V intelligence officer posing as a diplomat at the Permanent Mission of Cuba in New York. The intelligence officer would "clear" the drop or pass—make sure the FBI wasn't watching—and then walk it inside the Cuban Mission. From there, Ana's encrypted floppy disks went to the "Center," where Cuban intelligence operated inside the mission. They packed her disks, placed them in [redacted].

In 2000, Omar—Pedro Piñero Sanchez—managed Ana from Havana. As the FBI investigated her, Omar was the one sending the messages. Soon, he told her, she would have a new handler, "Mr. X."

As of this writing, you can find Pedro on Facebook. According to his Facebook profile, he works as a journalist and executive producer at Cuba Films. I reached out to see if he wanted to talk with me, but he declined.

Guess he doesn't want to help with the movie either.

At the beginning of her espionage career, the Cubans gave Ana two standing collection requirements: we want any information about an imminent military attack and any hint of an assassination attempt

Photo by Author

*Pedro Pineiro, Montes' final Havana-based Cuban intelligence officer handler who would have drafted high frequency messages to her after 2000 up to her arrest.*

against Fidel or Raúl. Beyond that, Ana dictated to the Cubans what she thought they needed to know.

Every day—for nearly seventeen years—Ana went to the "war machine" and memorized the three most important things she thought the Cubans needed to know that she had learned that day. At home, she either wrote down or typed all her notes into her intelligence diary. Later, she typed her intelligence into first the Tandy, and then the Toshiba.

After encrypting the disk, she waited for the next lunch meeting.

No cool James Bond spy camera.

No secret rendezvous with a copy machine to make copies of classified documents.

No downloading classified information onto a thumb drive.

Memorized.

No technology can detect evidence inside someone's mind.

After Ernesto was recalled to Cuba after the *La Red Avispa* arrests, Ana traveled every six months or so to an island to meet the Cubans. During these trips to a Caribbean Island, Ana offered only high-level strategic intelligence. It's hard to memorize six months' worth of information, and she couldn't sneak classified notes through airport security.

Steve and I needed to develop assumptions to help drive our investigation while keeping open minds that our assumptions might be wrong.

Sometimes, we get our assumptions wrong.

Steve and I didn't know how Ana got her intelligence to the "illegals." We had no facts. We had to come up with an operational assumption so we could aim our investigative techniques and surveillance at something reasonable. We knew there were "illegals" in the mix—hell, we read some of Ernesto's encrypted high frequency messages. But how did she pass the intelligence?

Dead drops?

Brush passes?

Shopping carts? (Don't laugh: Kendall Myers used shopping carts.)

We just didn't have facts.

Like any decent investigators, we looked at how Cubans handled other agents: *La Red Avispa*. The distance from Miami to New York to Cuba was too great for quick trips. The Wasp Network typed and encrypted their intelligence onto floppy disks, and then they [redacted] to the New York area. A diplomat/intelligence officer then cleared the post office boxes after getting word a package with disks arrived, and then they walked it into the Center to get it to Havana.

We assumed there was zero chance Ana would conduct a dead drop in Rock Creek Park.

Mail?

Maybe. Maybe *La Red Avispa* was the norm. We had the Gs watch her drop each of her bills at each mailbox she frequented—only to learn she was pretty good at paying her bills on time.

We failed to understand how alone she was in her secretive life. Isolated in her cause. So compartmented about her real self because any small revelation could end her liberty. No one could come in—not her family, not her boyfriend, not her friends, and certainly not her coworkers.

None of them knew the true Ana Belén Montes.

Only the "illegals" knew her at all.

Because she so desperately needed friends, Ana told the Cubans she would meet her handler for lunch every other couple of Sundays at a Chinese restaurant. There, they would sit down for two to three hours, and Ana would hand over top secret information encrypted on floppy disks.

Over General Tso's chicken and some dim sum.

They talked about the information she passed him on the encrypted disk: "the Eagle" (the White House) "met with the Cow" (State Department) "and they decided…" or some other bullshit code words so their fellow diners wouldn't get suspicious.

Just two friends having a long lunch on a Sunday. Talking about eagles, cows, and other barnyard animals.

Think about it: Does it make sense to meet in public and have a lunch with a Cuban "illegals" officer?

Should we have included that possibility as one of our assumptions about how she got the disks to her handlers?

We didn't consider it. We figured it was too dangerous—that they would fear being caught in the act.

Or was it dangerous?

Let's play devil's advocate (and with that, I now welcome you to the complicated world of counterintelligence): Say—hypothetically—one of Ana's coworkers stumbled upon this operational lunch meeting. Even, say, a Scott Carmichael, or a Reg Brown. Do you think it's suspicious—in D.C. of all places—for a single Hispanic woman to have lunch with a single Hispanic man speaking Spanish over dim sum? (Let's assume your average gringo doesn't know the Spanish words for barn animals.)

Nope. Not even close. It happens all the time in our nation's cerebral capital.

Hiding in plain sight.

Ana committed espionage in broad daylight. Not in a dark alley, a dank tunnel, or a wooded park.

Over Chinese food. On a Sunday afternoon.

Why Chinese food? Because apparently Chinese restaurants stay open for lunch longer.

Mind: blown.

Assumption: destroyed.

The world of counterintelligence is hard. Far from black and white. There are shades of gray in counterintelligence that Sherwin-Williams could never dream about.

This would not be the last assumption we got wrong.

# 19

# We Have All the Time in the World

We knew we needed to act quickly. The bosses at DIA were growing impatient. We continued our surveillance, and we sneaked into her apartment a couple more times, but every ninety days, we had to renew the search warrant. Ana was past due for another polygraph, and we hoped to ensure that didn't happen because we didn't need a FISA judge to see two passed polygraphs, even though, by now, we knew we had a Robert Hanssen and not a Brian Kelley.

On August 15, we watched as Ana made another phone call to a pager in New York City, but we still couldn't prove who owned the pager. We knew it had been bought at a mom-and-pop store in New York City, but we couldn't show up there with a National Security Letter to identify the buyer—lest the seller tell the buyer about a visit from the FBI.

Two days later, Ana and Roger flew to Cape Cod to meet some of his family. Obviously, she still worked with the Cubans, but we needed to understand how.

Without the opinion of a real federal prosecutor, we weren't sure we had enough—we thought we had to catch her in the act. We searched everywhere: In her safe deposit box, where we proved beyond a reasonable doubt that she had been, in fact, born—that's where she kept her birth certificate. In her red Toyota Echo, we found she was just as meticulous as she was at her desk. We found her cell phone, but nothing glaring, sans the "driving" gloves—for a Toyota Echo. That was odd.

In her office, no one involved in the case saw anything unusual, besides the Shakespeare quote taped in plain view in front of her desk. Her emails checked out. She hadn't downloaded any files. She didn't look at anything she wasn't supposed to see. We had the authority to listen to her phone calls, but we heard nothing. Our full surveillance wasn't enough to figure out what was in her head.

But everywhere she went, she carried a purse, which was the one place we hadn't yet been able to search. Brilliantly, Steve cooked up an idea: let's steal her purse. We started intense planning sessions. Once again, Steve and I would need an excuse to be somewhere we shouldn't be because we didn't want her coworkers to grow suspicious.

We figured that if we could find the decryption key she used to decipher the messages, we could listen and read live as transmissions came in over the radio. We already had some messages, but they were just numbers—strings of numbers. Without the key, the Cuban-generated key, those messages remained encrypted: we couldn't crack the code. Which makes sense, right? The Cubans wouldn't send out a system that could be easily deciphered or their spies would have been arrested long before the FBI sent Ana Montes to a meeting so they could steal her purse. While Kevin didn't think highly of the Cubans' encryption code, I disagree: the key is good.

Somewhere, she had to keep a list of call signs. If she heard a call sign from the list come in over the radio, she knew she was meant to listen to that message. She would write down the letters from that message, and then she'd use the code to translate the message from letters to words.

If we could read the messages, we could catch her in the act: we could follow her to a meeting or see her follow an order or something—something we could take to court that wouldn't give away any secrets to our enemies.

In retrospect, the idea that she kept a floppy disk in her purse and then daily walked past guards at work—where they could conduct a random bag check and discover her secrets—was a bit of a stretch. But we needed to leave no stone unturned.

As it turned out, we already had enough, but we didn't know that yet.

To steal a purse, we didn't need a court order because there's no expectation of privacy in a government office.

So we set up a meeting. But we had to make sure she didn't take her purse along.

Yes. This is what FBI guys think about all day.

Scott figured if the meeting started long before lunch time, she wouldn't take her purse with her because she wouldn't plan to go directly from the meeting to lunch. That wasn't the whole plan. On the day of the theft, Scott ensured Ana would be required to give a presentation to the attendees. He knew that if she didn't feel her presence was required, she would ditch the meeting. Ego: Her work, in her mind, was far too important for her to attend the meetings that every other minion in the building attended. If she was presenting, she couldn't refuse. She also needed to stay in the room for the entire meeting—at least an hour or two.

We met in the copy room at 8:30 that morning.

Josh Mosley, an enlisted sailor who specialized in communications, pretended to search for a computer glitch in Ana's office. DIA security called Ana's cubicle mate to tell him his car had been hit in the parking lot. (It hadn't.) Steve went in posing as an IT guy, which is pretty funny since neither of us were any good at IT. Steve looked at her computer and sort of kicked it a couple of times then he tucked the purse into a toolbox and went to the copy room, where I was set up.

I called Steve the "purse snatcher" for months. It was certainly better than "urban sod farmer."

I don't remember the purse. It could have been Gucci and covered with rhinestones, but I think it might have been brown. But it could be that that's how I think of purses when I think of purses, which, honestly, I don't. It was a purse. It had pockets. It seems like it was pretty generic and reasonable. I dug through the pockets. I don't remember what was in there. Women's stuff. Keys. Kleenex. A wallet with a bunch of cards in it. Real pocket calendars, which now are antiques.

Scott and Steve stood at the door. We made photocopies of everything—we were, after all, in the copy room. After a couple minutes, I had a panic-induced epiphany: maybe I should have had "Flaps and Seals" with me?

*Shit.*

*What if I put her credit cards back in the wrong place?*

We didn't have time to do this properly. There's a methodology, and usually the guys from Flaps help. But I didn't have any of that, so I just hoped she didn't always put her driver's license in a pocket on the right, but I had put it on the left.

You know where your driver's license is, right?

In her purse, we found a prepaid phone card, the same one we knew had been used at the pay phone the previous day, and a slip of paper with a (917) area code number and a series of numbers that looked like a coded message. The paper felt odd too, not normal. Maybe it was spy paper, or "water-soluble paper," as it's known in the espionage world. Throw it into a toilet and it disappears. Obviously, I couldn't take it and send it to the lab for testing—Ana would notice its absence—so not anything we could take to court. It seemed like straight-up spy craft, but it wasn't enough to prove her guilt. We didn't find any floppy disks, and we didn't find a key to the code. And the numbers were just numbers—we couldn't prove it was a message if we couldn't even read it.

Another dead end.

But still awfully suspicious.

We still didn't have the matrix, but we could tie her to our pay phone surveillance. We had watched her walk to a pay phone to use it. And then one of us would use it to make a call to a specific number. Then we would serve a National Security Letter on the phone company and say, "Give us all the calls from this day." Then we'd dig through them, and we could see that our person made a call at 1:15 p.m. to this particular number, and the call before that was Ana's. She consistently called numbers with a New York area code: (917).

We searched her purse two days after we had seen her make a phone call—and the prepaid phone card she used was in there.

If you weren't a drug dealer in the 1990s, a pager number may not seem that important, but it was consistent with how we knew *La Red Avispa* communicated with the Cuban Mission to the United Nations in New York. And we couldn't read it. In the hands of even an average defense attorney, this would have been child's play.

We had a trash cover team. Trash covers provide one of the most fun yet disgusting of FBI investigative tools: You go through the trash. You find ridiculous things. It's gross.

In hindsight, perhaps Steve and I should have mixed in a male agent with the all-women trash cover team. Once, while heading back from a trash cover, Molly, Amy Landman, and Liana Davila were driving in a pimped out, tinted-window Bu-car. They came up on a stop light, and a guy looked over and said, "What are you guys, like 'Charlie's Angels' or something?"

Of course, the nickname stuck.

For months, we had Ana surrounded with surveillance. We read her emails and phone messages, and any time she picked up the phone at work or at home—or her cell phone—we had the authority to listen. I had been in and out of her apartment almost as often as Roger had.

But that doesn't tell you what's going on inside someone's head. I felt this constant fear that she would notice something was out of place after we had been in her house.

*Oh shit*, she might think. *I didn't put that there.*

Ana lived in a paranoid place already, so what would she do if she thought she was under investigation? We constantly tried to gauge where she was at: We listened to her calls to family. Normal? Cool. We watched her go to the gym. Was she listening to the *Rocky* theme (that's a Philly thing, so doubtful) and stress-pumping the elliptical? Skipping the gym entirely? Just doing her normal thing? We had a baseline of her behaviors, so any different behaviors would have stuck out.

We needed her not to flee. And we knew the DIA was running out of patience with our case. If they decided to fire her, we would lose any ability to learn with whom she worked and how.

By now, my nightmares, which previously involved Richard Jewell and Brian Kelley, were replaced by Edward Lee Howard—the CIA case officer who defected to Russia after he learned the FBI was on to him. He got off scot-free.

At home, my wife was pregnant. And we'd just discovered Jen had a congenital heart condition. Our son Ethan was due to arrive in mid-September, and I was excited, terrified, and stressed beyond anything I had experienced before.

We sensed the diary on the computer was important, but we didn't know how good it was. Even with the diary, we thought we needed to catch her in the act—watch her meet with her handlers, see her slip a floppy disk in a mailbox, take a vacation in Cuba...something.

Anything.

# 20

# Empty Sky

The day began as it had every day since August 27: I kissed my newborn son Ethan and marveled at how my life had changed forever. I was now a dad, albeit a rather worthless dad given that Jen did most of the parenting at this point—though I did help with diapers.

Ethan had been due to make his entry into the world September 15. Thank God the kid showed up two weeks early.

That morning, I left the house at 6 a.m. so I could work out at the office gym. Then I went to my desk to work on the case.

Coffee and bagel in hand, I noticed how clear and blue the sky looked from my desk. By 8:30 a.m., I was fully involved in writing something for the file. At 8:46 a.m., word spread that a plane had hit the Twin Towers in New York. I went into the office of a sister-squad's supervisor, Rudy Guerin, where CNN played on his TV. Turning off his office lights to see better, we began to process, like everybody else, what the hell was going on.

After the second tower was hit, I called my mom to coordinate help for Jen as I assumed we would be sent to New York. Mom and dad lived outside of Harrisburg, so it would be a two-hour drive. Without hesitation, they were in the car and on their way down to help, driving in the opposite direction of a procession of cars leaving the D.C. area and heading north up Route 15.

I don't remember how we learned a third plane had hit the Pentagon, but I saw black smoke rise from my window: my office faced the Pentagon, which sat three miles away. I knew I was not going to New York.

Word spread quickly that a fourth plane was not responding to the FAA and was headed our direction. As I scrambled along doing God-knows what, I ran into one of my squad mates, Zach, who expertly handled the physical surveillance on Ana. He wore his FBI-issued gas mask and the FBI bulletproof vest lovingly referred to as "Big Blue."

"Dude," I said, needing a moment of levity, "that's not going to stop a 747."

Washington Field handles international terrorism cases in the Middle East. With little real information to go on, we all presumed our field office was one of many likely targets. In the fog of battle, management sent the entire office to the basement, thinking it was the safest area in the building. By this point, both towers had fallen, and we realized that if a plane hit our building, the basement would be topped with a skyscraper's worth of rubble.

I'm not saying it was a mutiny, but the rank and file reached a collective *fuck this* conclusion. We did not stay in the basement long.

In the meantime, Washington Field management ordered us to look for witnesses who had seen the plane hit the Pentagon, as well as any security cameras that might have recorded it. That it was a plane and not a bomb seemed obvious, but considering the fucked-up, QAnon-inspired conspiracy theories that arose afterward, I'm glad we gathered that evidence.

Once in Pentagon City, I teamed up with two newer agents. Because I had seniority, I guess that made me in charge, but we were all making it up as we went along that day. Looking around, it was clear the east-side rooms of the Sheraton Hotel near Columbia Pike had a direct view of where the plane struck, so I suggested we head there to look for witnesses.

Parking in front of the building, we walked in to talk to hotel management. Pretty quickly, they identified a customer who had seen the plane hit. She was staying in a room on the east side of the hotel. We went up and knocked on her door, which she opened, tears flowing. Her drapes were wide open, and we could see smoke billowing from the Pentagon. She told us she had heard about New York, opened her drapes, and turned on her TV. Then she heard what sounded like a low-flying jet, so she glanced out her window in time to catch American Airlines Flight 77, which had originated at Dulles airport thirty miles away, deliberately crash into the headquarters of the US military. On the flight were sixty-four people. An additional 125 Americans inside the Pentagon perished in front of her eyes.

As I gathered her contact information for the report, I gave her a hug.

We both needed it.

Looking for more witnesses, the other agents and I went up to the eighth floor to the hotel restaurant, which has impressive views of Washington. As I looked east, I imagined a different target. Following the path Flight 77 took down Columbia Pike, I imagined the terrorists' target wasn't the Pentagon, but the White House. From this angle, and straight up the South Lawn, no office buildings guard the president's home—the plane would have had a path for a direct hit. The White House would have been a far greater gut punch to the United States had it been destroyed. The 9/11 Commission disagrees with my theory, but I guess we'll never know.

With no more witnesses to be found, I went back to my desk at Washington Field and met up with Steve. Having no further assignments, we decided to head over to the Pentagon on our way home.

The roads were eerily empty. Only law enforcement officers and first responders traveled on I-395. Washington Field had set up a command post at the Navy Annex, which is where the US Air Force Memorial now sits. We stood together looking down at the still-burning fire and watched as the navy lowered the flag there.

"We're supposed to prevent this," Steve said, tearing up. "Our government, *this* is what we are supposed to prevent."

I didn't fully grasp what he meant at the time. But he had picked up the mood of the whole Bureau.

As the day ended, I rocked my son to sleep, and I began to cry. It would be the first of many tears I shed about 9/11.

Ana Montes was the last thing on my mind.

She should have been the first.

# 21

## It's the Kiss of Death

On September 11, the Cubans sent Ana a message, just as they did every Tuesday night. Her secrets would go to a man who would happily feed them to America's enemies.

But Ana couldn't receive the messages. She had to work late—everyone did. And Roger was in town, because he couldn't leave.

"I couldn't get home," he said. "I was supposed to go home and work. You got to show up—it's all hands on deck. I couldn't get a flight."

Three days after the attacks, Ana got another promotion: acting branch chief. She was on a battle damage assessment team. Consequently, she would know exactly how the United States planned to attack Afghanistan in its search for Osama bin Laden.

We needed to act fast—we didn't think we had the case tied down yet, and there was no way I wanted this woman to go free.

Because Roger had been staying with Ana after the attacks, she couldn't pull out the shortwave radio and listen to her messages either Tuesday or Thursday nights.

As Ana quietly panicked, Roger linked up with other guys across Southern Command who also needed to get back to Miami. Remember what it was like after 9/11? No flights. The skies were eerily quiet. Traffic was jammed. People were desperate. There's a friggin' musical—*Come From Away*—about people not being able to get home.

Roger went to the airport and got a one-way rental car, which was one of the last available at Reagan National Airport. Four guys rode back to Miami—they spent the night in one hotel room in South Carolina because that was all that was available.

"We got home the one way we could—and the one-way rental cost a fortune. Then we started working. I don't remember anything after that."

Meeting after meeting, and the emotion of all of it: He'd spent his career making sure America was safe. And it seemed as if everyone on the East Coast had lost someone they knew in the attacks.

After being promoted, Ana left her office Friday afternoon—an office where both a regular and a secure phone sat on her desk—and she drove home in her car, where she kept her cell phone. Arriving at home, she walked past her landline. Twenty minutes later, she walked through the pedestrian gate on Connecticut Avenue at the National Zoo three blocks from her house, and then a short distance more before turning around and retracing her steps back to the gate.

Ana never conducted surveillance detection routes, or SDRs, contrary to what's been reported. She made this pay phone call at an unusual location, but the Cubans had told her not to play any games to see if anyone was following her because she hadn't been trained in the art of surveillance. Perfecting surveillance skills, and especially countersurveillance, takes months of training and practical experience. Ana had neither, and goofy circles and sudden stops would have done nothing but make her look suspicious. Instead, the Cubans had given her a long route to walk so their experts could, presumably, follow along.

On this day, we followed her. She then walked to a pay phone near the entrance and made a call to a pager in New York City. She made a second call to the same number.

Saturday night's high frequency message was a repeat of the September 11 message she had missed, but, party girl that she was, Montes was home alone. The Cubans repeated a message to her:

"Better not now."

Sunday afternoon, she walked to the Cleveland Park metro station, boarded the train, and traveled a couple of stops north. She thought she had an important meeting, but the Cubans had canceled it after the attacks.

Remember her hot date with the tall, non-smoking, fit man the Cubans set her up with? Well, after she said she wasn't into him, because he was, in fact, not any of those things, the Cubans figured they could still be friends. Ana and Pedro Piñero, her handler in Havana, had been talking about who would serve as her next illegal officer—handler—in the United States. "It's a bummer things didn't work out," Pedro said to Ana through a high frequency message, or something along those lines. "But would you be okay if he became your handler?" Security-wise, the guy already knew her identity.

"Of course," Ana told Pedro through pay phone calls to the New York beeper.

Both agreed to a first professional meeting in the United States, and they set a date for September 16.

So Ana sat on a train, on her way to a meeting that had possibly been canceled because of the terrorist attacks. She feared she had misunderstood a message that seemed to be the Cubans calling off the meeting. She got off the train and, nearby, found a pay phone. But this time, she did something different: She picked up the phone, started to dial, and then put the receiver back on the pay phone. She then walked away from the pay phone and circled the area.

She paused.

She thought.

She looked torn—as if, perhaps, she was making a life-or-death decision.

Less than a minute later, Ana walked back to the phone, picked up the receiver, and this time dialed the New York area beeper number—the one we found in her purse—again and entered an encrypted message into the pager.

Cuba has always been known as the Pearl of the Antilles, both because of its beauty and the availability of natural resources. Ana worried that Cuba might face an attack.

She hesitated, and then she made the call: "Danger Perla."

We knew Russia would love to have our attack plans for Afghanistan and that Castro would gladly hand them to his Russian allies, as well as his newly minted friends, the Taliban. No way in hell were we going to let that happen. Americans had been killed just because they were Americans. You can believe in a cause all day long, but you don't betray your country for it. Ana could have made a legitimate difference with her position, and yet she instead worked against her post.

Photo by FBI

*FBI surveillance photo of Montes sending a text message ("danger Perla") to a Cuban-controlled pager on September 16, 2001—five days after the 9/11 terrorist attack—telling them she believed Cuba was in danger of being attacked by the US.*

It must have been pure anguish. She thought she had found her sweetheart, and she hoped to leave DIA and the career she abhorred. Because of Roger, she would say, "Goodbye comrades! I've done enough for you, and I need to see where this is going." She knew Roger would never stand for her betrayal of our country.

But 9/11 sealed her fate: The Cubans wouldn't let her out. She was far too valuable.

From here, things started moving fast for us.

On Monday afternoon, I had a meeting at headquarters with Ana Maria Mendoza and an attorney, Homer Pointer, from the National Security Law Branch. Homer was a retired Navy JAG attorney. Steve and I had a mixed relationship with Ana Maria, who was our headquarters case manager. She had been a squad mate of ours before the Montes investigation: Ana Maria, herself Cuban-American, could micromanage like nobody else, but she was also a passionate and energetic ally for us.

We planned to talk about amending the FISA to allow us video surveillance authority inside Ana's home. I had asked Kevin Leuenberger and TacOps to put cameras in some items she had in her bedroom so we could covertly switch them out after we had the legal authority. The cameras would give us evidence.

Obviously, the cameras would have also captured anything else that went on in her bedroom.

Main Justice expressed concern about this intimate authority because Ana was a "Sonia" and not a "Sergio." Early in the meeting, Homer mentioned that Jim Baker, who headed DOJ's Office of Intelligence Policy and Review, and whose office presented our FISA applications to the FISA Court, had made a snarky comment about not wanting "a bunch of FBI agents sitting around drinking beer, eating popcorn, and watching Montes get undressed."

This set me off.

"Homer," I said, "I don't have time to watch my own wife get undressed, let alone this fucking woman."

In hindsight, Baker was right. As he would only months earlier tell FBI executive Mike Rochford as he applied for a FISA against Hanssen, "Mike, my job is to protect the American people from the FBI."[65]

Sometimes history can be hard to overcome.

We would propose assigning women—"Charlie's Angels"—to watch Ana's footage, and then the "Angels" could tell Steve and me if there was any video of her using the shortwave radio.

Reasonable compromise.

Still, I was terrified: Scott had told Steve and I that Admiral Wilson—the head of DIA—that morning had said there was no way in hell he would give her access to the war plans, and that he wanted her out of the building by Friday—arrest or not.

"This is it," Wilson told the FBI.[66]

Ana Maria and I went round and round, and Homer sensed that he needed to play the role of marriage counselor. DIA decided that Montes would not get access to the war in Afghanistan. As a matter of national security, the FBI agreed that the time had come.[67]

"Pete, it sounds like we need to get you guys in front of prosecutors," Homer said.

"Yeah," I said.

"Okay," he said.

Headquarters set up a meeting for the next day. By this point, Steve and I had never spoken to anyone in the criminal division at Main Justice—we weren't allowed. When we arrived, at least fifteen people filled the room. Steve and I were a last minute invite even though we had worked on the case for ten months. Bill Doherty—"WD"—started the briefing and then said Steve and I could fill in the details.

Steve opened his folder, then looked at me and rolled his eyes: *Glad we got a fucking invite.*

Toward the end of the briefing, John Dion, chief of the DOJ's Counterespionage Section, asked what DIA thought. John had been a part of every major espionage case since the early 1990s. He was a legend.

"DIA has run out of patience," Steve said. "They plan to fire her by Friday."

Dion leaned into Doherty and whispered something. Bill shook his head in agreement.

"Sounds like there is a conspiracy case here," I remember Dion saying. "I want you both to start working with the US attorney's office in D.C."

At this point, I admit I was confused. I turned to Duncan Wainwright, who was our office's legal counsel. Duncan was sharp, blunt, and always dressed—tie undone and top button undone—as if he had just walked out of a fight with FBI headquarters. He was just the kind of attorney you wanted on your side.

"What the fuck just happened?" I asked Duncan as we walked out.

"Your case just got thrown over the wall," he said, meaning we were moving from a counterintelligence case to a criminal case. The "wall" was a policy put in place by the Justice Department to prevent, in large part, what Hoover had done.

Now, I got it.

On the evening of Thursday, September 20, President George W. Bush traveled to Capitol Hill to address a joint session of Congress, as well as the world. It was a solemn, yet policy-driven, speech, and would become the opening statement in the United States' global war on terror.

"Whether we bring our enemies to justice or bring justice to our enemies, justice will be done," he said, putting the world on notice. I watched the address live at home, tears filling my eyes.

"And we will pursue nations that provide aid or safe haven to terrorism," Bush said. "Every nation in every region now has a decision to make: Either you are with us, or you are with the terrorists."[68]

For years, Cuba has been on the US State Department's list of countries that sponsor terrorism.

Ana also had the president's address rolling on TV. I called into the listening post to talk to the FBI translator who, like Lucy, would be on duty. Our team of translators probably knew Ana better than anyone: They read every email, listened to every phone call, and analyzed every whisper and moment from our microphones in her apartment. And they hated her more than I did, perhaps because of the betrayal to their mutual Hispanic heritage or because they just despised the Cuban government. They were a huge asset for our team.

"I don't think she's paying attention," a translator told me. "It sounds like she's doing other things."

*Listen or don't listen, Ana, I don't give a fuck. Tomorrow your life changes.*

*Forever.*

# 22

## Wanted Dead or Alive

On September 21, Steve and I sat in a conference room in the DIA's inspector general's office. I woke up that morning excited.

And a tad cocky.

I felt excited because I was about to make the biggest arrest of my career. And cocky because I knew we would get a confession from Ana.

I'd sat down with my wife the night before and said, "Listen, I'm going to have some news for you tomorrow, and it's a big deal.

"It's the reason I couldn't go to all of your appointments with you, and the reason I haven't been able to tell you what I'm doing every day, and the reason I've been so stressed."

"Stressed" doesn't capture it. I had cocooned myself off from her, which wasn't fair to either of us, but even looking back now, it's hard to imagine how I could do it differently. I had compartmentalized each bit of my life, but as she was giving birth to our child—creating a life—we had to focus on the investigation and saving other lives.

The possibility of Ana handing all our plans to Cuba played like the now defunct ticker tape of headlines on CNN through my mind. As Jen spoke of dreams, as I held Ethan, as I drank my coffee, I thought: If we don't arrest her, then Cuba, and then Russia, and then the Taliban, and God knows who else will learn everything there is to know about Afghanistan. More young people will die. No one could know (well, beyond all the historians who predicted it) what would happen in the Middle East, but I knew there was one piece under my watch.

"We're going to arrest a woman for espionage," I told Jen. "It's going to be a big fucking deal."

I promised I would be able to tell her everything, just as I'd done years before when I was a cop—when both of us would come home from work and talk about our days and let go of some of the stress. But this case had been particularly hard. I worked long hours, and I know I wore, on my face and in my posture, the weight of the possibility of Ana leaking information that could potentially lead to the loss of more American lives. I worried about Jen's health, and I worried that I hadn't been engaged enough during our pregnancy with Ethan.

"Wow," Jen said. "Okay."

Our son was two weeks old.

"That's nice," she said. "I think I hear Ethan crying. Can you bring him to me so I can nurse him?"

So much for the big deal.

My wife was also exhausted.

I'm sure I took all of that into the conference room with me. Since our meeting at headquarters with the Justice Department, I focused on the arrest plan and sorted out how we would search her office, her home, her car, and her safe-deposit box. Steve wrote up the arrest warrant—his Mona Lisa—with Assistant US Attorney Ron Walutes.

There was no question Ana's espionage had taken place in D.C., but the Eastern District of Virginia—known as the "rocket docket" because cases shoot through so quickly—had prosecuted most of the major espionage cases over the years because so many spies live and work in Virginia. I worried our case wouldn't get the time it needed. But Ron was a highly experienced prosecutor. And he'd worked closely with FBI Director Robert Mueller III when "Bob," as Ron called him, prosecuted D.C. murders when he worked at Main Justice.

No one else called Mueller "Bob."

Steve and I had one final meeting with Ron on Thursday to talk about the arrest and our plan to get Ana's confession.

"Do what you can, but don't kill yourself," he told us. "We have enough."

He told us we'd brought the case to him "gift-wrapped."

After Ron, we had one last meeting to get final approval. The Tuesday after 9/11, we—our squad, everyone else with a need-to-know—sat in a fifth-floor conference room at the field office so we could brief the SAC—the special agent in charge—of the Washington Field Office, Tim Bereznay. We all knew Tim, or knew of him, of course. He was probably a foot taller than everybody else, but introverted. Young-looking guy. He smoked. A lot. He smoked so much that he had this raspy old Russian-dude voice—like you're talking to Rasputin or something.

"Are you going to have the Gs bumper-lock her?" he asked, his tone measured. He did not want the Gs to lose her as she drove to the office on her last day of work.

"Uh," I said, "I guess so."

"Tell the Gs don't lose her," he said. "Period."

Got it, boss.

Meeting over.

With the plan approved, Steve and I went outside for what would be our final smoke break. My smoke breaks with Steve make up some of my favorite memories from that case.

But this time, we were solemn.

A family—a family that included two FBI colleagues we'd never met—was about to learn that Ana—a sister, a daughter, a person they trusted—was a traitor. Her life was a farce. Anything she had ever said was suddenly suspect. Worse, her actions would undoubtedly reflect on her family, and they were patriots.

I felt certain they wouldn't want us to lose Ana either—that they would see her as nothing but a viper.

I pulled the surveillance team leader aside to reinforce that, should we lose Ana Montes within the next twenty-four hours, my head would be served up on a plate—chicken-fried Pete—to the Mad Monk. Who I respected a great deal and who was completely right: if we lost Ana Montes, it was going to be a no-good, very bad day for Pete.

But I couldn't shake the feeling that she was 95 percent sure she was under surveillance. Ana picked up on the small stuff. Ana paid close attention to details. And Ana was already paranoid.

But maybe she wasn't quite sure. You don't just choose to leave the country: You choose to leave your cute co-op in a lovely neighborhood. You choose to leave your boyfriend. You choose to leave your mother. She knew she couldn't come back in three months when things settled down: leaving meant a final decision. At that point, she was sure that she loved Roger. She was sure she needed to save Cuba from George W. Bush. She was sure that Osama bin Laden was keeping the US government busy.

She chanced it.

At the same time, Ana was a creature of habit, which was great for our team. If she came out of her building with a suitcase, the alarm bells would sound. If she caught a taxi, we'd know something was up. If she didn't go to the gym, I'd wonder if she was calling travel agents. I mean, you could set a clock to her patterns.

The surveillance team would follow her, just as it had done for the previous ten months. They would tail her as she went to work Friday, September 21, 2001. Ten days after the attacks.

The next morning, Steve and I drove out to DIA. We had the arrest warrant. We had handcuffs.

We arrived at 9 a.m. and went to an office not far from the IG's conference room. Molly was close by because Montes was a woman and we would need a woman agent to pat her down and then process her: mug shot, fingerprints, and all. Although this sounds like a mundane task, it was a reward for Molly for going through Ana's garbage that summer.

Steve and I had come up with a pretext—basically a line of bullshit—to get a confession from her that we didn't need.

Never in my vast seven-year career had I ever known so much about a person I was about to interrogate. I had been in her apartment, listened to her phone calls, read her emails, and had people follow her every errand. I was an expert in Ana Montes.

In the IG's conference room, I went over my notes: "Sonia," "NELEBANIOS," the BYEMAN message, the shortwave radio, her Cuban handler Oneido, the pay phone calls. I planned to throw it all on the table, slamming my hand for effect.

Steve? He took a nap.

Well, it was more of a "rest." He'd been up late with Ron writing the warrant. And after 9/11, we were all drained.

"Pete," Steve said, without opening his eyes. "Remember what Walutes said? We don't need a confession."

But on a personal level, I needed it. My whole year had been Ana Montes. I needed her to throw up her hands and say, "Wow. You got me. Gig's over."

As we waited, a nurse sat nearby. Ana had passed out several years before when she learned she was being promoted. We knew she was seeing a therapist and taking medications. I thought this was a woman who might faint upon hearing she was under arrest for espionage.

Man, I was naïve.

At 9:50 a.m., her boss, Dave Curtin, asked her to meet him in the IG's office, which was on a different floor from her cubicle.

"Hey Ana," he said, voice casual. "The IG wants to talk to you again. He wants to meet you in their conference room." No big deal. She'd been there before: When she had reached out to the reporter at

*Soldier of Fortune* magazine without permission, Scott had used it to delay her polygraph by sparking an investigation. It wasn't a big deal, normally. It's not as if she handed him classified documents. But it can result in administrative action—a note in her file that advised her not to do it again. No one was going to fire this model employee—the "Queen of Cuba"—for a quick conversation asking a journalist about his story.

The receptionist sent her into the conference room.

We heard a faint knock at the door. We rose in unison to answer it.

"Hi," Steve said. "I'm Steve, and this is Pete. We're FBI agents."

We invited her to sit. Steve sat on one side of the table, and I at the other. One chair remained at the end of the table. She took her seat. BLUE WREN—the less-than-sexy code name I'd chosen, with Steve's I-could-care-less blessing, for Ana from a list of what was available that day in the FBI's archaic computer system—sat before us for the first time.

"Ana, Pete and I work Cuban counterintelligence matters out of the FBI's Washington Field Office," Steve began. She sat between us with her hands closed in front of her face and her elbows pressing hard into the table. Laser-focused on Steve, he had her full attention.

She didn't know she was under arrest. But she was in a room alone with two FBI agents, and she's a smart person. She had been planning for this day since she started working for the DIA. She had played out the scenario in her mind every night for years—enough so that she bought tapes to listen to try to calm her anxiety. But she knew she didn't feel anxiety about unreasonable fears. *What if one day I meet the FBI and it's on their terms, not mine*? I'm sure she played out the scenario so she would know how to behave when it happened. She had prepared for this meeting for years—long before we knew her name.

I don't know what I expected, exactly. I had this vision of her collapsing as we told her why we were there. I may still have been thinking in terms of how I expected a woman to act, which hadn't helped us in our investigation at all.

Steve continued.

"We've developed some information from a defector from Department M-I-2 that had alluded to a penetration agent within the Department of Defense."

She knew. As soon as Steve said, "Department M-I-2," I watched a red rash grow up the side of her neck.

*Holy shit*, I thought. *Look at that!*

She knew Department M-I-2 handled Cuba's spies in the CIA, FBI, and Defense Department—the enemy services.

She knew.

Steve couldn't see it. I had never seen anything like it before, but if I'd had any doubts about Ana, they disappeared in that moment.

I took a slow, deep breath.

Steve did most of the talking—senior guy, closer to her age. He acted as if we needed her help: We're looking for a defector. We've been fed some clues that lead us to believe there's been a penetration of the US government within the DIA. He gave another detail, another clue as to what was up.

She regrouped. The rash disappeared. She sat stone-faced with her hands crossed in her lap, staring at Steve as he talked.

But as he brought up another bit of information about Cuban intelligence, the rash appeared again. It was all I could do not to yell, "Holy shit, Steve! Check this out!"

When it came time, I planned to drop the "Listen, we don't need you to say a thing about what you've done, we know it all. But we're going to rip Tito and Lucy and Roger's life apart. We're going to talk to every neighbor, coworker, and friend you know because we aren't so sure they weren't involved in what you did."

And that was bullshit.

All she had to say was "Leave them alone, they had nothing to do with this." This simple sentence would have been incriminating. But Ana didn't let us get to this part.

Once again, Ana took control of the room: She didn't cry. She barely registered a response, as if she had been waiting seventeen years for such a scenario—as if she had thought about it so often that she listened to anti-anxiety tapes in her corner apartment in Cleveland Park.

"Am I under investigation?" she asked.

"Yes," Steve answered.

"Well then," she said. "I need to speak with an attorney."

"Hello" to "lawyer" took all of four minutes.

"That's fine," Steve said, almost apologetically. "I'm sorry to tell you, but you're under arrest for conspiracy to commit espionage."

I stood up, told her to turn around, and then I handcuffed her with the same cuffs I had used since my first day in Coatesville. I would use them only once as an FBI agent.

I wouldn't say she was proud. And she behaved exactly the opposite of how I would have expected her to act. She was stoic. She was resigned but composed. Ana would not break down in front of two FBI agents she did not consider to be her equals.

We had arranged for her arrest to not be the sideshow at a circus by making sure it didn't happen on the same floor where she worked. We didn't want to embarrass her with a "perp walk," knowing that one day we would sit down with her face-to-face.

As we walked her through the building toward the back exit, she was calm. Just three people in suits heading into the elevator. Most people didn't even notice the handcuffs.

Photo by FBI

*Montes' mug shot taken by SA Molly Flynn just after her arrest on September 21, 2001.*

# 23

## For Your Eyes Only

Using the keys our source had provided to me for the covert entries, the squad "hit" the doors at the co-op. Well, maybe "hit" is a little bit of an exaggeration. They pretty much just walked into the newly vacated apartment No. 20 to begin the tedious work of looking for evidence.

"Man, pretty strange to be walking in the front door without worrying about getting caught," I said, as Steve and I walked up the front steps to Ana's brick building. He laughed.

It was September. The same black squirrels—or their ancestors—that Ana would have seen celebrating the mating rituals of spring had fattened up for winter, acorns cached beneath each tree.

As we had begun our interview with Ana at DIA, Molly had sent word to execute the search warrant. She knew Ana would not be back. In fact, Molly, Steve, and I drove Ana to our field office to "book" her like the criminal we knew her to be. Steve remembers watching Ana look back at DIA almost longingly—as if she knew she would never see it again.

I've always wondered if Ana felt relief. She no longer had to worry about getting caught.

Back at her apartment, we would not have to be like the squirrels, scurrying quietly about, hoping no one would hear us and working quickly before the neighbors—or Ana—came home from work. This would be no "black bag job." Painstaking. Thorough.

Messy.

Every book, nook, and cranny.

And man, did they find some *good* shit.

The radio? Of course. It still sat near the window. The Toshiba laptop still lay hidden under the bed, the twenty-five-foot mono earpiece not far away.

The third "Angel"—Liana—led the search. She missed out on taking Ana to jail, but I think she enjoyed the boxing, bagging, and tagging as she coordinated gathering evidence to send to the Washington Field Office's evidence room.

So many times we had been in that tiny apartment, but our searches had produced only a nibble, a taste. This day, the team found enough to convince my pal the judge that we might have had a weak case for a search, but the judge shouldn't lose any sleep over approving it.

So much good stuff, and with the Potomac River so nearby…

In one closet, we found a collection of old purses, money wallets, and leather-ish portfolios with notepads and folders.

We had opened the closet door during previous searches, obviously.

But while Ana's personality would allow for nothing less than a spotless apartment, she didn't dust inside her closets. Each bag had a thin layer, which meant if we had touched anything, she would have noticed. I remember panicking when I realized I was leaving big Pete-finger smudges during our Memorial Day search. The bags would have to wait.

This was a good day. The team was there, doing what they do, with everyone understanding that without each member, the case would have gone nowhere. Steve and I, as co-case agents, had provided the strategic guidance and operational planning, but we and the rest of our squad reported to Diane, our squad supervisor. As the case grew, so did the number of people working on it, including people who got called in for extra duty to do some thankless tasks. The "Angels"—Molly, Amy, and Liana—went through Ana's trash. Zach handled all liaisons with the surveillance teams. Brad, the new guy, helped me identify all of Ana's neighbors at the Cleveland co-op so we could find someone who would help us covertly enter her apartment. Tré—a nickname—served as our squad's unofficial legal counsel. He was as "by the book" as an FBI agent could be, which was probably good since I still had visions of free coffee. Tré also solved the "NELEBANIOS" riddle. Mauricio worked with our team of translators, and Henry staffed the listening post.

"Hey, boss," Tré said, interrupting as I reflected proudly about the team, "you need to take a look at this."

He handed me one of the pleather portfolios. The manufacturer had added a flap to keep stuff...you know—notes, receipts, disappearing messages.

Photo by FBI

*Montes' clandestine communication plan written on water-soluble paper found inside this billfold during FBI criminal search warrant on September 21, 2001.*

Under the flap, Tré found Ana's communications plan written on paper similar to what I had found in her wallet the day Steve stole Ana's purse. Based on the piece of paper, we could tell what frequencies Ana used when she listened to messages from the Cubans, what days of the week she would receive those messages, and when she sent her own messages. She'd also written down the (917) area code pager number we knew she had called from the pay phone near the zoo.

She had written a lot of numbers—codes—that represented words.

And finally, we found the matrix. It was set up in a crosshatch, like a game of tic-tac-toe, with the numbers zero to nine, as well as all the characters of the alphabet. We had no idea how to use it.

But it sure looked like spy shit.

(*Looks like spy shit. Smells like spy shit. Good thing we don't step in it.*)

I did feel, as I left Pete prints everywhere, a bit of remorse: if we had opened that portfolio during a previous search, we would have been golden. I felt both elated and a tad embarrassed.

But we had it now. And man was it *good.*

We found something I was glad we hadn't seen before: in Ana's closet, where she kept her linens, the team discovered a Walt

Photo by FBI

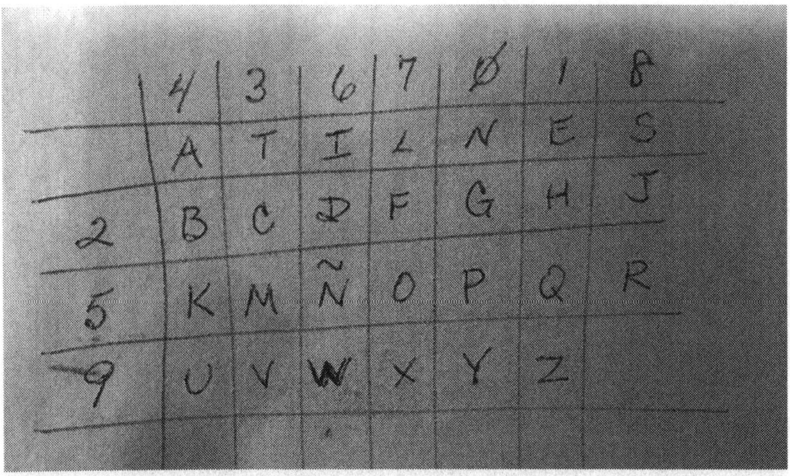


*One-time encryption pad Montes used to communicate with Cubans from late 1998 to September 16, 2001.*

Whitman book and an Encarta CD-ROM tied together and hidden among the sheets.

*Now that's odd....*

In the kitchen, they found a can of Pledge. This was no surprise, though she obviously hadn't used it on the purses. But somebody shook the can and realized it seemed hollow. It was, and it had a fake bottom.

*Lemon-scent spy shit.*

They found one last item, one that still haunts me: an old leather bag that contained maps of major cities around the world. Paris. Mexico City. Madrid.

And four, crisp, one-hundred-dollar-bills.

Damn.

She had a getaway bag.

*Why didn't she run?*

She also kept an old typewriter ribbon inside the bag.

*Odd.*

Photo by FBI

*Bag found during criminal search warrant that contained maps of cities around the world, four $100 bills, and an old typewriter ribbon. On the ribbon was an unencrypted message Montes typed to the Cubans that contained classified information.*

Analysis of the ribbon would later reveal a diary entry she had sent the Cubans. The message began something like this: "Hey, having issues with my laptop and encryption today, so I have to send this message unencrypted. Today I learned [national defense information, national defense information, national defense information]." What she had learned at work, and presumably sent to the Cubans, was classified Secret and typed—old school—on a never-to-be-used-again, typewriter ribbon that should have long been thrown away. Why she kept it hanging around remains a mystery to me to this day.

She could have walked to the Potomac from her place. I mean, it would have been a bit of a hike, but she was definitely doing her cardio. In Washington, nobody would have said anything about a woman tossing evidence off the Key Bridge. Hell, she might have run into some pals.

A competent defense attorney could have explained away most of our finds that day, but taken in sum, Atticus Finch himself would have been sunk trying to argue innocence for his client.

I simmered in pride that day—for the team. Steve and I had been pulled from the 9/11 investigation to work Ana. In my mind, working Ana was working 9/11. But the rest of the squad had been running leads, taking calls, and doing whatever they were asked to do related to the attacks, in addition to helping with our case. Though they were tired, they acted as if it were a privilege to be sprawled out on Ana's hardwood floors digging through old purses.

This was the FBI I was proud to have joined.

Hours we were there. Two full days. Steve and I helped Saturday, and everything felt electric and good, but only because we all understood the potential for future damage. The past damage made all of us feel sick.

That said, the team looked exhausted, so we ordered pizzas for everybody. As we ate, we took a break and shot the shit, telling stories about funny things that had happened during the case.

Ana in her driving gloves. Me digging through receipts at RadioShack.

Steve the purse-snatcher.

After the past ten months and 9/11, it felt good to sit with my people and relax a bit. They deserved a helluva lot more than pizza.

As we ate, we heard a knock on the door. Perhaps the "nosy neighbor?" I cracked the door a couple of inches. The lovely person on the other side of the door politely introduced himself as a reporter from the *Washington Post.* He wanted to know if I cared to comment on why the FBI was camped out in a tiny apartment in a quiet D.C. neighborhood.

He'd followed a resident of the building inside.

"You'll have to speak with public affairs," I said, firmly, giving him my best Agent Mulder. Johnny Utah. Whatever. I shut the door and grabbed another slice.

The next day, the reporter had written a piece about Ana, the search warrant, and the posse of FBI agents eating pizza in her kitchen.

Top Secret: FBI agents get hungry. Real hungry.

But the FBI makes a nice target.

On the seventh day, we rested.

With no work to do, I tackled my overgrown lawn, which hadn't been mown since before 9/11. As I plowed through what was sure to be a two-cut mow, I stared up at the blue. I saw an airplane, which struck me as odd.

*Damn,* I thought. *I guess we're getting back to normal.*

I gazed, lost in the contrails, thinking about the humans on board.

*Shit,* I thought. *I forgot to do something.*

After we put Ana in handcuffs, the FISA was dead. And I had been warned. Ana Maria at headquarters told me—strenuously emphasized to me—that we needed to turn off the FISA collection as soon as the arrest occurred.

The microphones.

The telephone taps.

The email surveillance.

So, this was back in the day.

*You've got mail.*

I had called Kevin to tell him to shut off the microphone and telephone taps, but I forgot that Ana's AOL mail had to be shut off through AOL. It was Sunday, and that part of AOL was off. Because of my mistake, we had unintentionally over-collected two days of Ana's emails while she sat in a D.C. jail.

Monday morning, I called Ana Maria.

*I told you so*. I could hear it in her voice.

She began to lecture me on the seriousness of this.

*Sigh*.

I know. I know. But you should have seen my lawn.

Ana Maria directed me to open the emails and see what we had captured. Which made absolutely no sense to me.

"Why would I do that?" I asked. "Isn't it better if we over-collected to tell the court we over-collected, but that we didn't open and read anything?"

Arguing with Ana Maria often felt like taking on a pit bull: She felt passionately about both management and investigations. Behind the scenes, she worked continually—the only refuge her daily dawn run on the National Mall. Managing a big case like BLUE WREN took everything—that she hadn't already spent managing Steve and me.

So this was just going to have to be another bend in the curve, a saying I came up with for situations just like this (and one for which Steve teased me for making zero sense).

In the end, I opened the emails sent to Ana after her arrest.

Coupons. Probably from RadioShack.

Alas, there was no email from the Cubans saying, "Hey, you okay?"

Ana Maria told the Justice Department about the over-collection, and there was not another word said about it.

This is oversight. This is why FISA is good.

# 24

# Their Children's Hell Will Slowly Go By

I interviewed Ana's mother the day after we arrested her daughter. "I cannot believe that people would go through other people's belongings," she said, referring to me and our black bag jobs and purse snatching.

*Mrs. Montes*, I remember thinking, *do you have any idea what your other children do for a living?*

But I have never been in a position where the FBI arrested my child for espionage. At the time, it wasn't at the front of my mind, but the more I interacted with her family, the better I began to understand just what Ana's arrest meant: Tito and Lucy feared guilt by association, and they both worked for the FBI. They wondered if they had missed the clues. And worst of all, they felt betrayed by their own blood.

The day before the arrest, headquarters called supervisory special agent Dell Spry: Ana's brother Tito and Tito's wife, Joan, worked in the same office as Spry, who, after leading the case in the Aldrich Ames espionage investigation, now led the counterintelligence squad in Spry's home state of Georgia.

The person from headquarters said they were just about to arrest a woman for espionage who worked for DIA and who was related to two of his agents.

"Okay," Dell drawled, as my source remembers. "Can you tell me the name of the spy?"

"Ana Montes," the supervisor from headquarters said. "Her brother is Tito Montes, and his wife is Joan."

"Are you joking?" Dell asked, sitting up straight. "Shit, Tito and Joanie are good friends of mine."

Dell made sure the pair would be in the field office the next day as Ana was arrested. They didn't need to hear about Ana from some reporter writing about pizza. After Dell learned Steve and I had made the arrest, he had Tito and Joan paged over the office intercom.

Because they were friends, they all often sat in Dell's office to shoot the breeze, Dell told me.

Dell breathed in deeply: "Tito, this is going to hurt."

I'm sure Tito thought a million thoughts in that moment—an accident, a death, a mistake—but not that his sister was a traitor. Dell paused, trying to come up with the appropriate words. He had undoubtedly thought through them many times, but now his friends, friends who cared about the United States just as passionately as he did, sat in front of him, thinking of every bad possibility. In the moment, he found no new words, no kind words.

"Tito," he started again, "your sister Ana has just been arrested on espionage charges after spying for Cuba."

Joan got it first. She let out a long breath. Tito slumped in his chair.

"You're full of shit," he said, sinking deeper.

"I wish I was, brother," Dell later told me he said.

"No, you're full of shit," Tito said, but this time as a question.

"I'm telling you the truth," Dell said.

"Dell," Tito begged, "please tell me you're full of shit."

Dell reached for a manilla folder on his desk and tossed it on Tito's lap. He'd put it together the night before, after the call from headquarters. "Secret" marked the red cover sheet in black. Tito opened the cover:

*Case Title: Ana Belén Montes 65J-WF-220371 FCI – Cuba.*

As he read, Tito grew resigned, heartbroken, he told me.

"Dell, we were raised morally," Tito said, working to keep it together. "All of us. I mean, my sister has always been the left-wing one in the family, but espionage?"

Dell shook his head. "Tito, this is not on you, man," he said. "This is on Ana. You're a good man."

"So, you want my badge and gun, right?" Tito said.

"No, we trust you, man," Dell said. "You still have a job."

Tito sank deeper, obviously not believing it, certain that his sister's stink would rub off on the rest of the family. Dell saw Tito didn't believe him.

"Come with me, man," Dell said. They walked down the hall to the nearest badge reader. "Now swipe your badge on the reader."

Tito swiped his badge.

The light flashed green.

Go.

"Your badge still works," Dell said. "You're still an FBI agent."

The two friends walked back to Dell's office, where Joan still sat, dazed.

"Now look," Dell said. "I love you both. I'm going to give you some time alone in my office to talk and get yourselves together.

"Take as much time as you need."

It would take Tito four months until he could laugh again.

I met Lucy the day the family came up to clean out Ana's apartment—after our team had already gone through it.

"We all flew up from Miami together," Lucy said. "I remember because it was about two weeks after 9/11. The anthrax attacks had just started, and everyone was terrified. And the security was very stringent at the airport—it was a nightmare."

Tito, still in shock, acted at first as if it was just another day at the office. He sort of buddied up to Steve and me, working the camaraderie people who work for the same agency often feel. He asked us what we did, what our jobs were, like he was just meeting another FBI agent and was trying to get to know us.

"Tito, we work Cuban espionage," I said sheepishly, not wanting to add more pain to the surreal fact we had just arrested his sister. For espionage.

Joan touched his arm and pulled him back a bit: "You can't do that. We have to keep some space here."

"This could be a big misunderstanding," she said.

Everyone was in shock. Tito acted as he would have the week prior, the week before his sister had been arrested for endangering the nation he daily worked to keep safe.

But Lucy didn't doubt what we had found during our investigation.

"I was absolutely stunned," she said. "But I believed it because the FBI doesn't make up stuff like that. And I know from experience, they have to have a whole lot of evidence to arrest somebody and charge them with espionage."

That wasn't the only reason. The arrest triggered bits of memory, things that had always seemed...

...odd.

"When they told me that, I thought, 'Yeah, that makes sense,'" she said. "Ana's always been kind of weird. It explained some things that she had said, it explained some odd behavior."

Once, Lucy told Ana that her Cuban housekeeper, who kept up on happenings back home, had mentioned how bad things had been—that people were suffering from malnutrition because they simply couldn't get healthy food. It was the "Special Period," and when the Soviet Union had collapsed, so had its aid to Cuba.

"'Well, they have everything they need,'" Lucy remembered Ana snapping. "It didn't seem factual or very empathetic."

Ana had been clear about her view that the United States had interfered without justification in Cuba's affairs.

Lucy hadn't worked counterintelligence for the FBI—and she certainly wasn't a Cuban spy catcher, instead working mostly drug cases for seventeen years as a translator. "I remember thinking at times, *Well, her supervisor must know how she feels.* But it's the United States. Everybody's free to have their own opinion."

She couldn't have known the Defense Intelligence Agency had called Ana in to ask about similar statements, and that they had made the same conclusion: Ana had a right to voice her opinion.

Ana didn't talk about her work with her family. At all. Tito might mention that he liked his job, and Lucy might talk about what she was learning—they were careful to avoid details—but Ana kept them at a distance.

"It was just odd," she said, a word she used often when describing her sister.

The day of Ana's arrest, Lucy met with two FBI agents at her house.

"I told them I would help in any way I could," she said. "And I did."

They asked her a lot of questions. She didn't have a lot of answers. She simply didn't know what Ana had been up to. "I was pretty sure my job was not in jeopardy, because I didn't know anything. I didn't hide anything. And I had been in the FBI long enough to know that I couldn't be punished for something I did not do."

If she had known anything, she would have informed the FBI long before Ana's arrest, she said.

Still, Lucy hoped the family would get word that Ana was a double agent, that she had been playing the Cubans for the benefit of the Americans, and that her sister's name would be cleared.

"Part of me still believed Ana was not the kind of person who would do these things," Lucy said. "We were not raised that way. I thought she was very ethical."

It took months for Ana's mother to believe she was a spy.

While the FBI interviewed Lucy at home, the special agent in charge of the Miami Field Office, Hector Pesquera, called in all the translators. Hector had led the investigation into *La Red Avispa*, so he knew about Cuban intelligence—and he had a no-nonsense personality. "A coworker told me he said my sister had been arrested for espionage," Lucy said. "He said my brother, Tito, and I had nothing to do with it—there were no doubts that we were innocent. They were to treat me the same as they had before my sister's arrest." And, she said, they did.

"They knew that if they had opened their mouths, they would have to deal with Hector," she said, and then laughed. "The people who didn't talk to me before the arrest still didn't talk to me."

She kept working on her translating cases. A few months after Ana's arrest, the FBI planned to put Lucy on a Cuban counterespionage case. "I said, 'No thanks,'" Lucy said. "'I really don't want to do this.' So they took me off."

But even with her instant realization that Ana had, in fact, worked as a spy for the Cubans, Lucy's willingness to empathize—her ability to allow space and grace, even in the face of betrayal—makes her wonder if the Cubans tricked and manipulated Ana.

In Lucy's mind, the Cubans saw a naïve, brilliant young woman and took advantage of her. "I think the Cubans are the greatest manipulators of human psychology," she said. "They had already evaluated her. They had already done their behavioral analysis. She was ripe for the picking for a lot of reasons."

Ana had a "lot of rage," Lucy said, but she was also idealistic and empathized with the underdog. "I think she also craved recognition. She was extremely bright—extremely bright. She could have been very accomplished in her career.

"The Cubans knew how to use that."

The rage. They knew how to use the rage.

"Why did she feel the need to punish people?" Lucy said. "Where did that need to punish everybody come from? In the United States, you're free to express your own political opinions. Why the need to break the law? She could have done a lot of things legally to help the Cuban people."

Dr. Eric Shaw, the psychologist I talked to who studies these cases, had a thought about Lucy and Ana's father: "It is no surprise that Ana had a sensitivity to, and defensiveness about, bullying US authority figures from her army psychiatrist dad, that colored the way she saw the world and US foreign policy."

Because she saw herself early on as a defender of the "abused"—her Mother—and as an adversary against bullies—her father—those traits likely became part of her personal and social identity. This probably left her vulnerable to political indoctrination as a student, as well as to Cuban recruitment because of her perception of US foreign policy in Latin America. Her rigid, obsessive personality characteristics only solidified these beliefs, while her narcissistic personality traits meant she felt entitled to act on these commitments because she knew better than everyone else: she was above the law.

Ana could have joined a nongovernmental agency. She could have worked for a relief organization. She could have campaigned for better relations with Cuba. But when Lucy asked Ana, after her arrest, why she had spied for Castro, Ana said anything except what she did would have been "wasted time."

"She told me she really thought that, being a spy, she was going to change something," Lucy said.

But even with the grace and space, Lucy doesn't believe the bullshit. Doesn't believe Ana worked purely out of the goodness of her heart. Doesn't believe Ana aimed for altruism. The Cubans wouldn't have picked her out of a crowd of students had she simply been a smart young woman with a heart of gold.

"Deep down, and she will never admit this, she enjoyed the feeling of power," Lucy said. "There's always been a hint of hypocrisy in why she did what she did."

Castro wasn't good to his people. Castro was a tyrant. Ana knew this. And she had no problem if Americans died because of her actions.

The US intelligence community said Ana was a narcissist, Lucy said. Narcissists believe they are the smartest people in the room—everybody else is an idiot. They believe they should be treated differently, as if they are special. They like to manipulate situations to fit their own needs. They maintain control. They are arrogant and need to be admired. They are so self-involved that they can't think about what other people need or want—and they don't understand how their behavior affects others. They like to be around people who feed their egos.

Like the Cubans.

While Ana could show empathy—extreme empathy, empathy that everyone could see—she could also be cold and uncaring, Lucy said.

Sister. A word filled with shared dreams and hopes. A word filled with love.

It's a word Lucy finds hard to use.

"My sister committed a very serious crime against this country, against the people of this nation. I feel they have the right to know what happened. She committed a crime against all of us."

In March of 2002, Ana's mother, Emilia, sent Ana a heartbreaking letter.

> *I defended you, and those who love you rejected the idea that you could have gotten mixed up in such a dangerous proposition, but now we have to accept the facts. Now we have no more doubts because you made an admission. You have no idea of our disappointment. Neither your siblings nor I would have considered such action, even though I disagree with the USA when it comes to Puerto Rican policies and other foreign policies. I am a citizen, and I learned when I was young that we owe loyalty to the nation. How or when did I fail you in teaching this principle? I feel guilty; I failed you when you took that road.*
>
> *Did it ever occur to you that I would not be happy with your actions? Maybe that is why you never confided in me. I would have*

*slapped you a good one and marched you to the big boss at the DIA to confess and get you out of that mess! And would have saved this country a lot of embarrassment, too.*

*I hate to tell you this because it will hurt: Ana Belen, you were misguided, and in following your own ideology, you have hurt your country and your siblings more than you will ever know.... Did you think of the consequences? Or how it would affect our lives? Did you think of me, whom you said you love so much? It never occurred to you that you would be found out? That you could lose your freedom or your life? I guess it was an exciting life and you had the temper for it. But was it worth all this pain? What are you leaving your nephews and nieces? You will be a footnote in American history, the first female spy. They will have to deny you if they want to have it easy in school. You had good intentions, but it has been said that the road to hell has been paved with good intentions....*

*Love you, your mom loves you as much as always.*

Ana's former boyfriend felt similarly betrayed, though he had contemplated cutting ties long before the 9/11 attacks, he says.

Roger moved to Washington from Miami and started his new job just as we arrested Ana.

"My mindset was that I had been over the relationship about a year prior to her arrest," Roger said.

He was young. He was in too deep. He didn't want to hurt her feelings. Because he lived in Miami, they only saw each other about once a month, which suited him fine. He knew he needed to end it, but he also knew that it could cause some discomfort at work.

Don't shit where you eat.

But, when we arrested Ana, Roger hadn't yet figured out how to tell her.

"The trauma was about the damage to national security," he said. The forced end of the relationship? Well, that part wasn't so upsetting. And no one, ever, blamed him. "My management, in particular—they were all just great."

Roger went to Ana's boss, Marty Shiner, with one question: Had they read Ana into the Special Access Program? You remember, the "four sentences."

When he found out they had, he felt depressed for about a month afterward, he said.

*My God,* he thought. *That puts this at a whole new level.*

The Cubans wouldn't have used that information directly—they would have used it as a commodity, something to sell to the Russians or the Chinese. "I think she was duped or in denial, but I think that's what her whole value to them was," he said. In other words, she wasn't helping the Cuban people. She was helping the Russians.

"It was well past the time of the Cold War," Roger said. "We weren't going to do anything to the Cubans. It was all about what you could get to sell to get oil or cash from the Russians."

But it cost the Americans too: They put a lot of money into that program. Millions. But once the Russians or whomever had access, "it was absolutely worthless," Roger said.

After Ana was arrested, Roger's boss became the head of the DIA.

"He was like, 'You can do whatever you want.'" Roger told me. "And I said, 'Well, actually, I want to get out of here.'" Roger got a job offer and he took it. "I think I just wanted some distance. It was like playing for the Yankees and you realize there's this massive cheating scandal going on. Not only did you lose the World Series, but you lost it because your teammates threw the game. Everything I had committed my whole life to, and we lost the game."

But even though he left the intelligence community, he didn't leave the government—not for more money in the private sector or more time with his kids. "I just feel like I owe it to the country to keep up the fight," he said. "I definitely would have been pushing some bullshit software somewhere if it hadn't been for her."

Roger's feelings about Cuba have only grown: "Those people are trapped in a prison," he told me over beers and dinner in Tysons Corner. "And when Castro died, the authoritarians held onto power, because they had no other choice—because they're going to get strung up if they release their grip for any significant amount of time."

His feelings about Ana are more nuanced.

"I feel bad," Roger said. "Just for the person she was. I don't feel bad that she went to jail for spying for Cuba."

It had been a while since I had seen him, but at no point did I ever believe he was in on Ana's espionage—or even that she used him for fodder at home any more than she did at work. I still believe she saw him as her way out, as the life she wanted to have.

But Ana had surrounded herself, by birth and by choice, with patriots.

She would spend the next twenty-five years alone.

# 25

# A Million Shards of Glass that Haunt Me from My Past

Ana could have faced the death penalty because of the Special Access Program information from the computer that she should have thrown into the Potomac.

Defense Secretary Donald Rumsfeld alluded to wanting just that.

A few months after her arrest, Michael Chertoff, who was the deputy attorney general at the Justice Department, reached out to let Rumsfeld know that the Justice Department had reached a plea agreement with Ana: twenty-five years in prison in exchange for a full debriefing and no trial.

"Over my dead body," Rumsfeld sent back his response to Chertoff.

This was early 2002, and Rumsfeld had a lot of political clout in Washington.

"Sometimes when people say that," Chertoff responded, "the Justice Department is inclined to send flowers."

At first, Ana worked with a public defender, which had all of us scratching our heads. But about a month after we arrested her, I read in the *Washington Post* (I guess I had forgiven them for the original pizzagate story) that Ana had hired Plato Cacheris, Preston Burton, and John Hundley.[69]

She hired *the* Plato Cacheris.

Boom.

That told me more than I needed to know about Ana Montes.

"Yes!" I shouted, as I slapped the newspaper on the table. If Ana had hired Plato—and was about to feed him her life savings, as well as the profit from the sale of her co-op—then, in my mind, she had confirmed that she was a spy.

I liked Plato. A lot. He was a fair and competent attorney—a well-fed D.C. powerbroker wrapped up in a Greek package. And, working as an FBI agent had…matured me. Gone were my days as a Coatesville cop who despised defense attorneys who dared to question the facts I presented in criminal cases. I had evolved: I now respected the role defense lawyers played in our legal system. A good defense lawyer means I have to know I'm right—so I have to do my job as well as I can—but it's equally important to me that only the guilty face time in prison.

Plato was a pro, and he had worked with some big names in the past. Aldrich Ames and Robert Hanssen had both hired him to defend them in their espionage cases. Plato had represented former US Attorney General John Mitchell for his role in Watergate. Fawn Hall, whose boss Ollie North had been instrumental in the Iran-Contra scandal, worked with Plato. And Plato had gotten an immunity deal for Monica Lewinsky in exchange for testifying against President Bill Clinton about their affair.

Plato's office faced the Mayflower Hotel, a D.C. gem with a lot of history—it's where President Franklin Roosevelt wrote, "The only thing we have to fear is fear itself." It's where the government debriefed Lewinsky. And, it's where FBI Director Hoover and his close "friend," Clyde Tolson—Hoover's deputy—used to meet at the

Carvery Restaurant and Coffee Shop for lunch. In fact, the hotel now has a bar called "Edgar" named after the teetotaler Hoover, and a private dining room called "Tolson."

Plato undoubtedly thought about that history as he passed the hotel each day. Plato, who died in 2019, may also have thought about his family's personal connection to the FBI: his brother James was a federal judge who sat on the FISA court beginning in 1993.

D.C. is a small town masquerading as the capital of the free world.

In this instance, Plato's experience with Hanssen would undoubtedly help him with Ana's case.

Robert Hanssen gave up the names of three Russians recruited by US intelligence who still operated in Russia. Based on his information, Russia arrested and executed the three Russians, which made Hanssen eligible for the death penalty. The CIA was willing to walk into an open courtroom with evidence of their assets' deaths because it didn't put any other agents in any danger. For Hanssen, negotiations with Plato meant life-or-death. In Ana's case, the Espionage Act of 1917 specifically designates "military spacecraft or satellites" for death penalty eligibility. Ana's case was a bit more complicated than that, but Plato sorted it.

On March 2, 2002, Ana—wearing the orange jumpsuit Scott Carmichael had imagined for so many months—pleaded guilty, in D.C.'s federal courthouse, to one count of conspiracy of gathering, transmitting, or losing defense information to the Cuban Intelligence Service.

Espionage.

She would not face the death penalty.

The four sentences we'd found on Ana's laptop about the Special Access Program would never see the light of day. It was a special department within the top secret classified world, and the Justice Department wasn't about to put it in court documents.

The Special Access Program should not be revealed—unless absolutely necessary—anywhere: public court rooms, on Fidel's desk, or on a computer under a bed in Cleveland Park.

The National Reconnaissance Office's information could never be released. So, the Justice Department and the FBI negotiated with Plato from the starting point of a maximum of a life sentence for Ana if she were convicted at trial. There's no magic formula here to come up with an objective amount of time for someone to serve after a plea deal. Plato got Ana to agree to twenty-five years in prison, if she pleaded guilty, in lieu of a trial.

Why twenty-five?

Because I had to get out of the FBI before she got out of prison.

In reality, it had nothing to do with me, but I was glad to hear she would be released after I retired—though I would still have to spend hours with her. In exchange for the leniency of a twenty-five-year sentence, she would have to allow FBI agents to debrief her: Steve and me.

(Ernesto, Ana's hander who was recalled to Cuba because he was too close to *La Red Avispa*, was fired from Cuban intelligence after Ana's plea in 2002.)

After her plea in court, Steve and I took Ana to the interview room on the first floor of our field office, which would become our home away from home for the next seven months. That first meeting included Ana's attorneys and Ron Walutes and senior trial attorney Michael Liebman from Justice's Counterespionage Section. While the small interview room could barely contain everyone, it sent Ana a subtle message: tell the truth.

Plato asked if Ana could make a statement before we started with the questions.

"Sure," Steve said, "the floor is yours."

Ana went into an opening diatribe about why she did what she did. Part soap box, part declaration of her intent to fully cooperate. As part of the plea negotiations, Plato had sent over a proffer of what Ana would be able to provide during a debriefing. The proffer, though general and high-level, teased the intelligence and counterintelligence nuggets we were about to learn.

She finally finished. She still believed in what she had done, but she would cooperate.

"So, how were you recruited?" Steve asked.

And she told us.

"I was recruited by Marta Rita Velazquez in 1984, who introduced me to a Cuban diplomat in New York named Millan Chang-German," she said.

With our first question, we learned a lot, including two names we had never heard before.

Usually, that's the big question: How and when and why did you start spying on your country? It usually takes some time to suss it out. But during that first session, we learned the Cuban Intelligence Service had already recruited her before she graduated from grad school—and that she went to DIA solely to help the Cubans. That never happens.

Marta heard that her old pal was talking and fled the country after the US government indicted her. She's still under indictment. She now lives in Stockholm with her diplomat husband. She spent several years there working as a teacher.

We still haven't been able to arrest her.

Ana, in addition to providing information that had already made the plea agreement worth our time, also let us know we'd fucked up.

"You know I made your surveillance, right?"

What?

No.

September 16, five days after 9/11, Ana made the emergency call to Cuba from a pay phone near her apartment: "Danger Perla." As she walked toward the pay phone, she heard one of our surveillance specialists say, "She's about to make a pay phone call."

The specialist was close enough to Ana that Ana could hear her on the radio.

Holy shit.

*First the broken lock, then the mail thing, and now this. Shit, I'm under investigation.*

Ana wasn't done. She described several members of the surveillance team: the guy on the skateboard. The old woman on the bench. All ghosts.

"So let me get this straight," I said, flabbergasted and seeing the befuddlement on Steve's face, "you messaged the Cubans five days after 9/11 that they were in danger of being attacked by the US just moments after you had made our surveillance?"

"Yes," she said. "I walked up to the booth, picked up the phone, heard your specialist say, 'She's about to make a pay phone call,' put the receiver down, and paced. I realized that if the message was important enough for the Cubans to get, it was worth the risk to me to send the message knowing I was under surveillance."

Say what you will, she was committed to her cause.

I had so many questions, just on a personal level: Why didn't she throw away the laptop? If she had, she would be a free woman now. After the arrest, we busted into her apartment building, blue jackets and all, to conduct a big, noisy search. And eat pizza.

Inside a vinyl folder, we found coded stuff: schedules, days of the week, frequencies. It was all there, including the cipher.

But we still couldn't figure out how to use it—not just me, Joe cop, sitting down trying to puzzle it out, but the guys who do this stuff full-time didn't get it either. I needed for her to tell me.

So, we brought the cipher in one day. "Hey, we got this from your house," we told her—she did know we had been in her place. "Can you show us how to use it?"

"Sure," she said.

She showed us how she used it to listen to phone calls, but also to transmit pay phone calls in code.

We brought in other things we found in her co-op, and she explained them. The book and the CD in the linen closet with the rubber band?

"What's up with this?" we asked.

"Oh, the Cubans asked me to find two things that were completely unrelated and put them together in a bundle and to hide it," she said.

"And then, if I ever thought I was under suspicion, I could give it to them, and they could analyze it to see if anyone had messed with it."

We hadn't. She had hidden it well enough that we didn't find it until after we arrested her. Which is weird, because it was such a strange bundle that I don't know how we missed it. If we had found it, I would have been like, "Whoa! This is weird." And I definitely would have put Pete-prints all over it and made a copy of the CD. But there was a lot to look through in a short amount of time—and it took us hours to go through her bookshelves.

At the time, we couldn't release the information we had used to get the FISA, which is why the plea agreement was so important. But we can talk about it now.

What was the name the Cubans called you during your meetings?

"Well, the first time I traveled to Cuba with Marta, they knew me as Ana Montes," she said.

Right. Before you were a spy, they called you by your real name.

Crazy.

"And they said," she continued, "'We'll never call you 'Ana Montes' again. Your new name is 'Sonia.'"

Ding. Ding. Ding.

We knew she wasn't trying to mislead us. Her handlers only knew her as "Sonia" Belén (or "NELEBANIOS")—we knew that. She answered correctly. We also knew Marta, the woman who first introduced Ana to the Cubans, used the code name "Barbara."

Ana got that one right too.

It was a test she passed.

If she did try to mislead us, she didn't do it on the questions we knew the answers to—and we asked her several questions throughout the debriefings, sprinkled in, so she wouldn't know they were coming. We knew giving her a polygraph was pointless. She had already beat a DIA polygraph nine years after beginning to commit espionage.

There were times when she was genuinely helpful, and I have to wonder if it was a relief, on some level, to just tell it. She had been holding it in for a long damned time.

One day, she explained what information she sent to the Cubans.

"I didn't need them telling me what was important," she boasted, that arrogance shining through. "I told them what they needed to know."

But remember the guy the Cubans fixed her up with who was supposed to act as her handler? The not-tall, not-athletic, not-non-smoker dude? "Mr. X?"

She said she couldn't remember his name.

She spent three days with him—this was a woman who memorized documents over lunch, but she couldn't remember Romeo's name?

Sure. Hard for me to believe, but it wouldn't have been his real name anyway. So, we just went with "Mr. X."

She hit us with, "I don't remember," a few times. She had been at it for seventeen years, so yeah, she probably didn't remember everything. But some of her answers surprised me. How could she not remember things she had done that affected so many people's lives?

Do you not remember? Or are you choosing to forget?

"Did you meet Staff Sergeant Fronius when you went to El Salvador?" we asked.

"I don't remember."

Fronius was the Green Beret killed during an ambush just days after Ana had visited. She told us that if she had, in fact, been responsible for his death, it was his own fault: He had made the decision to join the US military and he understood the risk he took. It's not my fault.

Wow. Fucking wow.

We learned during the debriefing that she had traveled covertly to Cuba to receive a medal, and that she was supposed to meet Fidel Castro, but it didn't work out. I presume they gave it to her, and she gave it right back because it's not the best thing to have sitting on the bureau. We didn't find it during our search, and we would have.

I suspect she earned that medal because, I suspect, she offered up information to cause Fronius's death. Can't prove it, but she never denied it.

We learned she had no interest in applying to the CIA because she despised what "the Agency" was doing in Central America. And—interestingly—the Cubans never pushed her to go there. She told us she was shocked by how easy it was to get into DIA after she applied.

Ana had also given the Cubans the real name of a covert US intelligence officer who lived in Cuba. They wrote to tell her that they "welcomed him with open arms." I interviewed him after we arrested Ana. Every time he turned a corner in Havana, he said, he felt as if he had his own personal Cuban ghost—a surveillance team member who followed his every move. But he never felt like he was in danger, he told me. In fact, one day, he and his wife drove two cars, with her following him. She got into a serious accident, and our US intelligence officer couldn't stop and circle back to help because of circumstances—but he knew the Cubans had stopped and gotten her aid.

When not rubbing human feces on the door handles of the homes of US diplomats in Havana, the Cubans, in spite of it all, can be caring and professional.

Of course, this was before "Havana syndrome."

That first debrief session led into what felt like hundreds of sessions with a woman who actively disliked me. You know, every once in a while, someone will show up on CNN or some talk show talking about how he was in the debriefings, and I think, *Who the fuck is that guy?* And then they'll start spouting off some information from the debriefings, and I think, *No. No, she didn't.* It's frustrating, particularly because those debriefings were so damned awful. Every day we went in there for several hours a day. Every day we were polite and mindful of her needs. Every day I shoved everything down into an emotional well and pretended like this was normal, this was fine. For the first month, it was Steve and it was me in that room and it wasn't anybody else.

And quickly, I started to hate Ana Montes.

In the aftermath of the 9/11 attacks, it's even possible I focused some anger on her. As far as I was concerned, there was no difference between her and Osama bin Laden: they both wanted Americans dead to prove a point. In some ways, I felt like she was worse: these were her people.

Those weekly meetings were painful. Her posture remained erect. Her manner was businesslike. If we tried to make small talk—"How are you?" "How's your mom?" "How's the food?"—she said, "Do you have questions for me?" She treated me like a dumb cop—like I wasn't smart enough to be in the room with her, though she was kinder to my older, more experienced, and more academic partner, Steve. They were closer in age, and he knew more about the Cubans and Central America because he had worked the Sandinistas. I couldn't spell "Sandinista."

*I'm in jail because of this idiot?*

Yep.

As FBI agents, we're trained to build rapport with whoever we're talking to, whether it's a victim, a serial killer, a child pornographer, or a traitor.

Ana's version of rapport? "Turn on your tape recorder and ask your first question."

It was a grind. It was painful. But we needed to remain professional because we needed her to tell us as much as possible. We tried to create an atmosphere where she would want to be transparent.

Ana wasn't in the local federal jail—the Alexandria, Virginia, jail—because Robert Hanssen was there. And so was Zacarias Moussaoui, the "twentieth hijacker," who was accused of being an understudy for one of the 9/11 terrorists if any of them were unable to make it to the attacks.

Side note: Every time Moussaoui called his mom in France, an FBI agent had to sit with him and listen to the conversation. So, randomly, I got sit-with-a-terrorist duty one day. Workday, so I showed up clean-shaven. He, of course, had the jihad beard.

"You a homosexual," he said, by way of greeting as I walked in. "You a faggot."

"I'm sorry," I said, "excuse me?"

"You clean-shaven," he said. "That mean you a homosexual."

Right, so a) Is that all you got? Because I'm going to head over to the PRIDE parade after this, manhood fully intact. And b) You're in a jail cell. I'm free. It's cool to be me.

So anyway, John Walker Lindh, the "American Taliban" guy who converted to Islam at sixteen while growing up in California and then fought with the Taliban in Afghanistan, was also there. These folks were in isolation at a jail—not a prison—which takes up considerable resources.

Given that there was no room for Ana at the inn, she went to the jail in Orange County, Virginia, where she was put in isolation so she could not talk to the other prisoners. She looked like hell, just not healthy. She had already been petite, but it seemed as if she was losing weight. She looked ragged, like she hadn't slept. I don't think you get good sleep in prison, and she had shitty bags under her eyes.

Jail is tough for hardened criminals. This was a University of Virginia grad, a twenty-five-year white-collar professional. I don't think it was an easy time for Ana.

But Ana remained stoic in her demeanor. Poised.

US Marshalls drove her up to the D.C. courthouse from jail. Molly and I—or somebody else—would pick her up to take her to the field office. She'd be in her orange jumpsuit with her hands handcuffed. The three of us would sit in this room, probably twenty feet by twenty feet, at a conference table. It wasn't necessarily inviting or comfortable.

We would take off her handcuffs, and she could walk around. She was probably 5'6" and weighed like 110 pounds, so we weren't worried about her attacking us, and there was no way for her to get out of the building—but that wasn't something we did with everybody. She could grab a bottle of water. She asked for fresh fruit, so we got her fresh fruit. I don't think the food was good or particularly healthy at the jail.

Every other day or every third day, we'd meet her at about 9 a.m. We'd be done at about 2:30 p.m. Done, done.

We tried to create a professional environment, and we treated her, not like a peer, but in a respectful way—not like a prisoner. I got her lunch and breakfast, asking her what she wanted. Steve did the primary questioning, for the most part.

The debriefings were humbling. I was a young FBI agent—I was overachieving in a big way, but I made some mistakes too. Young. Naïve.

When we took her into the conference room on the day of her arrest, I had prepared—but never got to use—some questions about her family, trying to get her to say something along the lines of, "My family wasn't involved in this" as a semi-admission of guilt. Instead, she asked for a lawyer. During the debriefing, I asked her to grade us—critique us—on our interview technique.

"I knew you didn't have anything on them," she said, "because I know my family, and I know they would never do what I did."

She knew they would dime her out in a heartbeat if they knew how she was betraying her country. Lucy would later thank me for arresting Ana because she would have been devastated to have to turn her own sister in if she had discovered her espionage herself—I imagine the Unabomber's family were much the same when they got ahold of Molly.

But something always bothered me: Ana knew she made our surveillance. She had the go-bag. She had the cash. Why didn't she even try to leave? She may have thought she wouldn't have gotten away with it—and she wouldn't have. But it would have been a clusterfuck. Because she would have gotten in her car and headed to Dulles International Airport. The surveillance guys would have said, "Hey. We're heading in the direction of the airport. Anything you guys want to tell us?

"Now we're parking at the airport..."

She wasn't getting on any planes, but we didn't have an arrest warrant. We could have detained her and interviewed her, but we would have had to let her go—just not in time for any flight she might have planned to take. We were not prepared to let her get on a plane.

My best guess is she wasn't 100 percent convinced she was under investigation—even after making our surveillance during the call on September 16. Maybe she was 95 percent convinced. And here's the thing: she needed to be 100 percent convinced. There was no fleeing the United States (assuming she could) and hanging out in Cuba for three months, and then calling Tito or Lucy and saying, "Hey, sorry I haven't called in a while. By the way, has anybody been asking about me? Like, maybe your colleagues?" No, her fleeing would have been a life-altering decision.

No turning back. And no more attending family get-togethers.

About halfway through the debriefings, Steve and I felt pretty frustrated. She was just not being cooperative, and the whole thing was miserable. So we told her.

"This isn't working," one of us said to her. "I know you're not happy. Being in jail fucking sucks. But you're being a huge pain in the ass."

That left eyebrow went up.

"You have to understand," she said. "This is torture for me."

I was offended. This was well before all the stuff came out about waterboarding and prisons in Iraq, but I knew enough to know we hadn't tortured her. We'd gone way out of our way to make sure she was as comfortable as we could make her, considering the circumstances, which were that she had spied for Cuba and gotten at least one American killed.

Torture.

Was your salad not good enough today, Ana?

"No, no," she said. "It's not how you're treating me.

"It's that I'm betraying my friends. And I don't have the courage to commit suicide to not betray my friends."

She explained that she had to take the plea deal because of her mother, and if she didn't take the deal, she would be in jail for the rest of her life. She would eventually get to see her mother, and her mother could take comfort in the idea that Ana would, someday, see her nieces and nephews again.

If she didn't cooperate, we could still throw out the deal. We would take it to court. She would go to jail for the rest of her life. She knew she had no choice but to play the game—and Plato, her lawyer, reminded her of that often.

She defused the situation, and I calmed myself down. *This is part of a process. It's a job we have to do, a game we have to play.*

The guys who debriefed Saddam Hussein? I'm pretty sure that was worse than debriefing Ana Montes.

Years later, Lucy would send an email to Steve.

"I always thought Ana was very lucky she was debriefed by the FBI," she wrote. "The despair inside prison is palpable. If it hadn't been for your humanity, I'm not sure she would have survived. Plato was grateful, and so am I. We all are. Thank you again."

She still had to answer our questions enough to fill the requirements of the plea agreement.

To make small talk, an endeavor that met no success, I tried to keep her a bit informed about the publicity around her case, like, "Hey, there was a story about you in the paper this morning. Do you want to see it?"

"No," she'd say, inevitably. "I don't want to see any of it."

But then there was *Cigar Aficionado*. I was pretty proud of that: Cuban spy. Cover of a cigar magazine. I liked cigars. Life is good. For whatever reason, I thought she'd be excited about it. I was feeling kind of proud about it.

"Hey!" I said. "Guess what?"

Yeah, read the room, Pete, read the room.

"You're gonna be on the cover of *Cigar Aficionado*!"

"What's that?" she said.

I don't know how to write the sound of a deflating balloon.

"It's a magazine for cigar lovers," I said, unable to hide my sarcasm.

And then, "What does my case have to do with cigars?"

"You know...Cuba? Cigars?"

Never mind.

(Ollie North was interviewed in the same issue about Iran-Contra, which helped me figure out who the Contras were.)

In any case, my attempt at small talk probably didn't help bridge the divide between us. But it also told me a bit about Ana: Smartest person in the room, but maybe not the top on the block when it comes to street smarts. Her world was tiny—laser-focused.

As we worked with Ana, I got to know Steve a lot better too. I don't know why we connected as well as we did—beyond the similarity to my dad—but neither he nor I connected with anyone else on the squad to the same degree. Confession: When he smoked, I often bummed one.

Or two.

All in all, we got along great. There were a couple of times when he pissed me off: First, when he brought Ana a pair of nail clippers. She was small, and I don't know that there was much she could do with them—she wasn't going to pick the lock on her handcuffs or use them as a weapon.

"Give me a fucking break, man," I remember saying. "If she wants to cut her nails, let the jail handle that." He did it to build rapport, but I thought it was being a little too kind to someone who had committed espionage.

She appreciated his kind gesture initially, but then started expecting it and stopped thanking him.

So much for the rapport building.

Steve pissed me off again one day when we took her to use the restroom on the way out for the day. Looking back, I guess it shows my own personal evolution, my ability to start to see the gray.

He asked me if he could have a moment alone with her.

*Good cop needs time alone.*

Then he ripped into her about her attitude, and about her perversity regarding the Cubans. "You know I'm tired of your bullshit," he told me he said to her. "You and I know the Cubans and how they oppress religion and free speech. It's a fucking regime—it's not a friendly government."

He told her she was a hypocrite, that she thought she was "altruistic" and "trying to help."

"But they're pieces of shit," he said. "They kill their own people."

"I get it," she said. "I understand. You're right. But it's not the United States' job to change the Cuban government. It's the Cuban people's responsibility to change the Cuban government."

*As if they could, Ana.*

I was pissed because, by that point, there wasn't anything he couldn't say in front of me. We trusted each other. We were partners. He didn't say anything I disagreed with. Back then, I didn't understand why he did that to me.

But in retrospect, it makes sense. Given that Ana and I didn't get along, my judgmental presence during his chewing of her ass would have been counterproductive. Ego aside, sometimes there is addition by subtraction.

It's odd to look back now. When we started, I hated her. I hated what she stood for. I hated that she had gotten at least one person killed. I hated that she had betrayed her country—and her family. It was brutal to sit with her.

On this, she and I agree about the debriefings: it was fucking torture.

I missed the days and the stress of the investigation, of trying to prove the case. Then, I didn't have to see, feed, or fake being nice to her.

Steve's woodshed session worked—for two days. Ana slept on it. At the next session, she told us that she agreed with Steve and that perhaps she had made a mistake in helping the Cubans. Steve and I felt like we had made some progress.

The following session, she told us she had followed her conscience and done the right thing.

Blah blah blah.

But even that makes sense: Twenty-five years is a long time to serve in a maximum security prison if you think you made a mistake. But if you believe in a cause—and you believe what you did was right—twenty-five years in jail is a justified sacrifice for that cause.

We often ate lunch together. Steve and I wanted her to be comfortable as we spoke, so I'd ask her what she wanted and go get it, and then we'd sit in the conference room and talk about anything but Cuba. I told Steve about my wife and about my new son and about how scared I had been, dealing with the plethora of health complications they both faced. Ethan. My God. That poor little guy was born with bad acid reflux problems, and he just puked constantly.

Constantly.

And we were talking to different cardiologists trying to figure out Jen's heart—should she have surgery? Ethan would be fine, but Jen's health was serious.

After that, Ana sometimes asked about them. She asked about Jen's heart and the health issues she had faced. She asked about Ethan's reflux. Asked if anyone was getting any sleep with our newborn. It felt genuinely empathetic.

She was kind when it came to my family.

I also knew she loved *Star Trek*, so she couldn't be all bad. But I kept thinking about the decisions she had made at a young age and all she had given up because of those decisions. I had to admire, in the most fucked-up of ways, her dedication to her cause and that she had done it purely based on principle and not for money or because she had been blackmailed—though let me reiterate that her crimes against people who served the United States are heinous.

Do I believe she should have come clean at some point? Yes. Absolutely. Do I think I could ever have betrayed my country like that at any age? Hard no. But I could see that Ana was a multifaceted person, and I did think it was sad that she hadn't used her formidable skills in a legal way to support her cause, a way that would have caused her less anxiety and allowed her to pursue a fulfilling life. Instead, she made a decision that could have earned her the death penalty.

I never saw Ana lose control. I never saw her cry. Not about Roger. Not about being arrested. Not about the knowledge that she would spend twenty-five years in prison. The rash that appeared when we arrested her? She got that under control twice.

Twice.

Ultimately, jail did not lead to remorse or a change of heart for Ana. If anything, it solidified her belief that she did the right thing: I helped my friends. I helped the Cuban resistance. I took on the man. This is the cost, as I come into the prime years of my life, of helping fight back against the imperialistic, big, bad United States. She sat in her cell thinking of all the reasons why she had given up the best years of her life—a, she believed, chance at love, and the possibility of sleeping without the assistance of meditation tapes.

But what do I know? Maybe it was the best sleep she'd had in years: she didn't have to worry about getting caught.

She probably knew that Castro himself had commented on her arrest. This is unusual—you never hear Vladimir Putin or Kim Jong-un acknowledging our arrest of a foreign spy, or Castro either, for that matter. But Castro came out and said that it was a shame that someone of Ana's moral character had to do what she did because of the "illegal" US embargo. Right, so if we didn't know she was a spy before, we now had it on the record from Fidel. A couple months later, a lower-level official said there would someday be a statue for Ana in Cuba. When you think about it, the Russians probably thought Hanssen was a scumbag because he betrayed his country for money. But Ana was altruistic—fucked up, but altruistic. She risked her life, her freedom, for nothing. No cash. No glory. The Cubans—perhaps—also saw her as a true friend.

During the debriefing, we studied her. We changed a lot because of her. And we're safer because she went to prison for twenty-five years.

In October 2002, at her sentencing, she showed no remorse.

"My way of responding to our Cuban policy may have been morally wrong," she told the judge. "Perhaps Cuba's right to exist free of political and economic coercion did not justify giving the island classified information to help it defend itself. I can only say that I did what I thought right to counter a grave injustice."[70]

I wonder if that's what she thought about in her jail cell, this idea that she's a moral hero. Or did she think about what it would have been like to have friends. Fun. A lover.

When we talked with Ana about top secret Special Access Program information, we had to go to a SCIF: a Sensitive Compartmented Information Facility. They look like a typical office from the outside, but like a windowless conference room inside. And they definitely don't look like a locked closet in a public hotel, or garages that house Corvettes.

I remember one time when Ana and I were in the room alone together, and the threat of the death penalty still bothered me—that she had risked it to give Castro access to the Special Access Program, potentially putting American lives at risk. Did she know what she had risked, herself? Did she know she could be put to death for the sake of a corrupt regime? But I felt uncomfortable bringing it up, first because we would be talking about her potential death, but second, because I didn't know how she would react.

Finally, I just asked her.

"I really, genuinely want to know…" I started, then regrouped. "You got read into this program. You provided these four sentences to the Cubans. What was going through your mind? Did you understand what you were doing? How significant it was?"

I asked her about the Special Access Program information—the classified information she shared with Castro.

"Absolutely," I remember her saying. My heart thumped hard, and I sat back in my little plastic conference room chair. She, as usual, sat with her back perfectly straight. "I knew how bad it was. It was one of the only times I paused before sending information."

She told me she knew it could earn her the death penalty.

"If it's that important," she remembered thinking, "then the Cubans should know."

But I knew what else was important to her.

When Ana talked about Afghanistan, it took everything I had to control myself. I'm a professional—I've been controlling myself for a long time. But I kept thinking about the picture of the "falling man" from the Twin Towers. That image stays with me. It haunts me. And while she obviously directly wasn't involved in that, she had been poised to hand our battle plans to Cuba.

Toward the end of our debriefings, I asked Ana a hypothetical question: Would you have continued to spy?

She believed the United States had a right to invade Afghanistan in self-defense after the 9/11 attack, she told me. And she believed she had a moral right to tell the Cubans how we fought a modern war in case the United States attacked Cuba. If Cuba gave the Taliban or al-Qaeda her intelligence, and that lead to the deaths of more Americans, "Then that's the risk they took," she told me.

I think she told us the truth about that because it was a hypothetical. We couldn't charge her with thinking about handing over battle plans, so there was no reason for her not to tell us.

She could have said, "Yeah, that's not a line I was willing to cross." And I would have been fine with that—I don't necessarily need to hear everything that's inside your head, lady.

Instead, she went right over the line.

That's some fucking cold shit.

I'm proud to be part of the team that put her away.

She would have given up her chance at normalcy, at a family.

At redemption.

She knew Roger well enough to know that she had lost him.

Roger, of course, didn't know the stakes on her end. He just knew it wasn't the right relationship for him, he told me. He did visit her in jail. It wasn't because he loved her or hoped to see her through anything. He felt strongly about national security, and I think he wanted to make sure she was no longer a threat.

Ultimately, he realized the case was locked down—the loose ends had been tied and Ana was going to prison—and he stopped coming.

She never tried to be protective of him with us: She didn't have to. There was no chance he was a threat, and she knew the FBI would figure that out. And he saw the same information Ana saw. The Cubans didn't need him.

But Ana had thought their relationship was stable. She had introduced him to her family. She had talked about marriage.

She had planned to tell the Cubans she was out.

"Would they have let you go?" I asked.

"I think so," she said. "They were my friends."

EPILOGUE

# A Blaze of Glory

A few years later, I visited Ana in prison in Texas. She had no window. She wore an orange jumpsuit. She told me she was angry that I hadn't let her know I was coming—that I hadn't given her a chance to prepare emotionally for it.

But before I talked with her, the staff gave me a tour of the prison.

It didn't take long.

They showed me the outdoor area: a basketball court surrounded by a fence that rose straight up, and then curved hard so that even Spiderman would have to think about it. As we walked down a hallway to see Ana's cell, an older, frail-looking woman walked past us. She looked as if she could have been my aunt—she was on her way to knitting class. That woman was Squeaky Fromme, of Charles Manson and Gerald Ford fame.

*This woman tried to assassinate a president?*

She looked broken.

When I reached Ana's cell, she seemed tired. Prison is a noisy, well-lit place, and she told her sister that it was like an insane asylum. Many of the prisoners have serious mental disorders. Some of them scream in the middle of the night. They attack each other. Every half an hour, as Ana sleeps, a guard shines a light at her as part of a well-being check. They've been doing it for twenty years.

Still, Ana glared at me.

Through me.

I had shown up unannounced.

When we arrived at a conference room to chat—she lifted a chair, then slammed it down. "Fine!" she shouted. "Ask your first question."

"Well," I said, "hello, Ana. How are you?"

"Fine," she said.

This may seem naïve to you, but I thought, because we had spent so much time together—because she had asked about my wife and kid—she might be, well, not angry.

"Look," she said. "I need time to prepare to talk to you."

I thought my charming personality would have won her over during the nine months of debriefing, but she still saw me as a dumb ex-cop who couldn't spell "Nicaragua."

I was very happy to leave when the visit was over. For several reasons.

"I visited her there, and it intimidated me," her sister Lucy told me. "I can only imagine going there from our upbringing, from our quality of life. I think she'll come out a lot harder than she was when she went in."

On January 6, 2023, she walked out of prison and took a one-way flight to San Juan, escorted by a US marshal. She was a model prisoner, of course. I don't think she'll go to Cuba—not immediately, anyway—because she wants to be close to her mother. Ana has kept up a correspondence with Lucy, but Lucy said she never got what she needed from the letters: a sense of regret. An apology. An acknowledgment that Ana did wrong.

"I've always written to her," she told me. "I still write to her. But the hard part's coming."

While Ana has been in prison, the family hasn't had to worry about where she fits—who's going to take care of her, who's going to spend time with her, whether she's going to be invited for Thanksgiving and Christmas.

"We're preparing for that," she said. "We're preparing for all of the differences.

"She wrote to my son about a year ago," Lucy said. "She told him she had done nothing wrong. There's no remorse."

Lucy's children had loved Ana as a favorite aunt. They loved her so much that Lucy took them to see her in prison once.

I asked her why she still talks to her sister.

"She's my sister," she said. "She suffers a lot in prison."

"When I was first told Ana had been arrested, I didn't know what to do, whether to communicate with her anymore or not," Lucy said. "FBI Miami supervisor Gino Giannotti told me, 'Be a sister to her. We'll handle the rest, Lucy.' So I've tried to let that guide me over the years. I've tried to be a sister to her. Prison is a terrible place. Yes, I hold conflicting feelings, but I also know it was not my job to investigate her; that was the job of the FBI. It was not my job to prosecute her; that was the job of the attorneys at the DOJ. And it is not my job to punish her; that was the job of the Bureau of Prisons."

Lucy stayed at the FBI, as did their brother, Tito. Both had long, proud careers.

"She's asked me not to speak to the media," Lucy said, "but I don't work for her. I worked for this country, as an FBI translator, and that's where my loyalty lies. I did it for thirty-one years, and that hasn't changed."

Her mother? The woman who admonished me for invading her daughter's privacy? She's still hanging in there, at age eighty-six, waiting for her daughter to get out. They talk on the phone twice a week. She's her mother. But she told Lucy Ana's actions weren't worth it—that Ana had wasted her life.

"She's spent the last twenty years saying, 'I don't understand why she did what she did,'" Lucy said.

Just weeks before Ana's release from prison, her siblings issued a statement:

"Our sister committed treason against this country and the people of our nation," they wrote. "None of us were ever aware of her actions at the time, and we have never agreed or supported her position in any way. We continue to disavow what she did and any statements she has made or may make. All four of us were raised to be law-abiding citizens, with a strong moral sense of right and wrong. Ana's decision to commit espionage was based solely on her own convictions and was not in any way a reflection of our parents."

Many people use "treason" to describe espionage. Ana's espionage doesn't quite meet the legal definition for treason—certainly treachery—but for her siblings to use such a strong word speaks volumes. Noticeably absent from the public statement is a "but we love our sister" sentiment. I have no doubt that, as a sibling, they do still love the sinner, but likely hate the sin she committed.

Elena, the senior analyst and team lead at the National Security Agency who connected the earliest dots, believes her efforts were marginalized, her career even more so, because she went outside the "need to know" rules for the case, she told me. To this day, she doesn't know why that hurt her—without her, it would have taken much longer to find Ana, I believe. Was it because she went around the FBI's case? Was it because she's a woman? Was it because she's Cuban American?

Despite the toll the case took on her career, Elena received a medal personally from the director of the Defense Intelligence Agency for her work: Elena helped break the case. I'm not sure I would laude her for her "bravery"—especially in light of how close she came to alerting Ana. But I have always had the deepest respect for Elena's tenacity and analytical skills, and I worked well with her. Nancy Drew would be proud.

Kevin is now a successful businessman who reached the highest level of his company for a Cuban immigrant. He now travels first class, rather than in a rubber raft.

I don't imagine any of us have ever felt finished with this case. There are still so many questions. Why didn't Ana meet with Fidel?

Did they not trust her? They gave her a medal, presumably because she helped get a Green Beret killed. But was she simply not that important to them?

After all, Kendall Myers earned a four-hour love fest with Fidel.

Was it because Fidel didn't like Puerto Ricans, as was suggested to me recently by a retired US intelligence officer?

Was it just a schedule conflict?

It may not matter. What matters is the damage she did to our country, our government, her employer, and her family.

I did learn, as I researched this book, people within Cuban intelligence knew about Ana who shouldn't have known about Ana. They knew her real name. They knew her work. And they told us about it. If I were a spy for Cuba, that would make me nervous. People in Havana know your name.

Good luck with that.

Ana seems to have learned only that she doesn't want to deal with anyone who might question her morality. The weekend Ana was released from prison, her attorney issued a statement on her behalf:

"I am more than happy to touch Puerto Rican soil again," she wrote. "After two rather exhausting decades and faced with the need to earn a living again, I would like to dedicate myself to a quiet and private existence. Therefore, I will not participate in any media activities. . . .

"I encourage those who wish to focus on me to focus instead on important issues, such as the serious problems facing the Puerto Rican people or the U.S. economic embargo against Cuba. February will mark the 61st anniversary of the economic embargo against Cuba, enacted by President John F. Kennedy and later tightened by the U.S. Congress.

"Who in the last 60 years has asked the Cuban people if they want the United States to impose a suffocating embargo that makes them suffer?"

Translation: no remorse.

Me? I've worked on resolving some things.

After the debriefings and after Ana went to prison, Steve and I went to the National Security Agency to talk about her case. It was a big deal—all hands, four hundred or five hundred people. I told my dad about it.

He sent me a handwritten card.

"I'm so proud of you," he wrote. "I wish I could have been there."

Jen and I had two more children, Emma and Katelynn. My children are everything to me. Jen had heart surgery in 2008, and while it went well, she had a stroke afterward that caused more problems. She still deals with health issues today.

*Photo released by Ana along with her statement on January 8, 2023, after her release from federal prison on January 6.*

But as a couple, we didn't make it. I will always love our time together, and I will always consider her one of my best decisions, but between the stress of my job and the stress of her health, we couldn't make it work. We co-parent well now, and I'm in a committed relationship with a woman I love very much.

Our kids are growing up to be fine humans. And I'm super proud that my daughter turned down an admission to Ana's alma mater, UVA. Not bad for a dumb cop.

The breakup of our marriage led me back to another love: music. For as much as I wanted to be Jon Bon Jovi when I grew up, the idea of playing music in front of people terrified me. I'm not exactly a wallflower, and I can easily play the roles required of me, but underneath, I tend toward shy and introverted.

No, really.

The weekend Jen and I split, she had a work party at our place. She and her coworkers performed a silly skit—they took a well-known song and changed the lyrics. My guitar remained under the couch, hidden away. I was not about singing or playing in front of people.

But a year later—and it was an incredibly hard year—I went to an open mic session in Clarendon. I don't know what happened, exactly, beyond a sudden need to take a risk. I'd been pretty dress-right-dress about things—I absolutely understood the being-an-FBI-agent assignment: first I need to do this, then I need to do that, and, along the way, I also need to take care of my family.

The need for risk may also have been a need for release, like a soda can that's been shaken too hard. Working the case. Convincing the judge we had the right person. Those hours and hours with Ana. The divorce. Somewhere along the way, I had lost something of myself.

I had lost that first dream.

So, I took a risk. I picked up my guitar.

"All right," I remember telling the crowd. The dozens of faces seemed to me like thousands. I swear I shook more than I ever did as a cop surrounded by drug dealers. "So, uh, the more you drink, the better I'll sound."

I'm sure that I had imbibed a couple by that point too.

The first song was personal, and they were polite about it. There was scattered applause—like that clapping you do without stopping your conversation or putting down your beer.

You know.

So I started into the second song.

Bon Jovi.

Wanted.

Dead or Alive.

The crowd perked up a bit.

Like a tent revival for the church of Bon Jovi, the crowd sang back: "Wanted…"

I was like, *Oh, this is cool. This is mine.*

*This is free.*

Now I perform pretty regularly at the vineyards and brewery near my house.

It's pretty neat.

Even if only three people show up, it's like there are fifty thousand in my head—and I'm right back where I started as a kid from Jersey with big dreams.

Of course, I wasn't done with Ana. I'll never be done with Ana. But I wonder if the music freed me to feel some things I had shoved down as a hard-assed FBI agent. During the debrief, I had a hard time feeling compassion for her. I still saw things in black and white.

But I look back now with some distance, with some life experience, and I remember that when we worried so much about my son and when my then-wife's heart problems could have killed her, Ana never forgot to ask about them. She showed genuine concern for our family.

In some ways, Ana makes me question all my relationships. I know a dichotomy exists in all of us, that people show us only what they want us to see, and we are all complicated: Hoover. Ana. Dad. Others. And yes, me.

I may never offer a handshake without wondering what I don't know about that person.

But Ana, the "Queen of Cuba," also taught me to be curious, to be open to the gray, even as I'm eternally grateful to all the people who worked hard to help lock her away.

# Endnotes

1 Raymond Bonner, "America's Role in El Salvador's Deterioration," *The Atlantic*, January 20, 2018, https://www.theatlantic.com/international/archive/2018/01/trump-and-el-salvador/550955/.

2 Kevin Sullivan and J.Y. Smith, "Fidel Castro, Revolutionary Leader Who Remade Cuba as a Socialist State, Dies at 90," *Washington Post*, November 26, 2016, https://www.washingtonpost.com/world/fidel-castro-cuban-dictator-dies-at-90/2016/11/26/f37bf3bc-b399-11e6-be1c-8cec35b1ad25_story.html.

3 Amby Burfoot, "Castro's Cuba: A Public Health Phenomenon in the '90s Showed the Effects of National Weight Loss," *Washington Post*, December 1, 2016, https://www.washingtonpost.com/lifestyle/wellness/castros-cuba-a-public-health-phenomenon-in-the-90s-showed-the-benefits-of-national-weight-loss/2016/12/01/c179c6fe-b68d-11e6-b8df-600bd9d38a02_story.html.

4 Richards J. Heuer Jr. and Katherine Herbig, "Espionage by the Numbers: A Statistical Overview," NOAA.gov, last modified November 28, 2001, https://www.hq.nasa.gov/office/ospp/securityguide/Treason/Numbers.htm.

5 Tim Johnson, "She Led Two Lives—Dutiful Analyst, and Spy for Cuba," *Miami Herald*, June 16, 2002.

6 Tim Johnson, "She Led Two Lives—Dutiful Analyst, and Spy for Cuba," *Miami Herald*, June 16, 2002.

7 Scott W. Carmichael, *True Believer: Inside the Investigation and Capture of Ana Montes, Cuba's Master Spy* (Annapolis, MD: Naval Institute, 2009), 49.

8 Jon Lee Anderson, "The Dream of Puerto Rican Independence, and the Story of Heriberto Marín," *New Yorker*, December 27, 2017, https://www.newyorker.com/news/news-desk/the-dream-of-puerto-rican-independence-and-the-story-of-heriberto-marin.

9 Jon Lee Anderson, "The Dream of Puerto Rican Independence, and the Story of Heriberto Marín," *New Yorker*, December 27, 2017, https://www.newyorker.com/news/news-desk/the-dream-of-puerto-rican-independence-and-the-story-of-heriberto-marin.

10 "U.S. Census Bureau Quickfacts: Puerto Rico," U.S. Census Bureau, accessed October 19, 2022, https://www.census.gov/quickfacts/fact/table/PR/PST045221.

11 Kanako Ishida, et al., "Child Maltreatment in Puerto Rico: Findings from the 2010 National Child Abuse and Neglect Data System," *Puerto Rico Health Sciences Journal*, U.S. National Library of Medicine, accessed October 19, 2022.

12 Andrea González-Ramírez, "In Puerto Rico, an Epidemic of Domestic Violence Hides in Plain Sight," Type Investigations, December 6, 2021, https://www.typeinvestigations.org/investigation/2020/06/30/in-puerto-rico-an-epidemic-of-domestic-violence-hides-in-plain-sight/.

13 Tim Johnson, "She Led Two Lives—Dutiful Analyst, and Spy for Cuba," *Miami Herald*, June 16, 2002.

14 Tim Johnson, "She Led Two Lives—Dutiful Analyst, and Spy for Cuba," *Miami Herald*, June 16, 2002.

15 Popkin, Jim. "Ana Montes Did Much Harm Spying for Cuba. Chances Are, You Haven't Heard of Her," *Washington Post*, April 18, 2013, https://www.washingtonpost.com/sf/feature/wp/2013/04/18/ana-montes-did-much-harm-spying-for-cuba-chances-are-you-havent-heard-of-her/.

16 Palacios Klinger and Carla Corina, "'Las Acciones De Ana Belén Constituyen Un Acto De Solidaridad,'" 80grados+, accessed October 19, 2022, https://www.80grados.net/las-acciones-de-ana-belen-constituyen-un-acto-de-solidaridad/.

17 James M. Markham, "Thousands in Spain Strike to Protest Political Violence," *New York Times*, January 26, 1977, https://www.nytimes.com/1977/01/26/archives/thousands-in-spain-strike-to-protest-political-violence-24.html.

18 "A Sourcebook," DIA Declassified, Office of the Inspector General of the Department of Defense, June 16, 2005, https://nsarchive2.gwu.edu/NSAEBB/NSAEBB534-DIA-Declassified-Sourcebook/; Markham, "Thousands in Spain Strike to Protest Political Violence."

19 Thom Patterson, "The Most Dangerous U.S. Spy You've Never Heard Of," CNN, August 8, 2018, https://www.cnn.com/2016/07/06/us/declassified-ana-montes-american-spy-profile/index.html.

20 "Aid to El Salvador." In *CQ Almanac 1981*, 37th ed., 184-86. Washington, DC: Congressional Quarterly, 1982. http://library.cqpress.com/cqalmanac/cqal81-1172150.

21 "Truth Commission: El Salvador," United States Institute of Peace, September 17, 2021, https://www.usip.org/publications/1992/07/truth-commission-el-salvador.

22 "A Sourcebook," DIA Declassified. Office of the Inspector General of the Department of Defense, June 16, 2005. https://nsarchive2.gwu.edu/NSAEBB/NSAEBB534-DIA-Declassified-Sourcebook/.

23 Roscoe C. Howard, "United States of America v. Marta Rita Velazquez," Antipolygraph.org, George W. Maschke, accessed January 10, 2023, https://antipolygraph.org/documents/marta-rita-velazquez-arrest-warrant-and-indictment.pdf.

24 "A Sourcebook," DIA Declassified, Office of the Inspector General of the Department of Defense, June 16, 2005, https://nsarchive2.gwu.edu/NSAEBB/NSAEBB534-DIA-Declassified-Sourcebook/.

25 Ana Montes, debriefings with Steve McCoy and Peter Lapp.

26 Roscoe C. Howard, "United States of America v. Marta Rita Velazquez," Antipolygraph.org, George W. Maschke, accessed January 10, 2023, Page 12, https://antipolygraph.org/documents/marta-rita-velazquez-arrest-warrant-and-indictment.pdf.

27 Roscoe C. Howard, "United States of America v. Marta Rita Velazquez," Antipolygraph.org, George W. Maschke, accessed January 10, 2023, Page 13, https://antipolygraph.org/documents/marta-rita-velazquez-arrest-warrant-and-indictment.pdf.

28 Roscoe C. Howard, "United States of America v. Marta Rita Velazquez," Antipolygraph.org, George W. Maschke, accessed January 10, 2023, Page 11, https://antipolygraph.org/documents/marta-rita-velazquez-arrest-warrant-and-indictment.pdf.

29 "A Sourcebook," DIA Declassified, Office of the Inspector General of the Department of Defense, January 10, 2023, Page 11, https://nsarchive2.gwu.edu/NSAEBB/NSAEBB534-DIA-Declassified-Sourcebook/documents/DIA-37.pdf.

30 "A Sourcebook," DIA Declassified, Office of the Inspector General of the Department of Defense, January 10, 2023, Page 11, https://nsarchive2.gwu.edu/NSAEBB/NSAEBB534-DIA-Declassified-Sourcebook/documents/DIA-37.pdf.

31 "A Sourcebook," DIA Declassified, Office of the Inspector General of the Department of Defense, January 10, 2023, Page 10, https://nsarchive2.gwu.edu/NSAEBB/NSAEBB534-DIA-Declassified-Sourcebook/documents/DIA-37.pdf.

32 "A Sourcebook," DIA Declassified, Office of the Inspector General of the Department of Defense, January 10, 2023, Page 24, https://nsarchive2.gwu.edu/NSAEBB/NSAEBB534-DIA-Declassified-Sourcebook/documents/DIA-37.pdf.

33 History.com Editors, "The U.S. Invades Panama," History.com, A&E Television Networks, February 9, 2010, https://www.history.com/this-day-in-history/the-u-s-invades-panama.

34 "A Sourcebook," DIA Declassified, Office of the Inspector General of the Department of Defense, January 10, 2023, Page 10, https://nsarchive2.gwu.edu/NSAEBB/NSAEBB534-DIA-Declassified-Sourcebook/documents/DIA-37.pdf.

35 Andrew H. Malcolm, "The U.S. and Panama: The Toll; Deaths of 23 Americans in Panama: Their Dreams Cut Short," *New York Times*, January 8, 1990, https://www.nytimes.com/1990/01/08/us/us-panama-toll-deaths-23-americans-panama-their-dreams-cut-short.html.

36 "A Sourcebook," DIA Declassified, Office of the Inspector General of the Department of Defense, January 10, 2023, Page 10, https://nsarchive2.gwu.edu/NSAEBB/NSAEBB534-DIA-Declassified-Sourcebook/documents/DIA-37.pdf.

37 "A Sourcebook," DIA Declassified, Office of the Inspector General of the Department of Defense, January 10, 2023, Page 2, https://nsarchive2.gwu.edu/NSAEBB/NSAEBB534-DIA-Declassified-Sourcebook/documents/DIA-37.pdf.

38 "A Sourcebook," DIA Declassified, Office of the Inspector General of the Department of Defense, January 10, 2023, Page 13, https://nsarchive2.gwu.edu/NSAEBB/NSAEBB534-DIA-Declassified-Sourcebook/documents/DIA-37.pdf.

39 "A Sourcebook," DIA Declassified, Office of the Inspector General of the Department of Defense, January 10, 2023, Page 12, https://nsarchive2.gwu.edu/NSAEBB/NSAEBB534-DIA-Declassified-Sourcebook/documents/DIA-37.pdf.

40 "A Sourcebook," DIA Declassified, Office of the Inspector General of the Department of Defense, January 10, 2023, Page 28, https://nsarchive2.gwu.edu/NSAEBB/NSAEBB534-DIA-Declassified-Sourcebook/documents/DIA-37.pdf.

41 Scott W. Carmichael, *True Believer: Inside the Investigation and Capture of Ana Montes, Cuba's Master Spy* (Annapolis, MD: Naval Institute, 2009), 21.

42 Ana Montes, debriefings with Steve McCoy and Peter Lapp.

43 Scott W. Carmichael, *True Believer: Inside the Investigation and Capture of Ana Montes, Cuba's Master Spy* (Annapolis, MD: Naval Institute, 2009), 10.

44 Author TWC, "The Forgotten Lynching of Zachariah Walker Was One of Our Most Shameful-and It Was in the North," The Weekly Challenger, June 1, 2017, https://theweeklychallenger.com/the-forgotten-lynching-of-zachariah-walker-was-one-of-our-most-shameful%E2%80%8A-%E2%80%8Aand-it-was-in-the-north/.

45 "The Lynching of Zachariah Walker Historical Marker," Explorepahistory.com, accessed February 11, 2023, https://explorepahistory.com/hmarker.php?markerId=1-A-3DB.

46 Kathleen Brady Shea and Nancy Petersen, "Hope Growing Anew in Forlorn Coatesville," Philadelphia Inquirer, May 7, 2007, https://www.inquirer.com/philly/news/local/20070507_Hope_is_growing_in_Coatesville.html.

47 Michael P. Rellahan, "Coatesville Murderer Duron Peoples Speaks from Prison of Past and Coming Life," *Daily Local*, August 19, 2021, https://www.dailylocal.com/2014/10/23/coatesville-murderer-duron-peoples-speaks-from-prison-of-past-and-coming-life/.

48 Scott W. Carmichael, *True Believer: Inside the Investigation and Capture of Ana Montes, Cuba's Master Spy* (Annapolis, MD: Naval Institute, 2009), 14.

49 Scott W. Carmichael, *True Believer: Inside the Investigation and Capture of Ana Montes, Cuba's Master Spy* (Annapolis, MD: Naval Institute, 2009), 14.

50 Scott W. Carmichael, *True Believer: Inside the Investigation and Capture of Ana Montes, Cuba's Master Spy* (Annapolis, MD: Naval Institute, 2009), 11.

51 Scott W. Carmichael, *True Believer: Inside the Investigation and Capture of Ana Montes, Cuba's Master Spy* (Annapolis, MD: Naval Institute, 2009), 17.

52 "Joint Committee on Foreign Affairs Debate - Tuesday, 15 Feb 2005," Houses of the Oireachtas, February 15, 2005, https://www.oireachtas.ie/en/debates/debate/joint_committee_on_foreign_affairs/2005-02-15/3/.

53 "Former State Department Official and Wife Arrested for Serving as Illegal Agents of Cuba for Nearly 30 Years," The United States Department of Justice, July 13, 2022, https://www.justice.gov/opa/pr/former-state-department-official-and-wife-arrested-serving-illegal-agents-cuba-nearly-30.

54 Scott W. Carmichael, *True Believer: Inside the Investigation and Capture of Ana Montes, Cuba's Master Spy* (Annapolis, MD: Naval Institute, 2009), 35.

55 Scott W. Carmichael, *True Believer: Inside the Investigation and Capture of Ana Montes, Cuba's Master Spy* (Annapolis, MD: Naval Institute, 2009), 23.

56 Scott W. Carmichael, *True Believer: Inside the Investigation and Capture of Ana Montes, Cuba's Master Spy* (Annapolis, MD: Naval Institute, 2009), 40.

57 Malcolm Gladwell, *Talking to Strangers: What We Should Know about the People We Don't Know* (Boston, MA: Little, Brown and Company, 2019), 60.

58 Scott W. Carmichael, *True Believer: Inside the Investigation and Capture of Ana Montes, Cuba's Master Spy* (Annapolis, MD: Naval Institute, 2009), 74.

59 "COINTELPRO 2.0: Chicago Committee to Defend the Bill of Rights," Chicago Committee to Defend the Bill of Rights, January 2, 2021, https://www.ccdbr.org/issues/cointelpro-2-0/.

60 "Senate Select Committee to Study Governmental Operations with Respect to Intelligence Activities," U.S. Senate, February 26, 2021, https://www.senate.gov/about/powers-procedures/investigations/church-committee.htm.

61 "United States Senate Select Committee on Intelligence," Federation of American Scientists, April 26, 1976, Page 5, https://www.intelligence.senate.gov/sites/default/files/94755_II.pdf.

62 "U.S. Constitution — Fourth Amendment | Resources — Congress," Constitution Annotated, U.S. Congress, accessed March 21, 2023, https://constitution.congress.gov/constitution/amendment-4/.

63 Ronald Kessler, *The Secrets of the FBI* (New York: Broadway Paperbacks, 2012), 7.

64 Ronald Kessler, *The Secrets of the FBI* (New York: Broadway Paperbacks, 2012), 13.

65 Lis Wiehl, *A Spy in Plain Sight: The Inside Story of the FBI and Robert Hanssen—America's Most Damaging Russian Spy* (New York: Pegasus, 2022).

66 "A Sourcebook," DIA Declassified, Office of the Inspector General of the Department of Defense, June 16, 2005, https://nsarchive2.gwu.edu/NSAEBB/NSAEBB534-DIA-Declassified-Sourcebook/; Markham, "Thousands in Spain Strike to Protest Political Violence."


67 I spoke with several retired FBI senior executives who don't recall, and don't believe, Admiral Wilson personally gave them, and thus the FBI, a deadline to arrest by September 21. They say Admiral Wilson (admirably) was patient throughout the FBI's investigation and never gave the bureau a deadline. My recollection, which seems to be supported by the Defense Department Inspector General report, from Steve and my interaction with Scott at the time, as well as an interview Admiral Wilson gave author Jim

Popkin in Code Name Blue Wren, was that he did insist that the case be wrapped up quickly after the September 11 terrorist attack and before the beginning of the war in Afghanistan.

68 "President Bush Addresses the Nation," *Washington Post,* April 8, 2023, https://www.washingtonpost.com/wp-srv/nation/specials/attacked/transcripts/bushaddress_092001.html.

69 Bill Miller, "Analyst Hires Veteran Espionage Lawyers," *Washington Post,* October 5, 2001, https://www.washingtonpost.com/archive/local/2001/10/05/analyst-hires-veteran-espionage-lawyers/3531d816-efd5-4a66-9dc3-193e1611c65f/.

70 Antonio de la Cova, "Statement by Ana Belen Montes, Who Received 25-Year Sentence for Spying for Cuba," *Miami Herald,* April 8, 2023, https://www.latinamericanstudies.org/espionage/montes-statement.htm.

# Acknowledgments

I want to start by thanking my super talented co-writer Kelly Kennedy, who really was my #secretweapon. I could not have done this without you, and there is no person I would have wanted to co-write this story with. Having the distinction of being the only woman who has ever served in combat both in the military and as a journalist, you understood my commitment to public service and the impact of this kind of treachery on our military. I am honored you joined me to help tell this great story. It was nice to have a partner, again.

The quote "Success has a thousand fathers" is widely attributed to President John F. Kennedy. With that, I share credit of the identification, arrest, prosecution, and conviction of Ana Montes with every person in every agency who had a hand in the outcome. The truth is there is not one person, and certainly not one agency, that deserves full credit. Professionally, my great fortune was to have been part of such an important investigation at such an early stage in my career. While I was a cop, my only goal was to get into the FBI. Beyond that, I can't say I had lofty ambitions. Obviously, I wrote this book from my point of view, but I have trouble catching colds let alone spies—I'm certainly no "master spy catcher." I want everyone who worked this case to know how immensely proud I was to have worked with them. I say this every chance I get: this was a "we" case, not a "me" case. I hope I honored all of you and captured the true nature of this inter-agency and team accomplishment.

Steve, thank you for picking me to be your partner. We made a great team, and you are a friend. Our skills, talents, and personalities meshed well, and I was honored to be your partner.

To everyone at the Bureau who helped make this possible, including Molly Flynn, Diane Krzemien, Albert "Tré" Resolute III, Liana Davila, Henry, Brad, Amy Landman, Mark Gomez, Dan Cloyd, Doug Marshall, Kevin Leuenberger, Rusty Rosenthal, Homer Pointer, Duncan Wainwright, Ana Maria Mendoza, Bob and Rob, Bill "WD" Doherty, Jake, Zach, Dave, Treva, Steve, all the "G's," and the incomparable Stu Hoyt. To anyone I missed, my apologies and I sincerely appreciate all you did to support the FBI's case.

To everyone at Main Justice's Counterespionage Section and Office of Intelligence Policy and Review, as well as the US Attorney's Office in D.C., especially John Dion, Michael Liebman, Fran Townsend, Jim Baker, Ron Walutes, and Grace, thank you for all your help, oversight, and support getting us to the "wall," over the "wall," and then through a plea agreement. The American people should better understand the Justice Department's independence, oversight of national security cases, and steadfast loyalty to the rule of law and our Constitution.

Thank you to Plato Cacheris and Preston Burton. It was an honor to work against you (so to speak). You represented your client well and made us do our job better.

A very special thank you to Lucy Montes for your cooperation, friendship, and fact-checking on your family's history. This story, especially regarding your family's history, was made accurate because of your help.

Thank you to Elena for your professionalism and help with writing. I admire you and was really proud to work with you.

To Joanie Andrzejewski and Ana "Mimi" Colón, thank you for your valuable insight and photographs.

I very much appreciate Roger's help with this manuscript. I hope the American people better appreciate a more accurate telling of your perspective, as well as your loyal service to our nation. You are a true patriot.

Thank you Andy Guzman and John Kavanaugh for insights I hadn't known.

Thank you to everyone in the US intelligence community who helped make this case, including the [redacted], NSA, and DIA. This was a team effort, and the American people should know that the intelligence community unselfishly came together to solve a big problem. Each of these agencies deserves to share the credit for this success.

To the family of Staff Sergeant Gregory A. Fronius, as well as Carlos Costa, Armando Alejandre Jr., Mario de la Peña, and Pablo Morales who were all killed during the Brothers to the Rescue shootdown, my deepest condolences. Please know I wish we had evidence that would have helped with a longer prison sentence. Their sacrifices are not forgotten.

Thank you to Dr. Eric Shaw, Brian Latell, and Randy Pherson for your insights on Montes, and a special thank you to Frank Figliuzzi for your advice and counsel.

Thank you Malcolm Gladwell, Meghna Rho, and all at Pushkin Industries. I am very excited about our continued collaboration.

Thank you to Betsy Glick, who introduced me to Frank Weimann, my agent. Frank, you were the perfect Philadelphia guy via New York to have in our corner, and I appreciate all you did through the headwinds to sell our (inside) version of this story. A special thank you as well to Elizabeth Wachtel at William Morris Endeavor for your continued interest and help in sharing this story with an even broader audience.

I am incredibly grateful for the trust Kevin and Mandy, as well as a couple of others, gave me that allowed me to tell a lot about the Cuban Intelligence Service, as well as your journeys from adversaries to fellow Americans. All of you are true American patriots, and

I invite more of your former collogues to follow in your footsteps. They would be "welcomed with open arms."

Thank you to Post Hill Press, especially Alex Novak, Ashlyn Inman, Barbara Pepe, Cody Corcoran (love the book cover design!), and Alex Sturdeon, as well as Blackstone Publishing (audio book) for taking a chance on this story. Your faith in us is greatly appreciated.

A heart-felt thanks to Kandi at FBI pre-publication. You're a gem to the FBI, and I hope the Bureau knows how fortunate it is to have you.

A huge thank you to the "CA." You are a total badass. I thank you for being my champion, and for your service to our national security.

Thank you to my mom, dad, and siblings and their spouses for all your support and love over the years (How 'bout them Eagles?!?!)

I could not have written this book without the love and support of my partner and confidant, Amanda. You have been a true blessing in my life, and I love you dearly. Thank you for putting up with the me, and for your ever-so-patient listening to me tell parts of this story (usually multiple times) over glasses of wine.

To Jen, thank you for giving us our three "goos," who are growing up to be really good humans.

While the Montes investigation was the highlight of my professional career, it pales in comparison to my real accomplishment: my children. I love you all with all my heart, and I can't wait to watch as you achieve even greater things and write your own life's story. Know that your mom and I will always be your biggest fans.

Finally, the FBI and the intelligence community has received a lot of unfair criticism from certain circles since 2016. To be clear, the FBI is not a perfect institution—that unicorn doesn't exist. But the Bureau is filled with loyal, hardworking men and women who wake up every day with three goals: protect the American people; uphold the Constitution; and go home safe to their loved ones. They are sons and daughters, husbands and wives, parents, friends, and neighbors. All took an oath to the Constitution—one which Montes betrayed—to protect our communities and defend our nation from enemies, both foreign *and* domestic. While they are doing just that, they are trying to find soul mates, keep marriages together, start and raise families, and squeeze in enough time to cut their grass so their neighbors don't get pissed at them. The FBI is far from perfect, but the FBI I know strives every day to do the right things, for the right reasons, in the right ways. I hope and pray I have done those who served, continue to serve, and will serve honor in this book.

***Peter J. Lapp***
*June 2023*

# About the Authors

**Peter J. Lapp** retired as a special agent for the FBI after twenty-two years either investigating or managing counterintelligence investigations involving Cuba, Russia, and China. Before joining the FBI, he worked as a police officer in the Coatesville and West Whiteland police departments in Pennsylvania. He earned his bachelor's in criminal justice at West Chester University and his master's in criminal justice at St. Joseph's University. He served several years in the Army National Guard as an infantry officer. After retiring from the FBI, Lapp founded an independent consulting firm and conducts keynote speaking to help organizations mature their insider-risk programs. Lapp now lives in Loudoun County, Virginia, and performs on the winery circuit as a singer and guitarist. His daughters say he's not internationally well known; he's only "county famous."

**Kelly Kennedy** is the author of *They Fought for Each Other: The Triumph and Tragedy of the Hardest Hit Unit in Iraq*, as well as co-author of *Fight Like a Girl: The Truth Behind How Female Marines are Trained.* She served in the U.S. Army from 1987 to 1993, including tours in the Middle East during Desert Storm, and in Mogadishu, Somalia. She is the managing editor of *The War Horse*, a nonprofit investigative and long-form journalism newsroom affectionately known as the ProPublica of military news. She has worked as a health policy reporter for *USA Today*, as well as reporting for *Military Times*,

*The Chicago Tribune*, *The Oregonian*, and *The Salt Lake Tribune*. As a journalist, she has embedded in both Iraq and Afghanistan. She is the only U.S. female journalist to both serve in combat and cover it as a civilian journalist, and she is the first female president of Military Reporters & Editors. In her spare time, she dances ballet and completely loses her military bearing.

Printed in Great Britain
by Amazon

58942320R00152